Palgrave Historical Studies in Witchcraft and Magic
Series Editors: **Jonathan Barry, Willem de Blécourt, and Owen Davies**

Series Foreword

The history of European witchcraft and magic continues to fascinate and challenge students and scholars. There is certainly no shortage of books on the subject. Several general surveys of the witch trials and numerous regional and micro studies have been published for an English-speaking readership. While the quality of publications on witchcraft has been high, some regions and topics have received less attention over the years. The aim of this series is to help illuminate these lesser known or little studied aspects of the history of witchcraft and magic. It will also encourage the development of a broader corpus of work in other related areas of magic and the supernatural, such as angels, devils, spirits, ghosts, folk healing, and divination. To help further our understanding and interest in this wider history of beliefs and practices, the series will include research that looks beyond the usual focus on Western Europe and that also explores their relevance and influence from the medieval to the modern period.

Titles include:

Jonathan Barry
RAISING SPIRITS
How a Conjuror's Tale was Transmitted across the Enlightenment

Jonathan Barry
WITCHCRAFT AND DEMONOLOGY IN SOUTH-WEST ENGLAND, 1640–1789

Edward Bever
THE REALITIES OF WITCHCRAFT AND POPULAR MAGIC IN EARLY MODERN EUROPE
Culture, Cognition and Everyday Life

Ruth Bottigheimer
MAGIC TALES AND FAIRY TALE MAGIC
From Ancient Egypt to the Italian Renaissance

Alison Butler
VICTORIAN OCCULTISM AND THE MAKING OF MODERN MAGIC
Invoking Tradition

Johannes Dillinger
MAGICAL TREASURE HUNTING IN EUROPE AND NORTH AMERICA
A History

Julian Goodare (*editor*)
SCOTTISH WITCHES AND WITCH-HUNTERS

Julian Goodare, Lauren Martin and Joyce Miller (*editors*)
WITCHCRAFT AND BELIEF IN EARLY MODERN SCOTLAND

Louise Kallestrup
AGENTS OF WITCHCRAFT IN EARLY MODERN ITALY AND DENMARK

Jonathan Roper (*editor*)
CHARMS, CHARMERS AND CHARMING

Alison Rowlands (*editor*)
WITCHCRAFT AND MASCULINITIES IN EARLY MODERN EUROPE

Rolf Schulte
MAN AS WITCH
Male Witches in Central Europe

Andrew Sneddon
WITCHCRAFT AND MAGIC IN IRELAND

Laura Stokes
DEMONS OF URBAN REFORM
Early European Witch Trials and Criminal Justice, 1430–1530

María Tausiet
URBAN MAGIC IN EARLY MODERN SPAIN
Abracadabra Omnipotens

Robert Ziegler
SATANISM, MAGIC AND MYSTICISM IN FIN-DE-SIÈCLE FRANCE

Forthcoming:

Lizanne Henderson
WITCHCRAFT AND FOLK BELIEF AT THE DAWN OF ENLIGHTENMENT

Liana Saif
ARABIC INFLUENCES ON EARLY MODERN OCCULT THOUGHT

Palgrave Historical Studies in Witchcraft and Magic
Series Standing Order ISBN 978-1-403-99566-7 Hardback
978-1-403-99567-4 Paperback
(*outside North America only*)

You can receive future titles in this series as they are published by placing a standing order. Please contact your bookseller or, in case of difficulty, write to us at the address below with your name and address, the title of the series and the ISBN quoted above.

Customer Services Department, Macmillan Distribution Ltd, Houndmills, Basingstoke, Hampshire RG21 6XS, England

Witchcraft and Magic in Ireland

Andrew Sneddon
Lecturer in International History, Ulster University, Coleraine

palgrave
macmillan

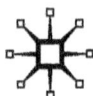

First published 2015 by
PALGRAVE MACMILLAN

Palgrave Macmillan in the UK is an imprint of Macmillan Publishers Limited, registered in England, company number 785998, of Houndmills, Basingstoke, Hampshire RG21 6XS.

Palgrave Macmillan in the US is a division of St Martin's Press LLC, 175 Fifth Avenue, New York, NY10010.

Palgrave Macmillan is the global academic imprint of the above companies and has companies and representatives throughout the world.

Palgrave® and Macmillan® are registered trademarks in the United States, the United Kingdom, Europe and other countries.

ISBN 978-0-230-30272-3

This book is printed on paper suitable for recycling and made from fully managed and sustained forest sources. Logging, pulping and manufacturing processes are expected to conform to the environmental regulations of the country of origin.

A catalogue record for this book is available from the British Library.

A catalog record for this book is available from the Library of Congress.

Typeset by MPS Limited, Chennai, India.

For my sons, Andrew and James Sneddon and in memory of my father, Andrew Sneddon (1948–2015)

Contents

Acknowledgements

I have collected many debts in writing this book. First of all, I thank the Arts and Humanities Research Institute at Ulster University, as well as the History Research Cluster, for research leave during which parts of this book were completed. I would also like to thank the Library staff on the Coleraine Campus, Ulster University, for their help in sourcing secondary material from far-flung libraries. I would also like to thank Dr Billy Kelly, Dr Gillian Kenny, Dr Leanne McCormick, Professor Don MacRaild, and Professor Martyn Powell for looking over drafts, and Professor Sean Connolly, Dr Peter Elmer, Dr Neal Garnham, Professor David Hayton, Professor James Kelly, and Dr Nerys Young for providing sources and/or looking over work in the past that in one way or another has been incorporated into this book. I am also grateful to Dr John Privilege who made the Magus-funded 'Supernatural in Ulster-Scots Language and Literature Reader' project such a rewarding and enjoyable experience. My current and past PhD students, Dr Nigel Farrell, Jodie Shevlin, John Fulton, and Cara Hanley, have provided invaluable support at public events and long chats about witchcraft and magic and Irish history in general. I also thank my mum and dad, my sister Sharon and my brother-in-law Steve, and Jim and Vivian McCormick for their continuing support. I apologise to my sons James (who was born while I was writing this book) and Andrew for seeing a lot less of their father over the last year or so, as it is often impossible to adequately balance the demands of modern academic life, publishing, and home life. Thank you, and one day you might read this book, and understand why your dad kept scuttling off into the study (in reality, a requisitioned dining-room). I also thank Jonathon Hinder, Graham Jackson, Stephen Scarth, and Peter Moore for their friendship and taking an interest in my work. Most of all, my heartfelt thanks goes to my wife Leanne, who proofread the entire manuscript – and without her this book could not have been started, far less completed.

Notes on Spelling, Dates and Irish Names

Spelling

When quoting from primary source documents or publications, grammar, punctuation, and spelling (as much as the maintenance of sense allows) have been kept as in the original. Capitalisation has been modernised and the abbreviation 'ye' has been written as 'the'.

Dates

The dates given in this book are given in the form related in the primary sources and as such are based on the old-style calendar. However, the year has been taken to begin on 1 January and not 25 March as was the custom before 1752.

Irish Names

Historic Irish names are presented in the manner they appear (where possible) in the DIB or ODNB.

List of Abbreviations

BL   British Library, London

BNA   *British Newspaper Archive*, http://www.britishnewspaperarchive.co.uk

BNL   *Belfast Newsletter*

DIB   *Cambridge Dictionary of Irish Biography*, http://dib.cambridge.org/

ESTC   *English Short Title Catalogue*, British Library, http://estc.bl.uk

FJ   *Freeman's Journal*

ILD   *Irish Legislation Database*, http://www.qub.ac.uk/ild

INA   *Irish Newspaper Archive*, http://archive.irishnewsarchive.com

JHCI   *Journals of the House of Commons, Ireland* (20 vols, Dublin, 4th ed., 1782–94)

JHLI   *Journals of the House of Lords, Ireland* (8 vols, Dublin, 1779–1800)

NIN   *Nineteenth Century Newspapers from the British Library*, Gale Online

NLI   National Library of Ireland, Dublin

ODNB   *Oxford Dictionary of National Biography*, http://www.oxforddnb.com

OSMI   *Ordnance Survey Memoirs of Ireland*, edited by Angélique Day, Noirin Dobson, Lisa English, and Patrick McWilliams (40 vols, Belfast, 1990–8)

PHS   Presbyterian Historical Society, Belfast

PRONI   Public Record Office of Northern Ireland, Belfast

TCD   Trinity College Dublin, Library Special Collections

UTC   Union Theological College, Belfast

Introduction

The early twentieth century saw the publication of a pioneering overview of Irish witchcraft by Church of Ireland clergyman, St. John D. Seymour,[1] which was well received at the time by readers and critics alike,[2] and remains an essential tool for students of the subject. Seymour's book related salient cases of witchcraft, magic, and dealings with the devil, in a country that he admitted had largely avoided the ravages of early modern witch-hunting. Its great strength, and one that has ensured its cultural currency, was that it was based on a wide range of primary printed and manuscript material, some of which was destroyed in 1922 during the Four Courts fire in Dublin in the Irish Civil War. Combined with the destruction of records in the seventeenth and early eighteenth centuries, almost all of Irish administrative and criminal manuscripts (relating to the main criminal courts of Quarter Sessions, Assizes and court of King's Bench) up to the mid eighteenth-century are now lost, along with probate material and Church of Ireland parish and institutional records.[3] As Neal Garnham has pointed out, Irish historians have no option but to rely on 'aggregations of examples drawn from the contemporary press, or the wealth of anecdotal evidence contained in the private papers of prominent individuals'.[4]

A consequence of lack of sources is that academic history of witchcraft in early modern and modern Ireland is under-researched in comparison to England and most of continental Europe.[5] Other Gaelic or Celtic regions of Britain (Wales, Isle of Man, and the Highlands and Islands of Scotland) have also been better catered for in terms of historical scholarship.[6] From the latter half of the twentieth century onwards a handful of popular books were published which brought Irish witchcraft to public attention. These studies often lacked adequate referencing, failed to put witchcraft in its wider historical context and were content with providing narrative accounts of infamous trials and the activities of notorious 'wise-women'.[7] The little academic work undertaken was largely concerned with establishing why there was little witch-hunting in Ireland, with only Professor Ronald Hutton and the author showing an interest in the nature of early modern Irish witchcraft belief and how this might have differed from the British Isles.[8] Some case studies of Irish witchcraft trials, such as that of Florence Newton in Co. Cork in 1661 and the 'Islandmagee Witches' in Co. Antrim in 1711, have also been produced.[9] Professor Raymond Gillespie, however, has done more than any historian to map the magical, moral universe of early modern Irish people, suggesting that belief in witchcraft, ghosts, divination, prophecies, and astrology, along with the regular intervention in earthly affairs by spiritual essences such as God and the Devil, Angels and Demons, formed a core part of both Catholic and Protestant popular religion in Ireland.[10] It is only relatively recently that the late eighteenth and nineteenth century has been examined in relation to the non-Christian supernatural, with various writers arguing that it formed a core part of popular religion alongside official Catholic doctrine and ritual up until the late nineteenth century. Current historiography remains largely silent on Protestant witchcraft belief.[11]

This monograph is not only the first academic overview of witchcraft since St. John D. Seymour's book but differs from previous studies in a number of ways. Its arguments are informed by recent developments in the study of European witchcraft and popular magic, which guard against regarding the Irish experience as more exceptional than it was in reality. Although England is the main point of comparison used, as it shared almost identical legal and administrative structures, and the Irish Witchcraft statute of 1586 was based on the 1563 English Witchcraft Act (see Chapter 2), other Gaelic areas of Britain have been extensively referenced (Chapters 1, 6), as has Scotland. Scotland experienced severe, epidemic witch-hunting and was the country of birth or ancestry of many Irish Protestants, especially in Presbyterian Ulster (Chapters 1, 3, 5). Although the few witch-trials that occurred in Ireland are discussed in Chapter 5, along with the legal structures and legislation that made them possible, the heart of this book is a study of belief in witchcraft and popular magic in Ireland among the three main religious denominations (Presbyterian, Church of Ireland, and Roman Catholic). The book focuses on the period that fell between the passing of 1586 Witchcraft Act and its repeal in 1821, but the medieval period (Chapter 1) and the nineteenth and early twentieth century (Chapters 6, 7) are also discussed. By examining witchcraft and magic over such a long period of time, this book joins a growing body of research which traverses the usual chronological and conceptual boundaries imposed on the past by historians: the early modern era, the eighteenth century and (in Ireland) the pre-Famine period.[12] These studies generally regard modern witchcraft and magic not as 'survivals' of older traditions but as an evolving, protean corpus of beliefs, able to adapt in order to remain culturally relevant.[13] The present book is thus able chart change over time in relation to Irish witchcraft and magic much more accurately than otherwise would have been the case. For example, it explores how eighteenth-century, 'enlightened' Irish writers, in common with authors in other countries, re-wrote the history of early modern witchcraft trials for their own ideological ends. I have also endeavoured to note denominational difference (as well as convergence) and to avoid making unproblematic distinctions between malefic and demonic witchcraft beliefs of popular and elite cultures (Chapters 1, 4). Also, for the first time, both harmful magic and its beneficial counterpart are examined together, with one of the main arguments being that cunning-folk, or commercial, multifarious magical practitioners, were a recognisable part of both Protestant and Catholic popular culture in early modern and modern Ireland, just as they were in the British Isles and other parts of Europe. It is further suggested that that although their activities were illegal, from the sixteenth to early nineteenth century, they were largely ignored by secular authorities, if not their ecclesiastical counterparts, who considered them an important obstacle to the imposition of right religion (Chapters 3, 7). Finally, to compensate for the catastrophic destruction of official or public records, I have employed a wide range of new, under-used, and under-analysed primary source material, from surviving church records to private correspondence, to depositions, newspapers, periodicals, books, ballads, almanacs, and printed pamphlets. This process of record compensation, as any historian of medieval or early modern Ireland will tell you, is not just painstaking but often painful!

Scholars starting out on their academic career are already adding to what we know about the non-Christian supernatural in Ireland, with PhD theses currently underway that examine subjects and chronological spans not adequately covered in this book. Jodie Shevlin, for example, is examining Catholic attitudes to mediums, astrologers, ghosts, fairies, and the evil-eye in nineteenth-century Ireland.[14] While John Fulton's work explores witchcraft and popular magic among eighteenth- and nineteenth-century minority Protestant groups, such as Unitarians, Methodists, and Quakers.[15] The present book is therefore by no means comprehensive but breaks the hard ground of the academic study of Irish witchcraft, lays a foundation upon which future studies can be built, and dispels the myth that witchcraft and popular magic were not an important part of Protestant and Catholic culture well into the modern era. To use the words of sceptical witchcraft writer, and eighteenth-century Bishop of Down and Connor, Francis Hutchinson, in his last-ditch attempt to persuade authors to use his controversial, phonetic form of Irish: 'The ice is broken. The press is open.'[16]

1
Witchcraft Belief in Early Modern Ireland

Witchcraft belief in early modern Europe

Before examining in succeeding chapters witchcraft accusations and trials in early modern Ireland, it is essential to explore the belief systems that underpinned them, for as Robin Briggs has argued, witchcraft beliefs 'were the one absolute prior necessity if there were to be trials at all'.[1] The precise relationship between intensity of belief and prosecution rates in early modern Europe, however, is more disputed historical territory: some historians suggest that intensity of witchcraft belief directly affected prosecution rates,[2] while others argue that there is little evidence of such a relationship.[3] This chapter will in some way contribute to this debate and offer a culturally nuanced picture of witchcraft belief in early modern Ireland.

As Brian Levack has pointed out, it was not until 'the middle of the fifteenth century [that] the cumulative concept of witchcraft had acquired all of its basic elements'.[4] By the close of the sixteenth century, in almost everywhere in Protestant and Catholic Europe, belief in witches who destroyed property, person, and livestock using magical means, sometimes in combination with diabolism or Satanically inspired ritual or practices, was deeply embedded at all levels of society.[5] Early modern witchcraft belief has traditionally been divided by historians into elite and popular models. In educated culture, as reflected in works of learned demonology written by lawyers, theologians, and philosophers, witches were worshippers of Satan, men and women who had made an explicit pact with Satan in person at a witches' Sabbath attended by the Devil and fellow witches. They gathered, sometimes in great numbers, to dance, drink, eat (sometimes cannibalistically), and debauch, as well as to engage in the more bizarre aspects of what witches did: night-flying, the sacrifice of children and sexual intercourse with demons.

New recruits also renounced their Christian faith, paid homage to the Devil and were given an indelible Devil's mark as a sign of their new allegiance. All of a witch's magical power and knowledge of the dark arts came from Satan, and their attacks on Christendom were inspired or facilitated by him. Witches were thus pawns in an eternal, cosmic war between good and evil, dark and light, God and the Devil. It was, however, considered unorthodox by the learned to regard Satan as equal to God: the Devil, unlike God, was not an eternal being, therefore able to overturn the natural laws of the universe at will using miracles, *miracula*, but only capable of lesser wonders or illusions, *mira*. The Devil was only able to act with God's permission. God used Satan and witchcraft to punish individual sinners, warn mankind of the wages of sin, and test the faith of the Godly. Protestant demonologists tended to place importance on the demonic pact, and in contrast to their Catholic counterparts downplayed the witches' Sabbath. Popular culture of the masses, on the other hand, centred on its effects, or in early modern language, *maleficium*. In short, they were more concerned about the consequences of what witches did than how they did it or where their power came from. They also worried about how to best prevent, detect, and counter witchcraft attacks, and how to punish those responsible, not only to break a witch's spell, but to obtain closure, revenge or retribution. Harmful magic was, for most people, personal, and local, far removed from the idea of an international threat of a Satanic cult.[6]

The dichotomies of popular/elite culture, demonic/malefic witchcraft have challenged in recent years.[7] In England, witchcraft belief has been shown to have varied between individuals of the same social group.[8] James Sharpe for example has suggested that 'there was no single hegemonic attitude to witchcraft among educated men and women in England but rather a plurality of possible positions'.[9] Furthermore, both elite and lay cultures showed signs of cross-fertilisation.[10] Learned, European demonology not only drew some elements from literary traditions stretching back to classical times some aspects of it had roots in popular magical traditions, such as night-flight and the witches' Sabbath.[11] During the course of the seventeenth century, due to the influence of popular witchcraft pamphlets, sermons, and the impact of the trials themselves, popular conceptions in England increasingly afforded a greater role to the demonic, with Satan appearing to witches, taking their souls and, albeit infrequently, having sexual intercourse with them. The cannibalistic orgies described in continental trial records are absent in their English counterparts. However, something resembling a witches' Sabbath appears in English trials from the early seventeenth century onwards, in particular that of the Lancashire witches in 1612. One of the central motifs of English witchcraft belief from the late sixteenth century onwards, the familiar (a personal demon which took human or animal form, or occasionally shape-shifted from one to the other, and was given to a witch by Satan to perform harmful magic on their behalf), had its origin in elite concern over sorcerers and elite magicians in the middle ages. English witches named their familiars and fed them milk and bread, and they sucked on the witch's blood at the site of the Devil's mark, which was believed to take myriad forms, such as a flea bite or a mole.[12] Established as a method of detecting witches on the continent in the fifteenth century, searching for the Devil's mark appeared in England's first witchcraft pamphlet published in 1566. Thereafter, searching for, and the pricking of, the Devil's mark became a common procedure in trials, albeit one that could provoke fierce, socially and culturally contextualised debates concerning its worth as physical evidence of witchcraft.[13]

The late Christina Larner suggested that diabolism, in particular the demonic pact, was a central part of witchcraft belief in Scotland, and one of the driving forces in Scottish witch-hunting.[14] More recent studies have, however, downgraded the importance of these elements, suggesting that popular belief was a blend of demonological influences and *maleficium*-based notions, often rooted in community, familial or interpersonal rivalries and conflict, and that elite belief showed signs of cultural influence from below.[15] The importance of the demonic pact in most surviving documents between the passing of the Scottish Witchcraft Act (see next chapter) and its repeal in 1736 remains incontrovertible.[16]

Regional variation

Regional variation has also been highlighted as an important factor in determining what witchcraft meant for Scottish people. Ronald Hutton has argued that in the Highlands and Islands of Scotland, a Gaelic-speaking region with its own distinct traditions and culture, belief in malefic/demonic witchcraft was a weakened form of that current in England and other parts of Scotland, becoming weaker the farther north one travelled. In these Gàidhealtachd regions witches were less ferocious and physically repugnant than their lowland counterparts. Nor was witchcraft or magic viewed in these areas as an inherently evil force, with their main malefic activity focusing on magical pilfering of dairy produce, either directly or by transferring its abundance or goodness elsewhere. Along with the fact that these butter-stealing witches were easily countered by a range of counter magic, including a variety of rites, rituals, and amulets, Gaelic-Scottish witches were less feared than other purveyors of supernatural misfortune, namely those who unintentionally harmed by means of innate power located in the eyes (the evil-eye) and malevolent fairies.[17] This presence of a relatively weak witch-figure, and attendant attribution of uncanny misfortune to the 'evil-eye' and fairy attack, has been linked to a relative lack of witch-hunting not only in Highland Scotland but in other parts of Celtic Britain, Wales, Ireland, and the Isle of Man.[18] Lizanne Henderson offers a slightly different reading of Scottish-Gaelic witchcraft by suggesting that in the Gàidhealtachd regions witchcraft belief was essentially that of lowland Scotland, if rather less demonic and more concerned with the evil-eye, fairies, and charming cattle or stealing milk.[19]

This more benign, butter-stealing witch has also been found in early modern Isle of Man, where on May-Eve and May-Day they were believed to destroy or, more importantly, transfer elsewhere the pro-ductiveness ('the tarra' or 'increase') from household crops and cattle.[20] Along with newer ideas of malefic (if not necessarily demonic) witch-craft, which were imported into the country in the seventeenth century from England, the butter-stealing witch was also a common feature of popular culture in rural Wales up until the nineteenth century. They were thought to be particularly active in early May and to be able to transform themselves into hares and cats.[21] Butter- and milk-stealing witches were also found in Scandinavian territories from the middle ages onwards.[22] Nevertheless, shape-shifting witches, if not butter-stealing witches per se, who changed variously into (and back again from) horses, apes, cats, dogs, wolves, and even bees, can occasion-ally be found in parts of Europe which saw heavy witch-hunting, and may have even formed part of popular early modern witchcraft belief, despite being rarely mentioned in court cases. Rooted in folk tradi-tions of classical and medieval times, the concept of shape-shifting did not sit well with learned, elite writers of witchcraft, largely because it implied the theologically unorthodox position that the Devil performed *miracula* rather than *mira*.[23]

Witchcraft in Catholic Ireland: popular culture

Using modern, folklore sources, Ronald Hutton argues that a weak-ened, non-demonic, butter-stealing witch figure was also present in Catholic Gaelic Ireland, and that its presence was felt most in areas geographically closest to those 'affected by British settlement'.[24] In other words, the butter-stealing witch represented the partial and ultimately unsuccessful 'intrusion of foreign concepts' of early modern witchcraft into Gaelic Ireland;[25] a country that 'managed to absorb fervent Counter-Reformation Catholicism without also importing the stereotype of demonic witchcraft that commonly accompanied it'.[26] Hutton's departure from earlier treatments of witchcraft belief in Ireland thus should not be over-estimated, as both Raymond Gillespie and Elwyn Lapoint have argued that Catholic natives and Protestant settlers shared the malefic/demonic witchcraft beliefs characteristic of other early modern European cultures.[27]

In this chapter, I offer a different reading of Irish witchcraft beliefs to those provided by Gillespie, Lapoint, and, to a lesser extent, Hutton. I argue that belief in potentially harmful magic, in particular love magic, had a longer lineage in Ireland, stretching back before Anglo-Norman colonisation in the twelfth century polarised the country religiously, politically and socially along Anglo-Irish and Gaelic lines.[28] Furthermore, it is suggested that belief in butter-stealing witches was a distinct, resilient part of Gaelic-Irish culture.[29] Higher status and better educated Irish Catholics, both in the medieval and early modern periods, were, however, more likely to be influenced by European, elite views of sorcery and demonic witchcraft.

Sources for the study of medieval Ireland are rare,[30] but they demonstrate that the universe was viewed in supernatural and, more specifically, magical terms. People who used magic to harm were often feared and prohibited in Irish Penitential and legal codes, especially female sorcerers and male clerics who used love magic to control fertility or arouse or destroy amorous feelings in others.[31] The sixteenth canon of the *First Synod of St. Patrick*, a circular letter to Irish clergy written in the mid-fifth century by bishops Isernius, Patricius and Auxilius, censured older, pagan belief in witches (in this period, through the use of the feminine forms, '*lamia*' and '*striga*', harmful magic was associated with women), as well as anyone who made accusations of witchcraft.[32] The sixth-century *Penitential of Finnian*, the oldest Irish Penitential, also condemned harmful magic, specifically love magic:

(18) If any cleric or woman who practises magic have led astray anyone by their magic, it is a monstrous sin, but it can be expiated by penance. (Such an offender) shall do penance for six years, three years on an allowance of bread and water, and during the remaining three years he shall abstain from wine and meat. (19) If however such

a person has not led astray anyone but has given (a potion) for the sake of wanton love to someone, he shall do penance for an entire year on an allowance of bread and water. (20) If a woman by her magic destroys the child she has conceived of somebody, she shall do penance for half a year with an allowance of bread and water, and abstain from two years from wine and meat and fast for the six forty-day periods with bread and water.[33]

The *Penitential of St. Columbanus*, which was written after Finnian's, and in which the gender association between magic and women is not as strong, lists penances for those who harm by magical means, or those who used magic to 'excite love' or produce an 'abortion'[34]:

(6) If anyone has destroyed someone by his magic art, let him do penance three years on an allowance of bread and water, and for three other years let him refrain from wine and meat, and then finally in the seventh year let him be restored to communion. But if anyone has used magic to excite love, and has destroyed no one, let him do penance on bread and water for a whole year, if a cleric, for half a year, if a layman, if a deacon for two, if a priest for three; especially if anyone has thus produced abortion, on that account let each add on six extra forty-day periods, lest he be guilty of murder.[35]

Irish legal tracts from the eight century, which detail the system of law used in Gaelic Ireland, Brehon Law, prohibited the carrying of 'love charms', even 'without evil intent',[36] laying down stiffer terms of redress for victims of their use, especially when utilised to engineer a marriage.[37] It also prohibited using a 'charmed morsel' on a dog in order to determine the efficacy of 'a charm' or 'other enchantments',[38] taking human bones from church-yards in order to remove the 'marrow out of them for [the use of] sorcerers',[39] and causing impotence by means of 'bed witchcraft', effected by placing 'charms in the bed'.[40] While in the *Táin Bó Cúalnge*, an example of Irish saga literature of the branch known as the Ulster Cycle which describes the exploits of the Champions of the Red Branch and their King, Conchobar,[41] a shape-shifting sorceress threatens mythological hero Cúchulainn by variously turning into 'an eel', a 'grey she-wolf', and a 'hornless red heifer'.[42] A later medieval list of famous married women in Irish history and literature, *The Ban-Shenchus* (or history or lore of women), told of how 'the daughter of Mael Dun son of Aed (King of Munster)' ensnared 'the keen adventurous prince of the Ui Fidnehti … through her spells'.[43] Gerald of Wales, who first came to Ireland for a short period in 1183, before returning in 1185 with Henry II's youngest son John, in his most influential work, *Topographia Hibernica*, suggested that the culture of the native, Gaelic-Irish included belief in miracles, natural wonders, evil spirits, prophecies, curses, portents, and monstrous births.[44]

More importantly, Irish legal texts and their later commentators, dating from the early and later medieval periods, refer to women who turned themselves into hares to suck milk from the teats of cows on May Day and who also stole the profit from 'old milk' preventing it from being churned into butter. The former offence was taken more seriously than the latter because it was believed that when the milk was stolen directly from the cow using supernatural means the animal itself became bewitched.[45] Gerald of Wales noted in the twelfth century that 'it has also been a frequent complaint, from old times as well as in the present, that certain hags in Wales, as well as in Ireland and Scotland, changed themselves into the shape of hares, that, sucking teats under this counterfeit form, they might stealthy rob other people's milk'. He however went onto 'agree' with the theological position adopted by St. 'Augustine, that neither demons nor wicked men can either create or really change their natures; but those whom God has created, to outward appearance, by his permission, become transformed, so that they appear to be what they are not; the senses of men being deceived and laid asleep by a strange illusion'.[46] By the fourteenth century, even the flesh of a hare was believed to be imbued with magical efficacy. Norfolk-born Archbishop of Armagh, John Colton, prohibited, 'under pain of greater excomm[unication]', the 'diabolical' popular practice of using the 'flesh of a hare' as a 'medicine against various diseases' on the 'feast of preparation', the 'sixth holy day before Easter'.[47]

In early modern England, and elsewhere in Europe, it was widely believed at a popular level that malefic witches harmed cattle and stock and interrupted domestic or agricultural production.[48] In lieu of records written by the Gaelic-Irish, especially relating to those of lower societal levels,[49] the often deeply subjective accounts of Ireland by English commentators demonstrate that newcomers regarded Gaelic-Irish witchcraft as culturally distinct from the own conception of the witch figure. In these accounts, much of the harmful magic that had so concerned medieval, Gaelic Ireland, including that which related to fertility and relationships, is largely absent, save from the motif of the butter-stealing witch. In the 1580s, one-time resident of Limerick and agent of the English Counter-Reformation, Jesuit Fr. William Goode, in testimony included by English Protestant historian William Camden in his hugely influential *Britannia* (1586, trans. 1610), suggested that the Gaelic-Irish believed that when a house was looked at through the 'shoulder blade bone of a sheepe', and a spot or shadow appeared in the middle of it, the owner of it was 'a wicked woman and a witch' who would the 'next summer steale awaie all their butter'. As a counter measure, he reported, they would take some fire from the suspect's house, and if they found 'a hare amongst their heards of cattail on ... May Daye; they kill her, for, they suppose shee is some old trot, that would filch away their butter'. He also described the counter-magic adopted in the face of butter-stealing witches, such as the practice of taking away 'some of the thatch' that hung over the door of a suspected witch and casting it 'into the fire' to counteract its magical efficacy.[50] In the 1590s, Dr Meredith Hanmer, Church of Ireland clergymen and prominent antiquarian, condemned the 'wicked customs and observances' of the Gaelic-Irish, and specifically their belief in butter-stealing witches:

> On May eve they drive their cattle upon their neighbours' corn and eat it up. They were wont to begin from the East ... Unless they do so upon May Eve the witch will have power over the cattle all the year following.[51]

Hanmer's view of belief in butter-stealing witches was located in a particular view of the culture of the Catholic Irish majority. Elizabethan Ireland was marked by the continued failure to effect an Irish Reformation and periodic resistance to, and revolt against, attempts to bring the country under English rule, first through cultural and political assimilation and then conquest and colonisation.[52] Between the early and mid-seventeenth century, as Sean Connolly summarises, 'a better trained and more effectively supervised [Catholic] clergy, operating within a new, tightly organised diocesan and parochial framework, began the task of promoting a more regular pattern of popular religious practice purged of its more glaringly folkloric elements'.[53] Clergy influenced by the Counter-Reformation at various provincial Synods condemned popular magic and invocation, as well as dabbling in witchcraft and diabolism.[54] In this period, Gaelic Ireland remained Catholic and Irish-speaking, but although it had 'been largely demilitarised, and its political structures were being rapidly undermined by confiscation, legal redefinition and cultural assimilation', for their new English rulers 'cultural antagonism was reinforced by religious divisions', resulting in 'the stereotype of the Irish lower orders as irredeemably barbarous and wholly lacking in civic virtues, in thrall to a superstitious religion, and drawn by their idleness to a wasteful and unproductive pastoralism, with all the squalor and poverty which such a way of life entailed'.[55]

In 1691, Suffolk-born Anglican clergyman and historian, Laurence Echard, pointed out that the native, 'wild Irish', as opposed to 'the English' and 'the more civilised sort of Irish, who are very conformable to the customs and laws of our nation',[56] 'count her a wicked woman or a witch that cometh to fetch fire from 'em on May Day'. He further stated that 'they are of opinion, that if their butter be stolen', it would be restored by burning the thatch that hung over the suspect's door.[57] Echard may have been speaking of Irish butter-stealing witches in much the same way as his fellow countrymen a century earlier but he was living in a radically altered Ireland. The biggest religious and ethnic group remained the Catholic Gaelic-Irish and by the 1730s they made up around 80% of the estimated 2.5 million people in Ireland (the population had grown by around 25% in the previous 50 years), and their majority status was felt everywhere outside Protestant Ulster, especially in non-urban areas.[58] However, the Jacobean plantation, along with seventeenth-century immigration from England and Scotland, drastically increased the numbers of Protestants in Ireland, especially Presbyterians in Ulster.[59] By the very late seventeenth and early eighteenth century, a Protestant Ascendancy, peopled by communicants of the Church of Ireland, had been established which aimed to secure their religion and political and economic position through a series of Penal Laws that would remove competition and opposition from Irish Catholic and Presbyterian non-conformists.[60]

The evil-eye

Christina Larner has pointed out that in the Highlands of Scotland, as well as Southern Italy, 'known individuals ... are credited with possessing the evil-eye which is regarded as distinct from witchcraft and can cause unintended harm to the person "overlooked"'.[61] While Ronald Hutton, using medieval literary and modern folklore sources, has argued the unintentional evil-eye was an explanatory mechanism for misfortune utilised by the Gaelic-Irish in the early modern period, when in most other places in Europe, including England, malefic witchcraft performed the same function.[62] Jacqueline Borsje, however, has suggested that the Gaelic-speaking native population, as evidenced by the rich literature of the medieval period, conceptualised the evil-eye as being used both intentionally for nefarious ends and unintentionally by those unlucky enough to have inherited the gift, and has even linked the former to the activities of butter-stealing witches, who used it to steal the productiveness from milk; a contention she holds is also applicable to early modern Gaelic-Irish culture.[63] Fr. Goode in the late sixteenth century described a wise woman who cured livestock afflicted by the intentional evil-eye.[64] Physician Thomas Ady, writing some time later in the mid-seventeenth century, suggested that it was widely believed in Ireland that 'eye-biting witches' blighted cows by making them blind, a condition he explained away in the great tradition of English scepticism to which his writing belonged as being 'a common disease in that country'.[65] In 1683, Thomas Munck noted that the Gaelic-Irish inhabitants of Kildare protected their children from the unintentional evil-eye by spitting in their faces.[66] In 1584, another even more sceptical English demonologist, Reginald Scot, wrote that 'the *Irishmen* addict themselves wonderfullie to the credit and practice ... that not onelie their children, but their cattell, are (as they call it) eyebitten, when they fall suddenlie sick'.[67]

The notion that the evil-eye could be both intentional and unintentional was one also recognised in Irish Protestant culture, but here, as in other parts of Europe, it was firmly associated with malefic witchcraft.[68] Florence Newton was arrested in late March 1661 for bewitching (by means of demonic possession) Mary Longdon, a literate young servant to local gentleman, John Pyne in the English settler port town of Youghal, Co. Cork, which contained at that time around 2,500 people. Newton claimed that she had not 'bewitched' the girl 'but it may be that she had *over-looked* her, and there was a great difference betwixt bewitching and over-looking'.[69] Academic, theologian, and member of the Cambridge Platonists group, Henry More, who commented on the Newton trial in Joseph Glanvill's posthumously published late seventeenth-century compilation, *Saducismus Triumphatus* (London, 3rd ed., 1689), made no such distinction between 'over-looking and bewitching', or indeed the intentional or unintentional evil-eye.[70]

Fairy belief

Although the word 'fairy' itself is a later English import, the supernatural beings they describe, the *aes síde* (who were either immortal or at the least very long-lived), formed part of native Irish literary culture from the early medieval period, perhaps even before.[71] Throughout the early modern period, fairy belief in Gaelic-Irish culture provided a cogent explanatory mechanism for misfortune, even more so than butter-stealing witches or even the evil-eye: from the destruction of agricultural produce to death and illness in humans and livestock.[72]

In late 1678, in Co. Wicklow, Dr John Moore, an erstwhile London schoolmaster and recent purchaser of a local estate, was widely believed to have been abducted by a group of fairies on horseback, taken to a fairy fort and then to a feast in the woods. He was returned unharmed the next morning, believing he had been abducted because he had broken the fairy rule of speaking openly about an earlier abduction.[73] Church of Ireland clergyman, and correspondent to the Dublin Philosophical Society, Rev John Keogh noted in a letter of 1684 that a small, brittle pale, white 'fairy dart' or 'elf-shot', 'having some resemblance to flint' and possessing very small 'studs or prickles' on the edges, was produced by one of his Gaelic Irish neighbours in Co. Roscommon, as 'proof of the power fairies have to strike man or beast with some occult wound or distemper'.[74] He went on to describe another Co. Roscommon woman who 'some years agoe' having a cow that had died, gave its meat to the poor who, upon eating, found it to contain 'a piece of fairy dart'. The old woman in question was said to have kept the dart, claiming it contained medicinal and healing virtues, especially in ensuring 'the safe and sure' delivery of babies.[75] 'Elf-bolts' or 'fairy arrows' can also be found in early modern Scotland and were believed to induce sickness and death in animals. They were often used as protective or curative devices when discovered.[76] In early modern (and beyond), Gaelic-Irish culture, cunning-folk, along with specific rituals and magical protective devices, were often used to counter fairy attacks.[77]

Witchcraft in Catholic Ireland: elite culture

If European conceptions of malefic, demonic witchcraft were largely absent among the mass of the Gaelic-Irish population, and they tended not to make formal witchcraft accusations, it would seem that the Catholic elite, both in pre- and post-Reformation eras, were more influenced by traditional ideas of sorcery, demonology, and witchcraft. In Europe, before 1300, trials for harming using magical means were extremely rare.[78] The first three decades of the fourteenth century, however, witnessed sporadic outbreaks of sorcery-cum-treason plots in England, France, and Germany, in which prominent individuals were accused of using 'high' ceremonial or ritual magic to further social aspirations or to remove political rivals.[79] In the period that followed, 1330 to 1375, politically motivated trials tailed off but there were numerous trials for sorcery in Germany, France, Italy, and England, while the next 50 years saw an increase in Switzerland, Italy, France, and Germany in trials in which charges of diabolism also featured. These prosecutions were carried out against a backdrop of social disruption caused by the plague and in a new legal context that saw the adoption in local courts of inquisitorial procedure, making it easier and less dangerous for accusers to make formal complaints, as responsibility was now placed in the hands of judiciaries.[80] As Brian Levack has argued, 'prior to the 1420s, the concept of witchcraft as a crime involving both harmful magic and devil-worship was in the process of formation: therefore, it is problematic to speak of the prosecutions that took place during those years as witchcraft trials ... [as] most such trials ... were prosecutions either for simple *maleficium* or for ritual magic'.[81] In the century after 1420, however, there was an increase in sorcery trials (often involving diabolism), especially in Switzerland, France, and Germany.[82] Ironically, just as laws were put in place across Europe against witchcraft,[83] witchcraft trials in the period 1520 to 1560 began to slow, and in some places even declined. The next 20 years, however, saw the first indication, in Toulouse in France and Wiesensteig in south-west Germany, of the type of epidemic witch-hunting (characterised by large hunts and intense periods of prosecution) that would sweep through western and central Europe in the period 1580 to 1630: in Lorraine in France in the late 1580s and 1590s; in Spain in the 1610s; and in Wurzberg and Bamberg during the 1620s. Although this period saw the majority of all witchcraft trials, epidemic witch-hunting should not be overplayed, as most witches were executed not during large hunts but individually or as part of small groups of two or three people in sporadic trials. The mid- to late seventeenth and early eighteenth century is generally regarded as the period of decline in educated belief, of which more will be said in Chapter 6.[84]

Surviving primary sources suggest that later medieval, Catholic Ireland, specifically that part of society that associated itself with English law and customs, was not immune from the sorcery-cum-treason accusations, involving harmful magic in high places, that were present in medieval, pre-Reformation Europe. In Kilkenny in 1324–1325, wealthy Dame Alice Kyteler was accused by her stepchildren (from a number of different marriages) of using sorcery to murder their respective fathers. The accusations were inquired into by Franciscan Bishop of Ossory, Richard de Ledrede (Leatherhead), who accused Kyteler, and 10 male and female accomplices, of heresy (by virtue of her alleged dealings with the Devil) and sorcery. After interrogation and flogging, one of the accused, Petronella de Midia, gave evidence against Kyteler, who evaded arrest by fleeing to England. Her co-conspirators, however, were variously excommunicated, banished, and flogged, while Petronella was burned alive.[85] Accusations of sorcery, in which the demonic element was low, continued into the fifteenth century. In 1447, John Mey, Archbishop of Armagh, along with other prelates in the House of Lords, with the 'entire assent of the Lords spiritual and temporal and the commons of ... parliament', pronounced that King Henry VI should be 'certified' that an unnamed 'man of rank' had been 'slandered' by the 'subtle malice and malicious suits of certain persons' who wrongly accused him of harming and killing people using 'sorcery or necromancy'. They were further concerned that the good name of Ireland had been tainted by the allegations and were anxious to point out, 'that no such art was attempted at any time in this land, known or rumoured among the people, nor any opinion had or entertained of the same by the lay men in this land until now'.[86] Whether this statement that Ireland up until that point in time had been free from sorcery plots was a case of genuine ignorance of the Kyteler case or merely one of selective memory it is impossible to know. Accusations of sorcery reached farther down the social scale, as on the eve of the Tudor Reformation an un-named Catholic woman lodged a charge of defamation for being called a sorcerer at the consistory court of the Archdiocese of Armagh.[87]

By the mid-fifteenth century, the cumulative concept of witchcraft had penetrated educated Catholic culture. In 1544, Charles Fitzarthur sent an un-named 'witche' 'to the Lord Deputie', Sir Anthony St. Leger,[88] and in May 1571 'a woman accused ... of wychcrafte, [and] for enlardgynge of prysoners' was brought before Sir Barnaby Fitzpatrick (MacGillapatrick), second baron of Upper Ossory. Fitzpatrick was an outwardly Anglicised Gaelic Lord raised at the court of Edward VI and a loyal supporter of the English Crown but his lordship remained, culturally-speaking, a Gaelic dynasty presiding over an Irish-speaking, Catholic population.[89] Fitzpatrick claimed that the woman, upon 'beynge examined, dyd disclose a [w]hole pack of wyches, and they being apprehended, and examined dyd confess that the[i]r ch[i]efe wyche was a womane of' his step mother's, Elizabeth O'Connor, and together 'they were all sett on to do me harme and to destroye me'. Fitzpatrick was convinced he had only escaped from their 'dyvles practis' due to God's Providence. Having confessed to the charges laid against her, Elizabeth fled to Kilkenny, and according to Fitzpatrick 'entysed' his father, Barnaby (Brian) Fitzpatrick, first Baron of Ossory, to go with her.[90] Underlying this accusation was a tangled web of political rivalry and interpersonal and familial tension. Barnaby Fitzpatrick's relationship with his family, and his step-mother in particular, had become strained to breaking point from the mid-1550s onwards as he tried to wrest control of Upper Ossory from his father, who had increasingly distanced himself from the influence of the English crown. In 1564, in Upper Ossory, Barnaby and his Royal troops took to the battlefield against his father's soldiers, and five years later Elizabeth I made him regent of the lordship on the grounds of the first baron's mental incapacity.[91] In a letter written in 1571, Barnaby further claimed that Elizabeth O'Connor had not only turned his father against him but had been involved in the 'late rebellion of the Buttlers' and 'was confederate and assured to the rebels'.[92] In 1569, Sir Edmund Butler and his brothers joined forces with rebels, James Fitz Maurice Fitzgerald and Donal MacCarthy Mór, earl of Clanclare, in a revolt against the English crown and undertook an ultimately unsuccessful siege of Kilkenny. Butler's revolt, however, was not only in response to English colonisation and attempts to impose Protestantism on Ireland, but also represented a personal vendetta against local loyalists, including Barnaby Fitzpatrick, who once again fought on the side of the crown.[93]

In the seventeenth century, Catholic lay elites continued to level accusations of witchcraft attacks on humans. In September 1640, Catholic Katherine Manners, widow of the murdered George Villiers, duke of Buckingham, and new wife of Randal MacDonnell, the extravagant and subsequently heavily indebted second earl of Antrim, claimed to have been bewitched (causing her to miscarry) by a number of poor women living near Dunluce Castle, Co. Antrim, her main Irish residence from 1638.[94] It is probable that the accused women came from the pre-plantation town established a few decades earlier by Randal MacDonnell, first earl of Antrim, to accommodate around 240 families, from merchants to agricultural labourers, of mainly Scottish, Presbyterian heritage.[95] A woman with contacts at the top of the Dublin Administration, she ensured that Lord Deputy Sir Christopher Wandesford was made aware of her situation. Believing it would please Lord Lieutenant Sir Thomas Wentworth, earl of Strafford, his cousin and patron, as well as King Charles I, on 4 September 1640, Wandesford wrote to Wentworth's client and chief enforcer of his ambitious reconstruction of the Church of Ireland between 1633 and 1640, Bishop of Derry, John Bramhall. In the letter, he instructed Bramhall to use 'all possible meanes ... to discover this practyse' of witchcraft, and 'to assist S[i]r Charles Coote and Mr Arther Hill in this disquisition'. 'And to that purpose', Wandesford continued, he had added Bramhall's name 'to the commission of the peace for the countye of Antrym'.[96] In east Ulster, by the early seventeenth century, Justices of the Peace (JPs)[97] were responsible for the day to day maintenance of law and order, usually as a body of justices gathered together by the Sherriff in county towns such as Newry in Co. Down and Carrickfergus in Co. Antrim. The number of JPs in Co. Antrim in the 1630s was very small due to the fact there were a limited number of gentry of sufficient economic and social standing to impose their authority and fill available places. This partly explains why Wandesford gave Bramhall a commission, as well as to ensure that a case involving such a high-profile prosecutor was handled well.[98] When the political will that drove the investigation was withdrawn, the case was dropped. As 1640 wore on, both Wandesford and Wentworth faced parliamentary opposition to their administration, which eventually led to the latter's impeachment, arrest, and execution in May 1641. Bramhall himself, between 1640 and 1641, was imprisoned, impeached, and tried, as was the third main partner in Wentworth's reconstruction programme, the Archbishop of Canterbury, William Laud.[99] The political situation in Ulster worsened in the next few months[100] and Dunluce town was burnt to the ground by insurgents in January 1642. Katherine departed for England a few months later.[101]

Witchcraft in Irish Protestant culture

It is clear that Protestant settlers, from the two main denominations of Anglican and Presbyterian, from the mid-sixteenth century onwards brought their witchcraft beliefs with them to Ireland. These beliefs become particularly noticeable at a popular level from the mid-seventeenth century, primarily because they occasionally culminated in formal accusations of witchcraft and a handful of successful prosecutions of their fellow communicants and neighbours. These cases suggest that popular concerns over witchcraft centred on the tangible effects of *maleficium* rather than diabolism. However, the fact that some Irish witches were thought to own familiars and a number of victims became demonically possessed leads one to believe that among the mass of the Protestant population, witches were more than purveyors of *maleficium*. It also seems that human victims were more often than not the target of a witch's harmful magic rather than livestock, produce, or property.[102] Unlike their continental European counterparts, English witches were less likely to be accused of spreading epidemic diseases, creating bad weather (especially hailstones) which damaged crops and property, or interfering with procreation or sexual activity. Harming or killing humans by means of witchcraft was always taken particularly seriously in English communities, and by the end of the seventeenth century local legal elites were only prosecuting individuals accused of these sorts of crime, in contrast to their predecessors, who were more willing to proceed on accusations of the magical destruction of property or interference with domestic or agricultural produce. A particularly British form of witchcraft was that involving demonic possession where the witch summoned demons and commanded them to enter the bodies of victims and control their behaviour and speech. English witches harmed using innate power, the intentional evil-eye or a variety of magical means, including ritual curses, touching their victim, and the use of symbolic gestures, charms, spells, and magically imbued objects.[103]

It would seem that witches in Protestant Ireland harmed in much the same manner. In Co. Antrim in 1711, image magic, in the form of a knotted apron, was used to bewitch an elderly woman, Mrs Ann Haltridge, and later a young girl called Mary Dunbar.[104] Image magic was a technique that regularly appeared in English witchcraft cases and usually came in the form of waxen pictures resembling intended victims. The images were then melted or stuck with pins, and through a process of sympathetic magic the victim was subsequently harmed or killed.[105] Image magic that bears more resemblance to the Ulster variant, in the form of knotted strips of material, known to contemporaries as 'poppets', are mentioned in the witness testimonies given during the infamous witch-hunt in Salem, Massachusetts in 1692, where the accusations of a number of female demoniacs led to over 100 formal accusations and 19 executions.[106] Touching, cursing, and the intentional evil-eye were all said to have been employed by Florence Newton in 1661.[107] Protestant Irish witches also used spells and potions to harm and some did so by giving victims food or drink. In the small, Presbyterian town of Antrim, in May 1698, an educated, nine-year-old girl from gentry stock ate a sorrel leaf given to her by an elderly beggar woman, whom she had just furnished with bread and beer. Almost immediately, the girl became demonically possessed and began 'to be tortured in her bowels, to tremble all over, and then to be convulst, and ... to swon away and fall as one dead'.[108] The girl was taken to see a number of physicians, with which Antrim was unusually (for the time) well-stocked, who failed to cure her and presumably confirmed she was demonically possessed.[109] She was then taken to the local Presbyterian minister, Rev. William Adair, but he had 'scarce laid' his 'hands on her when the child was transformed by the daemon into such shap[e]s as a man that hath not beheld it with his eyes, would hardly be brought to imagine'. The demon in the girl then 'began first to rowl itself about, and nixt to vomit horse dung, needles, pins, hairs, feathers, bottoms of thread, pieces of glass, window nails draven out of a cart or coach wheels, an iron knife above a span long, egg and fish shells'.[110]

Elite belief in Witchcraft in Protestant Ireland

The scattered references to witchcraft in elite culture suggest it was more demonically and theologically informed than in plebeian culture. English author, soldier, and a man intensely hostile to Irish Catholicism, Barnabe Rich, writing in 1610, regarded the Gaelic-Irish as more susceptible to witchcraft and sorcery than Protestants due to the fact their perceived adherence to a superstitious faith made them easy prey for the temptations of the Devil:

> for the Devil hath ever been most frequent and conversant amongst infidels, Turks, Papistes, and such other, that doe neither know nor love God, then he can be amongst those that are the true professors of the Gospell of Christ.[111]

In doing so, Rich was espousing classic Elizabethan Protestant rhetoric that equated Catholicism with superstition and institutionally-sanctioned imposture of supernatural phenomenon. Furthermore, it became almost a literary and rhetorical cliché to link Catholics with magic and witchcraft. Protestants of this hue can be seen to have been in some way responding to Catholic propaganda in Marian England, which equated Protestantism with superstition.[112] Euan Cameron has suggested that Counter-Reformation Catholic theologians on the continent 'accused Protestants of being playthings of demons and sorcerers, and blamed them for the perceived rise of sorcery in the contemporary world'.[113] While in the late seventeenth century, high-church Bishop of Derry, Ezekiel Hopkins, saw witches as agents of the devil who had renounced their covenant with God:

> the most execrable idolatry that is, is that of entring into league and correspondence with the Devil; to consult and invoke him, and by any wicked arts implore, or make use of his help and assistance. And of this are those guilty in the highest degree, who enter into any express compact with the Devil; which is always ratified with some homage of worship given to him.[114]

In October 1693, Whig Archbishop of Dublin, William King,[115] wrote anonymously to Congregationalist minister Cotton Mather[116] to convince him that the best way for New Englanders, in the aftermath of the Salem witch-hunts, to protect themselves against 'Satan or any of his imps' was to turn their backs on non-conformity and be baptised and confirmed according to the liturgy of the Church of Ireland. The opening sentence of his letter belied the demonological nature of witchcraft beliefs: 'I have read over your account of witches in your plantation, I am much concerned to observe the power the devil has over your people'.[117] During the investigation into the bewitchment of Mary Dunbar in early eighteenth-century Islandmagee, Co. Antrim, Church of Ireland curate of the place, Rev. David Robb, presented 'a handsome discourse upon the danger of witchcraft, and the necessity of repentance, in order to obtain eternal life' to two of the accused Islandmagee witches.[118] At their trial held at Co. Antrim Assizes at Carrickfergus on 31 March 1711, one of the presiding judges, Tory Justice of the Common Pleas, Anthony Upton, also demonstrated a straightforward elite view of witches, as those who harmed using magical powers and 'were utterly abandoned to the Devil' and 'had renounced God'.[119] Dublin reprints of Protestant devotional works contained a demonological view of witches. Richard Allestree's classic devotional text, *The Whole Duty of Man* ..., first published in England in 1658 and printed for a second time for a Dublin audience in 1714, warned its readers that 'all dealing with the Devil is here vowed against, whether it be by practising witchcraft ourselves, or by consulting with those that do'.[120]

Certainly by the eighteenth century, members of the Irish protestant ascendency were collecting (and presumably reading) English and continental books on witchcraft,[121] unsurprising given the fact Ireland lacked an indigenous demonology or pamphlet literature.[122] During the latter half of the seventeenth-century, print culture grew dramatically in Ireland, indicated by the increasingly organised nature of the print trade, both in the provinces and the metropolis, an increase in the volume of the material printed, whether representing indigenous writing or 'pirated' copies of English works, and a leap in the number of books imported into the country from (mainly) England. English-speaking, educated protestant clergymen were thus in the intellectual and financial position to exploit this new literary culture.[123] As Stuart Clark has pointed out, there were sound theologically reasons for why books on witchcraft should find their way into the libraries of Irish Protestant clergy:

In the context of making a library for God it is utterly predictable that, in sixteenth- and seventeenth-century conditions, the devil should have a place in it too- and a prominent place. It was a commonplace of the time that in order to know God (and good) one needed to know the Devil (and evil)- more important still, that without accepting the existence of a devil one could not accept the existence of a God (the argument directed against 'Sadduceeism'.[124]

Bishop of Down and Connor, Francis Hutchinson's witchcraft-book collecting had a specific purpose: to facilitate his literary investigations into witchcraft, of which the pinnacle was his sceptical opus, *An Historical Essay Concerning Witchcraft*, published in 1718, two years before he was promoted to the Irish episcopate.[125] His large library in his mansion house on his impressive estate in Co. Antrim contained, by the 1730s, over 707 books in 712 volumes, of which 92 titles were dedicated to 'witches, conjuror's, devils, [and] oracles'.[126] It included John Webster's *Displaying of Suppos'd Witchcraft ...* (1677), Reginald Scot's *Discoverie of Witchcraft ...* (1584), Meric Casaubon's *Of Incredulity and Credulity in things Natural, Civil, and Divine ...* (1668), Jean Bodin's *De la Demonomanie des Sorciers ...* (1580) and Richard Baxter's *The Certainty of the World of Spirits and Consequently, of the Immortality of Souls* (1691).[127]

Conclusion

In this chapter it has been suggested that witchcraft belief in early modern Ireland was divided across cultural and religious as well as social lines. First of all, it has been contended that the female butter-witch, found in other parts of early modern Britain and who stole milk in hare form or appropriated its goodness by magical means, was not, as existing historiography maintains, a corrupt version of the malefic/demonic witch figure found in most of early modern continental Europe, but was evident in Ireland from at least the early medieval period. In medieval Ireland, butter-stealing witches formed part of a larger corpus of magical beliefs that were often focused on women who used magic to adversely affect fertility or engender or destroy relationships. Without this association, or indeed any connection, however tenuous, to the demonic, in the early modern period, and with their activities restricted to certain times of the ritual year and fended-off by a range of counter measures, butter-stealing witches represented a less threatening form of harmful magic. Early modern sources have confirmed Ronald Hutton's evaluation that the type of harm believed to have been inflicted on humans by malefic and/or demonic witches elsewhere in Europe was in Gaelic Ireland attributed to fairy attack. However, the role played by the unintentional evil-eye in inhibiting the uptake of malefic witch beliefs in Gaelic-Irish culture has been downplayed, not least of all because it was linked to the intentional activities of butter-stealing witches, as well as being present in Irish Protestant witchcraft belief. Furthermore, in contrast to previous studies, an examination of the Pre-Reformation era has demonstrated that Catholic elites, in particular those who by inclination or birth were more culturally English, were mostly concerned with politically-orientated sorcery plots. In the early modern period, being more influenced by continental demonology, Irish Catholic elites, especially the clergy, increasingly saw witchcraft accusation in much the same way as their Protestant counterparts, as agents of the devil who harmed and killed using a range of magical means. The Protestant settler population, of all social levels, brought with them a strong belief in witchcraft, albeit with diabolic witchcraft most heavily felt at higher social levels, from their native countries, especially Scotland, where belief was the driving force behind accusation. Before examining Irish witchcraft accusations, it is first of all necessary to explore the laws and legal machinery available to process them.

2
Witchcraft Legislation and Legal Administration in Early Modern Ireland

If a small minority of Irish Catholics and the majority of Irish Protestants in the early modern period believed in the type of malefic/demonic witchcraft feared all over Europe did it result in formal accusations for witchcraft and if so how were these handled? This raises the question, as to whether in Ireland, as in other parts of Europe, witch-hunting 'was essentially a judicial operation ... the entire process of discovering and eliminating witches, from denunciation to punishment, usually occurred under judicial auspices'.[1] These questions are considered in Chapter 4, but before this can be done we must first of all consider Ireland's legal system and in particular the Irish witchcraft statute of 1586, which has in the past been cited rather than studied, or indeed has it been placed within the context of the passing of witchcraft laws in other parts of the British Isles.[2]

Witchcraft legislation

Witch-hunting came relatively late to the British Isles, beginning after witchcraft became, in the late to mid-sixteenth century, a civil, statutory crime, as opposed to an offence that only concerned ecclesiastical authorities.[3] For example, although the pre-Reformation Scottish church arbitrated some witchcraft cases, witch-hunting only became serious post-Reformation, after the passing of the Scottish Witchcraft Act.[4] This Act was passed in June 1563 but drafted in December 1562 by a minister or ministers of the Fifth General Assembly of the Protestant Church and passed by the Scottish parliament in June 1563, a few years before the country witnessed its first witchcraft 'panics', such as that at Easter Ross in 1577. The Scottish Witchcraft Act was part of the new Protestant church's attempt to impose on the common people a new, theologically correct model of Christian belief and practice which included targeting surviving Catholic practices and popular 'superstition' involving fairy belief, magical healing, and popular magic. In fact, the Scottish witchcraft statute was not specifically aimed at malefic witches but charmers, the Scottish version of cunning-folk. The official theology of Protestant reformers regarded cunning-folk, just like witches, as gaining their power from the devil, and thus little different from malefic witches. The Scottish 1563 Act handed the death penalty not only to those guilty of practising popular magic but to those who consulted them. In practice, there was little thirst among ordinary people for the punishment of cunning-folk, and Kirk Sessions tended to punish them using public penance. Furthermore, although not intended as such by the radical Protestant reformers who drafted it, the Scottish witchcraft statute was used to prosecute demonic, malefic witches up until the early eighteenth century. As it failed to provide a useful definition for what the crime of witchcraft was, it was thus left to the courts to decide what a witch was, through custom and practice. It became practice for ministers (who were becoming more demonologically aware due to the republishing of continental texts) and the courts in the very late sixteenth and seventeenth centuries to define a witch as someone who had made a pact with Satan.[5]

By the sixteenth century, witchcraft and popular magic was of concern not only to the English government, but to ecclesiastical authorities and the malefic witch figure had been recognisable in popular culture for over a century. The first English witchcraft statute, and also the harshest, was passed in 1541/2 and imposed the death sentence for felonious invocation and conjuration of spirits by sorcery, and various magical practices associated with cunning-folk and malefic witchcraft.[6] Very few people were prosecuted under its dictates and it was repealed in 1547 by Edward VI along with other Henrician legislation.[7] In January 1563 the English parliament passed a new Witchcraft Act.[8] This was drawn up by the Privy Council to strengthen Elizabeth I's resurgent Protestant government, to enable the prosecution of those who used magic in a treasonable manner, in particular Roman Catholic plotters, and satiate those in the ecclesiastical hierarchy who wanted to clamp down on sorcery, witchcraft, and idolatry.[9] In common with the majority of continental witchcraft acts, when discussing witches, the 1563 Witchcraft Act employed gender neutral language.[10] The Act did not place emphasis on the demonic nature of witchcraft nor did it discuss a demonic pact, but instead concentrated 'on the physical harm that witches caused their victims ... [and] stressed supposedly verifiable, material grounds for conviction'.[11] Despite how the 1563 Witchcraft Act was interpreted by those who used it to make formal accusations, or the judiciary who based their prosecutions on them, this Witchcraft Act did not only, or even specifically, target the practices of the malefic witch but all magical practitioners, including commercial cunning-folk and conjurors of evil spirits. Consequently, it has been suggested that it should be referred to as the Conjuration Act in order to reflect its content more accurately.[12]

The 1586 Irish Witchcraft Act was almost identical in content to that passed in England thirteen years earlier[13] and thus could be regarded as an Irish conjuration act. It stipulated that those found guilty of causing illness or injury and destroying goods or livestock by magic, or anyone abetting them, would be imprisoned for a year and 'upon the market day ... stand openly upon the pillorie by the space of six houres'. During their six hour stint in the pillory, they were to 'confesse ... their errour and offence'. If a second offence was committed, or the victim had been murdered, they were to 'suffer death as a felon'. The Act also made the invocation or 'conjurations of evill and wicked spirites' for 'any purpose' a felony punishable by death. If accused of these crimes, peers of the realm were to be tried in the House of Lords 'as it is used in cases of felonie or treason'. For practising 'beneficial' magic, such as love magic, finding hidden treasure, or lost or stolen goods using charms, symbols, or incantations, the punishment was the same as for harmful witchcraft for a first offence. A second offence promised life imprisonment and forfeiture of all property to the crown.[14]

St. John D. Seymour, author of the first scholarly work on Irish witchcraft, argued that the 1586 Witchcraft Act was the result of the fact that two justices of the Assize, Lord Justice William Drury and Sir Edward Fitton, were frustrated by the lack of a witchcraft statute while on circuit a few years earlier.[15] The solitary surviving source relating to this episode informs us that in November 1578 the two men visited Kilkenny, in the centre of Thomas Butler, 10th earl of Ormond's lordship, and 'the jail being full' they immediately held court sessions, after which they executed 'thirty-six persons', including 'two witches by natural law', having 'found no law to try them by' in Ireland.[16] There is, however, no evidence to suggest that the framers of the Irish legislation were reacting to this trial or even had it in mind, and we know nothing about the age, gender, or names of the two 'witches'. As we shall see, witchcraft was only of sporadic concern to the educated elite before this time, and popular fear of witchcraft arguably came in the later seventeenth century when Protestants flooded into Ulster.[17] Furthermore, the only official concern shown with regard to popular magic came from ecclesiastical authorities.[18] It has also been suggested that the Kilkenny executions were an attempt by supporters of courtier and Lord Deputy, Sir Henry Sidney, to demonstrate 'the consequences of resistance to the social, political, and religious change the Elizabethan government in Ireland represented and required'.[19]

If the Scottish Witchcraft Act was an ecclesiastical measure conceived by concerned Godly, Protestant elites, and the English Act an official one passed for religious and political reasons, as well as catering to popular concern over witchcraft, the Irish Act was borne of a larger policy of the 'rolling-out' of the Elizabethan statute book in Ireland.[20] A politically deadlocked first session of the Dublin Parliament, which opened in April 1585, saw an old English majority in the House of Commons, and to a lesser extent the Lords, defeat key pieces of legislation introduced by the government of deputy, Sir John Perrot.[21] The 15 bills returned to the second session of the Irish parliament that reconvened in April–May 1586, Victor Treadwell has argued, 'were sufficient proof of the Queen's desire for a short, business-like session devoted almost exclusively to essential official measures'. Among these were 'three more extracts from the original compendium of English statutes: on witchcraft, fraudulent deeds and leasehold'.[22] As the witchcraft bill was one of the least controversial and complex handled that session, it passed quickly (in just over a fortnight) and easily through the Irish Houses of Commons and Lords and was given Royal Assent on 14 May 1586.[23] Bills that passed through parliament un-defeated or un-amended during this second session of parliament have been described by Stephen Ellis as 'innocuous commonwealth measures'.[24] This relatively easy passage of the Irish Witchcraft Act contrasted starkly with that of its English counterpart which endured a more torturous and controversial passage through the Westminster parliament.[25]

The 1604 Witchcraft Act brought in by the Westminster parliament during the first year of the reign of James I, who at that time at least took a personal interest in the prosecution of witches, was never extended to Ireland.[26] The 1604 Act was harsher than the Elizabethan if not the Henrician Witchcraft Act, as all witchcraft offences, not only those which ended in murder, carried the death penalty. Conjuring or invoking evil spirits had been banned under the previous act, but now owning evil spirits or familiars was made illegal. Love magic, treasure hunting, and damaging a victim's goods were to be punished by a year's imprisonment and stints in the pillory, but a second offence was made a capital crime. The *maleficium* of the witch was no longer the main focus of the legislation as it highlighted their demonic apostasy and the methods and tools witches used to harm, such as using dead bodies for magical purposes. In theory, if not in practice, the 1604 Act made it easier for witches to be convicted as all that was needed was an assertion (or their own confession) that the accused owned a spirit or a familiar.[27]

Why the harsher 1604 Act was not introduced into Ireland remains a mystery.[28] The fact that the Irish parliament had not sat since 1586, and would not do so again until 1613, may have been a factor.[29] There was also still virtually no public concern about the threat of witchcraft[30] in a country (especially in Ulster) wracked by political and religious divisions in the immediate aftermath of the bloody Nine Years' War and just before the flight of the Ulster Earls in 1607.[31] However, in October 1614, during the 1613–15 sitting of the Irish parliament, a bill was introduced into the House of Commons entitled, 'An Act for trial of Murthers, etc., in several counties'. It was read for the first time in November 1614, read a second time and put into a select committee in April 1615. The committee's report delivered to the House on 3 May by Sir Christopher Nugent concluded that the bill should go no further. Upon being put to a vote or division, it was read for a third time two days later but upon a further division it was finally quashed.[32] Surviving sources do not inform us of the grounds upon which opponents defeated the bill, or by how many votes, but what we do know is that it met its fate in a very religiously divided House of Commons, where 'in a house of 210, the Protestants numbered 108, the recusants 102'.[33] Furthermore, the whole final session of parliament had been marked by a deterioration in relations between the House of Commons and the Lords over jurisdictional issues, in particular the scope of their respective legislative functions.[34] The bill eventually passed into law during the next sitting of the Irish parliament, after a relatively smooth passage through both houses between November 1634 and February 1635.[35] The text for the 'Act for the Triall of Murders and Felonies committed in severall counties'[36] reveals it was framed to close a legal loophole based on jurisdictional limitations imposed on judiciaries. This loophole allowed killers (or their accessories) who 'feloniously stricken, poisoned, or bewitched' to escape prosecutions if their victim died in a county other than the site of the original crime. The inclusion of 'witchcraft' in the 1635 Act was comprehensiveness on the part of the legislation's framers: part of an attempt to list the main methods of murder or manslaughter, rather than an explicit attempt to curb its practice.[37] This sitting of parliament was marked by the Lord Deputy, Thomas Wentworth's attempt to modernise the legislative framework of the country, part of a bigger ambition to re-assert the King's will in Ireland by overhauling its state institutions and the imposition of land and religious reforms.[38] Formal accusations of malefic witchcraft, arising from a popular level, and handled by the machinery of the common law, were again still some way off in Ireland.

The legal system in early modern Ireland

Before examining Ireland's witchcraft accusations and trials in succeeding chapters, it is essential to examine the legal context in which the 1586 Witchcraft Act operated. As has already been hinted at above, the implementation by the Irish parliament of an essentially English witchcraft law (as opposed to the drastically different Scottish witchcraft law also passed in 1563) was part of a development, starting in the late fifteenth century and lasting up until the late eighteenth century, by which English laws were incorporated into Ireland's statute book. (This is not to say that the Irish parliament did not pass laws specific to Ireland and without counterpart in England, especially in the eighteenth century when its parliament began to sit regularly for the first time and became a relatively efficient legislative machine).[39] This copying of English legislation, at times systematically, was conducted within a legal context which saw the gradual replacement by the mid-to-late seventeenth century of Gaelic Brehon law and legal practices with English common law.[40] As Neal Garnham points out, Ireland and England by this time shared 'near identical systems of legal administration, prosecution and law enforcement'.[41] By the early seventeenth century, and in the wake of Gaelic defeat, emigration, and decline, Crown Courts had replaced Brehon legal structures for settling disputes. During the succeeding 100 years, despite periodic disruption due to conflict in the 1640s and between 1689 and 1691, county Assizes became Ireland's leading provincial criminal courts.[42] Assize towns came to life when the court convened, especially in the late seventeenth and eighteenth centuries, as people poured in to experience legal dramas as well as to shop, conduct business, participate in civic duties, and attend charity balls, taverns, feasts, markets, fairs, and auctions. The spectacle of the Assizes began with the arrival of the trial judges who had Royal commission to try criminals including felons and had been plucked from one of Dublin's three common law courts. Twice a year, Assize justices worked one of the five court circuits that divided Ireland, hearing all the cases JPs and grand juries had prepared for them. In theory, two justices were to be assigned to each circuit but in practice it was often only one.[43]

In England and Ireland in the seventeenth and eighteenth centuries, it was not the state who initiated prosecutions for criminal offences, such as witchcraft, but private individuals, usually the victim, or their relatives or acquaintances. Prosecutors were not usually poor, but male and Protestant, and legal proceedings began when prosecutors took their complaint to JPs who decided whether or not to take things any further. Taking into account regional variations, the office of JP was an established part of the Irish legal system by the early seventeenth century. It was abolished in the early 1640s and re-established in 1655. Irish JPs were male, usually Protestant (the 1704 Test Act specified they were to be communicants of the Church of Ireland), and drawn from the gentry class, as well as lawyers, clergy, and members of the aristocracy. Although, by the mid-eighteenth century at least, their numbers were theoretically large, the quality of JPs varied dramatically throughout the country, with many who held commissions not actively involved with dispensing criminal justice. Representing the bottom level of the judiciary, JPs were expected to screen initial accusations, gather evidence, and witness statements, and examine and commit suspects to gaol. If confessions were gained from suspects, this was to be done without the use of torture of the sort more likely to be used in countries operating according to Roman-Law principles.[44]

As Neal Garnham has recently suggested, 'the ideal of the self-policing society ... in which all male citizens served in turn to enforce the law ... did not work particularly well in England where it had evolved' and 'the same may have been the case in Ireland'.[45] Sheriffs appointed by the Dublin administration were ultimately in charge of law enforcement in the localities, but it was constables in rural areas, and parish watchmen, who were the first defence against crime such as burglary, murder, and robberies in Irish localities. Constables were unpaid and elected every year at the Quarter Sessions or Assize courts and although officially they were to serve for a year each they were frequently re-appointed. Although men of high social standing were exempt from sitting on the parish watch or acting as constables, Presbyterians and Roman Catholics were not.[46] In the later eighteenth century attempts were made to reform this system by increasing the numbers of baronial constables and equipping Dublin with something loosely comparable to a modern police force.[47] Would-be prosecutors of witches in Ireland, just as in England, had to negotiate a final hurdle before a trial, in that a grand jury had to be convinced there was enough evidence to

warrant one. Grand juries had, at a county level, a number of administrative, economic, political, as well as legal roles, and were composed
of between 12 and 23 men plucked from the wealthy, higher reaches of
county society. Grand juries often represented particular factions or family groups within the county and members were likely to sit on panels
over extended periods.[48]

If by the first decades of the seventeenth century, Ireland had a
legal system approximating that of England, by 1638 its largely legally
untrained JPs had a handbook, *A Justice of the Peace for Ireland ...*
(Dublin, 1638), written by English-born Protestant lawyer and politician, Sir Richard Bolton, which set out their main duties during session
and the form their proceedings should take. It included a useful guide
for hunting witches, which would further define the crime of witchcraft, if not popular magic. In the section, 'felonies by statute', it summarised in a straightforward manner the main offences laid out in the
1586 Act, minus the punishments they incurred: it was a judge's role
to pass sentence, not the JP; their role was merely to investigate accusations and pass the case, if the evidence warranted it, to the Grand Jury
to decide if it were to proceed to trial.[49] It was to aid JPs in the execution of these duties that Bolton included a number of points which he
believed indicated the presence of witchcraft. This was essential, he rea-
soned, because JPs, 'may not altogether expect direct evidence, seeing
all their workes are the workes of darknesse and no witnesses present
with them to accuse them'. He further stated that witches 'often have
pictures of clay, or waxe (like a man, etc) found in their house', and
instructed JPs to secure the 'voluntary confession' of the suspect because
it exceeded 'all other evidence'. Failing this, they were to gain sworn
testimony from victims and the children or servants of the accused.
There were told to search the house of the accused for ownership of a
familiar and search their body for a Devil's mark. If the victim had died
as a result of their bewitchment, the witch was to touch the dead body
to see if it bled.[50] Corpse-touching was an ordeal used both informally
and more formally by JPs and coroners and one given official approval
during the course of the seventeenth century.[51]

Bolton claimed to have based his section on the 'proofs' of witchcraft
directly from a pamphlet account of the Lancaster witch trial of 1612
written by Thomas Potts, *The Wonderfull Discoverie of Witches in the
Countie of Lancaster ...* (1613).[52] It is more likely that Bolton based his
musings on how to establish legal proof of witchcraft on a later edition
of *The Countrey Justice ...*, a handbook for working JPs first published in
1618 and compiled by Cambridgeshire JP, Michael Dalton. In addition

to a summary of the English 1604 statute, the 1630 edition of Dalton's book provided JPs with a detailed guide to the 'proofs' of witchcraft (including all those listed by Bolton), which he tellingly stated was based on Potts' pamphlet (as well as Richard Bernard's *A Guide to Grand Jurymen* ... (London, 1627)) and designed to overcome the fact that JPs were not to expect direct evidence of the crime.[53] The fourth edition of Bolton's book, *A Justice of Peace for Ireland ...*, was published in Dublin in 1750, replete with the section on witchcraft.[54] This is unsurprising since, as we shall see in Chapter 6, the 1586 Irish Witchcraft Act was not repealed until 1821.

Conclusion

Ireland by 1586 had a law to try as felons witches who harmed or killed using magical means, as well as a range of other, less overtly harmful, magical practitioners who used ritual magic to conjure up spirits, or performed the role of cunning-person. Although almost identical to the 1563 English statute, the 1586 Irish Witchcraft Act was not the product of the religious or political concerns that informed the framers of the Scottish and English witchcraft acts. Instead, it was part of a greater project on conquest and consolidation of Elizabethan power in Ireland, in which the rolling out of the English statute book and accompanying legal system played a principal part. This new legal system, in which transgressors of the 1586 Act were to be tried, would not be fully in place for nearly two decades. Furthermore, although the harsher 1604 English Act was not extended to Ireland, in the 1630s legislation was implemented by the Irish parliament that affected in theory, if not in practice, the dictates of the 1586 Act. It was in this decade that the main administrators of justice in the localities, JPs, would be provided with an easy guide to hunting witches. The next two chapters will explore how civil and ecclesiastical authorities interpreted the 1586 Act and to what extent they punished purveyors of magic, whether perceived to be harmful witches or beneficial cunning-folk.

3
Cunning-folk in Early Modern Ireland

Popular magic in early modern Europe

Cunning-folk were known by different names all over Europe: in England, wise-man and wise woman, wizards and conjurors; in Denmark, Kloge folk; in Germany, Hexenmeisters; in Scotland, charmers.[1] Even in England these multifarious magical practitioners were known by a number of interchangeable names, as Alan Macfarlane has pointed out: '"white", "good" or "unbinding" witches, blessers, wizards, sorcerers; cunning-folk or wise men'.[2] The all-embracing term 'cunning-folk' is often used to aid comprehension. The beneficial magic of the cunning-person and the harmful witch are inextricably linked and wherever in the world, both in the early modern and modern periods, one finds belief in destructive magic one also finds those dedicated to removing or counteracting it using beneficial magic.[3] Cunning-folk provided a range of magical services, such as love magic, fortune telling, thief detection, the finding of hidden treasure and lost or stolen property, and the diagnosis, detection, and cure of harmful witchcraft. They used an array of tools, from palmistry, horoscopes, and astrological charts, to almanacs, divination techniques, and spirit conjuration. In some areas, such as Scotland, France, and Portugal, cunning-folk also provided cures for a number of natural (as opposed to supernatural) diseases afflicting humans and livestock.[4] They were also present in seventeenth-century New England, specialising in fortune-telling, folk medicine, and counter-magic.[5] Although monetary gain was their prime motivation, the position of a cunning-person afforded social prestige, respect from peers, and power within communities as well as over individuals.[6] Distinct from 'high' magical practitioners associated with the culture of the literate and ruling elites, cunning-folk nevertheless imbibed some of their ideas and practices, from the later sixteenth century onwards, from learned magical books and manuscripts which served to impress a mostly illiterate client base. 'High' magic of the late medieval and early modern period is notoriously difficult to define but can be divided into two main branches: demonic magic concerned with the invocation and command of evil demons, once practised in courts of medieval European monarchs but later condemned for being at once dangerous and heretical; and natural magic which sought to understand and exploit occult relationships in Creation using Angel invocation, alchemy, and astrology; of which the last was arguably the least controversial.[7]

The activities of cunning-folk were theoretically illegal under the same laws that applied to malefic witches in most European countries. In practice, there was no large-scale prosecution under secular law of cunning-folk and very few executions, because even if local magistrates and elite groups displayed an appetite for such a course of action, accusations were very rarely brought forward against them, their activities being popularly deemed beneficial.[8] In Protestant and Catholic countries, on the continent and in the British Isles (as well as their colonial possessions), it was the ecclesiastical authorities, using the apparatus of Church courts, who were most concerned with the suppression of popular magic. The punishment for moral or religious offences meted out by them was less severe than in secular courts, as most cases were dismissed or the perpetrator was made to confess their guilt in front of the congregation, with the height of their powers being excommunication.[9] These attacks on magical practitioners by ecclesiastical courts formed part of a European-wide process of Christianisation, occurring during and after the Protestant Reformations and the Catholic counter-Reformation, whereby respective Churches censored beliefs and practices they believed undermined their doctrines, in a bid to gain greater control over the daily lives of the lay population.[10]

Not all popular magical practitioners, however, were specialists, or even commercial.[11] Owen Davies has recently distinguished between semi-professional cunning-folk, wandering petty-healers 'who earned a few pence treating ailments, including witchcraft, using herbs or a healing ritual', and more settled, amateur magical healers who 'had limited and specific healing powers conferred on them either by birthright ... by the possession of healing objects, or most commonly the possession or knowledge of simple written or oral healing charms which were often traditionally passed on contra-sexually, from male to female and vice versa'.[12] In combination with cunning-folk and healers, other types of magical practitioners plied their trade in both rural and urban early modern and modern England, from urban astrologers to itinerant fortune tellers and (by the mid-nineteenth century), respectable, town-based, mediums, clairvoyants, mediums, and phrenologists.[13]

Cunning-folk in early modern Ireland

The activities of early modern Irish magical practitioners remain largely untouched by academic historians and folklorists, as existing historiography tends toward the later period.[14] It will be suggested below that cunning-folk were a recognised, cross-denominational cultural phenomenon in early modern Ireland. This chapter will also provide an indication of how cunning-folk were treated by Church and State in a country where their activities were theoretically illegal.[15]

The English Protestants who arrived in Ireland during the Elizabethan conquest, Jacobean plantations, and afterwards, and were members of the Church of Ireland, as well as educated enough to leave us written evidence of their views, were hostile to the activities of cunning-folk, for much the same reasons as witchcraft writers across Europe.[16] Lord Deputy Sir Thomas Wentworth was convinced that those who used prayers, spells, and charms to cure the bewitched or possessed were guilty of witchcraft themselves and thus should be punished using the whole force of the law.[17] Wentworth's concern with superstitious beliefs needs to be seen in light of his larger religious reform agenda of the 1630s which included: boosting clerical incomes and estates of the Church of Ireland; purging it of the theological influence of Calvinism and replacing it with a more Armenian orthodoxy which had been gathering pace at the Royal court in England in the 1620s; and the recruitment of English clergy to either fill vacant livings or replace nonconforming divines, especially in strongholds such as Ulster.[18] Around the same time, the reputation of Dr Alexander Colville (died 1670), a Church of Ireland clergyman who held several, valuable clerical livings in the diocese of Connor, including the parish of Coole (Carnmoney), was tainted by rumours that he used spirit conjuration to find lost and stolen goods – an art he taught his servant who later fell afoul of secular authorities in Scotland.[19] A few decades later in his cattle management manual of 1673, Michael Harward criticised both 'the [Catholic Gaelic-Irish] natives; and many of our English-Irish lukewarm Protestants' for not taking prompt enough action when 'any disease happens amongst their cattle' and by using 'those who have charms, inchanted water, inchanted rings or bells'.[20] Harward regarded the use of popular magic to be essentially 'diabolical' and thus those who availed of it invited 'the loss of their precious souls, unless they repent truly'.[21] To avoid 'the hazarding your eternal happiness by using ungodly and diabolical means' to cure cattle, Harward prescribed an, albeit astrologically informed, 'natural way ... which God blesseth' that used 'juices, herbs, plants, and minerals'.[22] English-born Bishop of Derry, Ezekiel Hopkins, also writing in the late seventeenth century, condemned demonic witches who made explicit pacts with the Devil, as well as spirit conjurors and cunning-folk whom he regarded as having made an 'implicite' pact as the efficacy of their 'charms and incantations' were almost certainly derived from Satan.[23] The cheap Dublin reprint of high-church Anglican work, *The Whole Duty of Man* (1714), declared that the consultation of cunning-folk 'upon any occasion whatever, as the recovery of our health, our goods, or whatever else' was almost as bad as making a pact with the Devil directly for nefarious ends, as the former represented 'a forsaking of the Lord, and setting up the Devil for our God, whilst we go to him in our needs for help'.[24]

There was occasionally an overt anti-Catholic element to Protestant condemnation of Irish popular magic. In 1666, Sir Paul Davies and Lord Lieutenant, James Butler, Duke of Ormond condemned in traditional Protestant fashion[25] as 'wonders or tricks' the 'miracles' performed by 'Mr Digby' by 'virtue of some sanctity he derived from Father Finioughty' who lived 'most commonly in Connaught'.[26] Fr. James Finnerty of Tuam was a well-known exorcist and divine healer operating in the 1650s and 1660s, who passed on his 'art' to John Digby when living in England. After a brief sojourn in France, Digby sought out Finnerty in Connaught in the mid-1660s to persuade him to carry on with his training.[27] In a stridently anti-Catholic account of Co. Kildare sent to William Molyneux in 1684 for his natural history of Ireland, the native Irish of that county are described as being very 'much given to credit charms, spells, incantations' as protection against witchcraft and the evil-eye, and were encouraged by 'ignorant priests' who supply them with 'holy water, consecrated relicks, amulets etc'.[28] Immediately after a brief trip to Ireland to recover from a failed marriage and improve his financial situation, Anglican-Whig, London-based bookseller and author John Dunton, published *The Dublin Scuffle ...* (1699) about his experiences. In the book, Dunton described an 'old fryar, called Father Kereen' who was famed for being 'excellent good at helping cattle that were over-look'd or bewitch'd' using holy water; a service which provided him with 'such a sum of money, as might suffice for his support all his days'. Dunton went onto lament the fact that 'some of the vulgar are so superstitious as to believe' in Fr. Keeren's abilities.[29] These books and their authors were articulating a hostility to popular magic fundamental to European demonologists, that its efficacy (if any) was rooted in the actions or inspiration of Satan, and that those who practised it, or patronised those who did, made an implicit pact with Satan. Cunning-folk were consequently technically as guilty of witchcraft as malefic witches; some clerical writers, both Catholic and Protestant, regarded cunning-folk as even worse than harmful witches.[30] Molyneux, and to a lesser extent Hayward and Dunton, were drawing on another literary trope used by seventeenth-century English Protestant witchcraft writers to link Catholicism with popular magic. Specifically, they charged cunning-folk with the perpetuation of 'popish superstitions' perceived to be inherent in, as Owen Davies points out, the 'whole system of popular worship based around masses, sacraments, exorcisms, Latin prayers and the saints' and in the use of 'holy water, consecrated candles, crosses, [and] rosaries'.[31] This anti-Catholic rhetoric had some basis in fact, because cunning-folk often incorporated some Catholic prayer, holy objects, and exorcisms into their practices.[32]

In common with a minority of critics in England,[33] one Irish Protestant commentator stated that cunning-folk were common cheats who worked on the gullibility of their clients. In 1684, Church of Ireland clergyman Rev. Keogh noted with distaste the Catholic practice in Co. Roscommon of using cunning-folk to cure fairy struck cattle. He described how with his 'own eyes observed in a cow [that] which was said to be elf-shot ... that towards her hind quarter on one side of her the hide flagged inwards and was sunk into a hole ... which the dart had made through the flesh and bowells ... notwithstanding the skin or hide remained sound and intire with any hole in it'. He went onto describe the 'cure' used by a 'notable cow chirgeon', who was called on by the 'cowheard', was made of 'urin[e] and hen's dung ... together with a certain herb', all of which was thrust into the cow's throat and mouth. The cunning-man however 'was very secret in this other part of the cure and much wary lest I should know it but a little of it happening to fall after him in the administration was found ... and shewn to me which I perceived to be no other than ragwort'. Keogh then reported that the 'beast recovered' shortly afterwards.[34]

Cunning-folk and the courts

Due to the loss of Irish legal records, it will never be fully known how far this distrust of popular magic was shared by those who controlled the machinery of criminal prosecution, and how many people were tried and convicted under the 1586 Act, which made a wide range of magical practices illegal, just as in England and Scotland.[35] There seems, however, to have been little evidence of any secular concern with these activities. In fact, only one case is known of a prosecution for practising popular magic, but even this has a political edge to it. In 1609, Rev. John Aston, Church of Ireland rector of Mellifont, Co. Louth was tried before the Court of King's Bench in Dublin for 'being wholly seduced by the devil' into performing the year before, 'divers invocations and conjurings of wicked and lying spirits' to locate a lost silver cup and gold and silver buried treasure at Cashel and 'where and in what region the most wicked traitor Hugh [O'Neill, or Aodh Ó Néill, second] earl of Tyrone, then was, and what he was contriving against the said lord the King and the state of this kingdom of Ireland'.[36] Financial pressures, fear of religious reform, restrictions on their political power as Ulster Lords, combined with rumours that they were about to be arrested for treason against the English crown, convinced O'Neill and Ruaidhrí O'Donnell (Ó Domhnall), first earl of Tyrconnell and their dependants to flee from Rathmullen on Lough Swilly, Co. Donegal in September 1607 to the continent, eventually settling in Rome.[37] After the appearance at the King's court, Aston was imprisoned in Dublin castle and then 'by warrant of the King was sent into England' to be dealt with further.[38] It may have been the fact that Aston's divination involved the politically suspect O'Neill that brought him to the attention of the authorities. King James I's interest in witchcraft is well documented, especially cases with high political resonance: in the 1590s in Scotland (as King James VI of Scotland) he took a central role in witchcraft cases involving treasonable activity; and in England in the early part of the next century he continued to take an acute interest in witchcraft cases that seemed to pose a threat to his kingship while at the same time exposing a number fraudulent accusations.[39]

The fact that secular authorities in Ireland were little concerned with the judicial punishment of cunning-folk is also attested to by their involvement in witchcraft trials and accusations without subsequent or consequent legal censure. Cunning-folk supplied a range of counter-charms against the effects of witchcraft, and diagnosed its presence in and for suspected victims; a part of their business that increased after 1660 when many trained medical professionals (rather than those of non-conformist backgrounds) began to back away from supernatural diagnosis. They often identified witches (or at the very least confirmed a client's suspicion) by examining the victim's urine. Finally, cunning-folk assisted in the curing of bewitchment, by tackling the witch directly to compel them to remove their spell, either by physically attacking them, scratching their skin to draw blood, or by ensuring they were dealt with by the law. Various forms of sympathetic magic could be used remotely to coerce the witch, by inflicting physical discomfort, to remove their spell. A common method was the construction of a 'witch-bottle', a sealed container in which was usually enclosed the patient's urine (and sometimes hair or nail-clippings), along with sharp objects such as thorns or nails. The 'bottle' was then either buried or heated, and being symbolic of the witch's bladder, the sharp objects and/or the heat would cause searing pain, forcing the suspect to reveal themselves in order to seek relief. Other types of counter-magic were also used, including the burning of the thatch from a suspected witch's house or the clothing of a victim.[40]

Variants of these types of charms were in use in seventeenth- and eighteenth-century Protestant, settler Ireland. A seventeenth-century 'witch-bottle' containing liquid and nails was discovered in recent excavations of a house in Bow Lane in Dublin, and is now housed in the National Museum of Ireland.[41] In Youghal, Co. Cork, for the 'trial' of suspected witch Florence Newton in 1661 a tile was taken from the prison roof where she was remanded in custody and placed 'next to ... where the witch lay', before being carried to the victim's house and put 'into the fire till it was red-hot'. Some of the accuser's urine was dropped upon the tile and it was noted that as soon as this was done, 'the witch was then grievously tormented, and when the water was consumed she was well again'.[42] This counter-magic was employed at the request of Edward Perry, freeman of the borough of Youghal in 1655 and Mayor in 1674, who claimed to have learnt about it from William Lap after an 'Assize at Cashel'.[43] In Antrim town in May 1698, when local physicians and Presbyterian ministers failed to cure a demonically possessed young girl, her mother took her to Dublin to consult a cunning-man. Daniel Higgs, the author of a pamphlet detailing the case, stated distastefully that the cunning-man in question was 'believed by the vulgar to be verie famous in the curing' of bewitched persons.[44] The girl stayed several days in Dublin but when her condition failed to improve she was sent back to Antrim. Higgs consequently sought to cure her by 'naturall means, not omitting divine exercise'.[45] After much searching, he found a 'certain remedy proper to this malady' in a book, *Practica Aus Den Furnemesten Secretis* (Strassburg, 1579) by Bartholomew Carrichter, physician to Emperor Maximillian II and a follower of early sixteenth-century Swiss physician, alchemist and astrologer Paracelsus

(Philippus Theophrastus Bombastus von Hohenheim).[46] Failing to secure an apothecary in Dublin with the ability to prepare Carrichter's 'unguent and prescription',[47] Higgs took it upon himself to make the ointment himself from various animal and plant matter; a concoction which he claimed eventually cured the girl.[48] We know very little about Higgs, not even his profession,[49] but given the expense and time he devoted to looking after the girl it would seem he was of significant financial means.[50] Higgs was certainly well educated: in his pamphlet he quoted from the Latin text of Book VII of Ovid's *Metamorphoses* (as well as providing an English translation), and he was able to locate and consult Carrichter's esoteric magical treatise.[51] He was also conversant with current demonological trends, as his pamphlet not only provided readers with details of the girl's bewitchment and his role in curing her (see below), but consciously formed part of a literary crusade that dominated late seventeenth-century Scottish and English demonology. This anti-Sadducism demonology, written by luminaries such as Richard Baxter, Cotton Mather, Henry More, George Sinclair, and Joseph Glanvill, presented case studies of preternatural phenomena, such as ghosts, witchcraft and demonic possession, as empirical proof of the existence of spirits, and by extrapolation God. Together, they provided ideological ammunition for a war of words waged against 'atheists' who portrayed the Universe in mechanistic and materialistic terms.[52]

Counter-magic more associated with popular magic was used in another Co. Antrim demonic possession case just over a decade later. On 17 March 1711, Mary Dunbar, the demoniac who later had eight people convicted of her bewitchment at Co. Antrim Assizes held at Carrickfergus,[53] convulsed and later claimed that the circulation of the blood in her arm had been cut off, causing intense pain. Upon inspection, it was found that a 'black woollen string, with eight knots upon it' had appeared magically,[54] a 'fact' attested to by one of the men who had held her during her fits and who claimed to have seen 'nothing visible on her arms, when he took hold of them'.[55] The string was removed but a few hours later Dunbar fell into another fit and afterwards her cloth head-dress was found tightly wound round her thigh with 'seven knots upon it'.[56] Her mother, who had by that time joined her daughter, pointed-out that this 'was the same [head-dress] that she had given her that morning, and had seen it tied around her head'.[57] Two hours later, James Stannus, a member of the Larne (Co. Antrim) Presbyterian gentry, and Rev. William Ogilvy, Presbyterian minister of Larne, cut a length of blue string with five knots in it from Dunbar's arm.[58] This was followed by another fit and the discovery, by Armagh-born, Church of

Ireland curate of Larne and trial attendee, Rev. William Skeffington,[59] of more knotted string, first around the girl's neck and then her waist, causing intense pain in her stomach and back.[60] It was later discovered that these episodes were caused by an adverse reaction to the use of 'a counter-charm' procured by Dunbar's mother from 'a popish priest' and employed against her daughter's will during one of her fits. According to High Church vicar of Belfast and trial atendee, William Tisdall, the charm contained 'the first chapter of St. John in a paper' and was tied around the girl's neck.[61] The 'popish priest' referred to by Tisdall could have been Roman Catholic clergyman, Edmond Moore, whose ecclesiastical charges, in the early eighteenth century, encompassed the Larne area.[62] Certainly, charms such as these were in use in Gaelic-Irish Catholic culture in the early modern period,[63] as well as in England.[64] A few days after the written charm was used on Dunbar, a more effective protective charm was utilised, this time procured from a 'Scotch gentleman who had been troubled himself by witches'. The 'Scotch gentlemen' is not named in surviving records but his 'preservative' proved so effective that Dunbar was able to talk for the first time to one of the accused, Margaret Mitchell, without fitting.[65]

Popular magic and the Church courts

If secular authorities in seventeenth- and eighteenth-century Ireland were not concerned with beneficent magic, only its harmful counterpoint, surviving sources suggest that the ecclesiastical authorities in early modern Ireland were, however, concerned with cunning-folk. Although we have established that Church of Ireland educated laity and clergy were hostile to popular magic and cunning-folk it is impossible to know how far this was transferred into action by their church courts.[66] Church of Scotland church courts certainly policed the activities of magical practitioners up until the mid-eighteenth century, long after ecclesiastical counterparts in England (mid-seventeenth century), Sweden, and the Dutch Republic (end of the seventeenth century) had ceased to do so.[67] Raymond Gillespie has argued that in Ireland 'Presbyterian Churches tried to detect those practising divination and issued edicts against sorcery and those who used charms to cure the sick'.[68] I will argue below that what this amounted to was, in common with their Scottish counterparts, the use of ecclesiastical court structures to reprimand cunning-folk and occasionally their clients. Before doing so, it is necessary to describe Presbyterianism in Ireland in the seventeenth and eighteenth centuries.

Although Presbyterians, coming largely but not exclusively from Scotland, had been settling in Ulster in sporadic waves since the early seventeenth century, the last three decades of the century saw a surge in immigration, with the high point occurring in the 1690s with the arrival of between 50,000 and 80,000 people. This emigration was due to a series of bad harvests and famine in Scotland between 1695 and 1698, along with the promise of low rents in Ireland. By the 1710s, when emigration had tailed off, Presbyterians made up around a third of the total population of Ulster, standing at around 200,000 people. They were found in large numbers in counties Antrim, Donegal, Down, and Londonderry, but also in Armagh, Monaghan, and Tyrone. There were also small pockets of Presbyterians further south in towns such as Cork, Limerick, and Dublin. Although by political necessity loyal to the British crown as Protestants, Ulster Presbyterians at that time viewed themselves not as Irish or English but as the Scottish in Ireland. This is unsurprising since the Presbyterian diaspora in Ulster still had strong familial, economic, and cultural ties with Scotland. More importantly, their identity was shaped by their Presbyterian religion. The Presbyterian Church emerged distinct from the Church of Ireland in the aftermath of the political and social crisis of the 1640s, and between 1689 and 1707, the number of congregations and ministers doubled. This number grew by a further 30% during the next decade.[69] By the time of the establishment of the Ulster Synod in 1691, Presbyterianism in the province was, in the words of Sean Connolly, 'an autonomous and highly organised ecclesiastical polity', with elders and ministers who presided over Kirk Sessions and presbyteries that exercised moral discipline over their members' behaviour, from Sabbath-breaking and sexual impropriety, to popular magic, drunkenness, and dishonesty in business.[70]

The growing economic and political power of Presbyterians, along with the growth of Ulster Presbyterianism in religious and ecclesiastical terms, was regarded by many to be a great threat to the established church and state. As Ian McBride has recently pointed out, 'the fierce antagonism between church and Dissent ... was a central, persistent theme in the politics of Ascendancy Ireland'.[71] After James II had been defeated at the Boyne, the Presbyterians who had fought alongside Anglicans on the side of William of Orange were left in a precarious legal position, and it was during these years that animosity between the two denominations reached crisis point. The Acts of Uniformity of 1560 and 1665 had made attendance at an Anglican parish Church compulsory, effectively banned dissenting schools and colleges, and imposed a £100 fine on ministers administering communion who had not been ordained by an Anglican bishop. By the late seventeenth century, these laws went largely unenforced but any notion that they would be repealed was quashed in the Irish parliamentary sessions of 1692 and 1695. In England, religious toleration had been extended to all moderate Protestant non-conformists in 1689, while in Scotland a Presbyterian national church had been established. However, in Ireland elements within the Church of Ireland demanded that the seventeenth-century laws discussed above be more rigorously implemented; a call that reached a high point when their natural political supporters, the Tory party, were swept into power in late 1710. Although high-churchmen had been, from the end of the seventeenth century, using the apparatus of Church of Ireland Church Courts to sporadically attack Presbyterian marriage, funerals, and schools, this became more marked in the early eighteenth century. Moves were also made to prevent new Presbyterian congregations being set-up in Drogheda, Co. Louth (1708) and Belturbet, Co. Cavan (1712), and the subsidy given by the Crown to the Presbyterian General Synod of Ulster, the *regium donum*, was withdrawn. Although religious toleration was theoretically denied to them until 1719, there was no barrier to Presbyterians entering public office, and after the conclusion of the Williamite wars in Ireland they took increasing control of borough corporations in Belfast, Derry, and Carrickfergus. In Carrickfergus and Belfast, Presbyterians were made Mayor, with Belfast electing a non-conformist MP to the Irish parliament. Furthermore, many of the burgesses of borough corporations in Derry, Belfast and, to a lesser extent, Coleraine, if not Carrickfergus, were Presbyterian. Increasing political prominence was accompanied by an increase in militia officers, and Presbyterian JPs were suspected by 'hotter' Anglicans of protecting and favouring their co-religionists. Such fears were to some extent allayed by 'tacking' a clause onto the end of the Irish Popery Act of 1704, which excluded from the majority of munici-pal or crown offices anyone who had not taken the sacrament of Holy Communion according to the Church of Ireland. As a result, the office of High Sheriff became a monopoly for conformists, and Presbyterian members of corporations of Derry and Coleraine resigned en masse in late 1704, while those in Belfast lost their positions a few years later. Around 25 Presbyterian JPs resigned their commissions in 1704, which ensured a decline in Presbyterian influence in important arms of local government. Furthermore, although Presbyterian constables were not excluded from office by the Test Act, their election was now subject to the control of members of the Church of Ireland.[72] Unsurprisingly, the Test Act was fiercely opposed by northern Presbyterians, not least because it placed a stigma on a community that had fought for the maintenance of the Protestant interest in Ireland. More importantly, it convinced some of the already small number of substantial Presbyterian landowners to drift towards the Church of Ireland. Already distinct from Anglicans because of their religion, culture, and Scottish origins, Presbyterians became increasingly socially distanced from parish institutions and the associational life of towns after this time.[73]

The attitude of Presbyterian Church courts to magical practitioners and their clients is extremely difficult to discern not only because of the piecemeal nature of the extant records, but also because there is some confusion over terms. In England and Wales, the term 'charmer' referred to magical healers who cured ailments for no fee using a variety or magical means. In Scotland, the term 'charmer' at a popular level meant a commercial 'cunning-person' rather than a non-commercial magical healer.[74] Nevertheless, in Carnmoney, Co. Antrim, in 1672, a young servant, George Russell, was disciplined by Presbyterian ministers and elders for 'conversing and conferring with that spirit which appeared to him ... and conjuring it by drawing circles and other circumstances att the demand and direct[io]ne of the s[ai]d spirits'.[75] The demon who had tricked Russell into doing its bidding was also responsible for haunting his master, James Shaw, the Scottish-born Presbyterian minister of Carnmoney. Shaw died after a prolonged illness and his neighbours suspected both he and his wife had been murdered by a demon conjured up by the 'sorcery of some witches in the parish', who were never identified.[76] In February 1673, Antrim Presbytery set up a general committee to examine 'sorcerye' in the area, as well as agreeing to look into the case of W[illia]m Zaque, a cunning-man whose activities were supported by his Co. Tyrone neighbours but condemned by the elders of his congregation.[77] A few years later at Laggan Presbytery held at Omagh, Co. Tyrone, in November 1699, a 'Mr McGuichin' from the parish of Drummond asked the Presbytery its 'advice' on 'what to do with persons who use charmers and charms in curing the sick'. He was duly 'appointed' by the Presbytery to 'preach against' the practice.[78]

On 25 April 1703, John Craig and his daughter, Bessey, were cited to appear before Aghadowey Session, in north-west Co. Antrim, for the use of 'charming and spells'.[79] On the day of her hearing, 9 May 1703, Bessey pleaded guilty to the charges, but maintained the innocence of her father. She was duly 'rebuked sharply and dismissed' by the Session.[80] In the same session, Thomas Gray claimed he had been slandered by a woman named Martha Cockran and her son Andrew

Gray who had 'used that charm of turning key' to claim he had stolen some local goods. Andrew and Martha were summoned to appear at the next session, and Thomas Gray appointed to provide evidence 'to prove this charge'.[81] Along with the sieve and the shears, the 'turning key' charm was a common method of divination used by cunning-folk and the general public in early modern England (as well as in Puritan New England and the Isle of Man) to locate stolen goods and detect thieves.[82] Owen Davies has described this practice as 'either sticking the sharp end of some shears into the wooden rind of a sieve or balancing the sieve on some shears', before appealing 'to the Holy Trinity or to St. Peter and St. Paul' and calling out the names of those suspected until the sieve turned 'at the mention of the guilty party'.[83] Martha claimed that she had 'never used any charm' nor accused Thomas Gray of theft. Although the plaintiff was unable on the day of the hearing to provide any evidence to the contrary, Martha admitted 'her son, a child was guilty' and he was duly 'reproved upon the account that he declared he thought that there was no harm in it'.[84] In August 1703, cunning-men George Sheridan and John Stream were cited to appear before Carnmoney Session for making 'use of the Bible in their charming w[i]th key and riddle for recovering what they had lost'.[85] At their hearing the men admitted 'their sin in so profanely using the holy word of God', but mitigated their behaviour by professing their 'ignorance of the evil of it'. They were dismissed after having 'confesst they were rash, [and] promis'd to have a care of such things again'.[86] The perceived impious use of the Scriptures involved in this practice no doubt troubled the minsters and elders of the Session more than other forms of divination.

Six years later in April 1709, Nathaniel Gifford, and two other men, Brown and Friell, were similarly cited by Carnmoney Session for 'charming to get the stolen goods'.[87] Having failed to appear at the June and August Presbyteries, all three were cited to appear at the September meeting. Only Gifford appeared at the hearing, and was 'rebukt' for performing un-Christian, magical practices, before being dismissed.[88] In October 1731, a woman identified only by her forename, Agnes, complained to Carnmoney Session 'that Sam[ue]ll Dawson had difam'd her in calling her a witch'. Dawson assured the Session that he had called her no such thing but 'had a cow that … lost her milck and upon using some means to recover it … by the instruction of J[o]hn Laird, Agnes came to his house in a very great haste and said that her ears were burning out of her head'.[89] In other words, Dawson had used a counter spell supplied by cunning-man Laird to detect the source of his cows' bewitchment, the harmful magic of Agnes. The case was dropped by the Carnmoney

Session possibly because both parties would have been regarded by the Session as moral transgressors: Agnes for wrongfully accusing Dawson of slander and Dawson for employing the services of a cunning-person.

Non-conforming cunning-folk, it seems, even ran the risk of being rebuked by the ecclesiastical courts of the Church of Ireland. In the early 1720s, Bishop of Down and Connor, Francis Hutchinson, noted in his commonplace book, in order to remind himself to bring the matter to the attention of the Archbishop's court, that two non-conformists had used 'the sieve & shears' for the purposes of divination.[90] Bishop Hutchinson's decision to order dissenters to appear before an Anglican Church court could be considered excessive and in contradiction to his low-church, Latitudinarian principles, which were reflected in a 'tolerant' attitude to Protestant dissent and a preference for persuasive over coercive methods in efforts impose 'right religion' on the populace. He opposed, for example, high-churchmen in his diocese in the early 1720s prosecuting Presbyterians for fornication in their ecclesiastical courts because they had not been legally married in Church of Ireland church but by one of their own ministers.[91] His decision to prosecute cunning-folk using this apparatus can be understood more readily if one takes into consideration two things. First of all, sceptical witchcraft authors, especially clergymen such as Hutchinson, were often just as opposed to cunning-folk as demonologists and for much the same reasons as discussed above. Indeed, it is certain that his views on popular magic were derived from reading (and collecting) both continental and English demonological tracts, books, and pamphlets.[92] Secondly, the activities of the dissenting cunning-men could have come to his attention in a number of ways, not least while acting in his capacity as JP for Co. Antrim,[93] as they were technically guilty of a secular crime under the 1586 Irish Witchcraft Act.[94] Chief Justice of the Irish court of the Queen's Bench, Sir Richard Cox, certainly believed that 'spirit[ual] courts' could try certain moral offences which included certain defamation cases where moral rather than criminal transgression had been implied.[95] Taken in this light, Bishop Hutchinson's referral of the two dissenters to his Archbishop's church court could be seen either as leniency or a further confirmation that the secular authorities were not concerned with such matters.

Catholicism in Ireland and popular magic

If the clerical elite of both the Church of Ireland and the Presbyterian Church denounced popular attachment to magic and magical practitioners, and the latter even took direct action against perpetrators, this raises the question as to whether the Catholic clergy were as concerned with cunning-folk as their Protestant counterparts. Catholic clerics were certainly aware of their activities in early modern Gaelic-Irish communities. Counter-Reformation cleric Fr. Goode noted the services provided by a Gaelic-Irish cunning-woman in the late sixteenth century:

> against all maladies and mischiefs whatsoever, the [wise] woman have effectuall enchauntmentes, or charmes, as they suppose: divided and parted amongst them, each one her severall enchamment, and the same of divers forces: unto whom every man according as his mischance requireth, speedeth himselfe for helpe.[96]

Goode went onto say that cunning-folk generally 'say alwaies both before and after their charmes, a Pater-Noster, and an Ave Maria'.[97] Goode also described how Irish 'wise' women were employed to cure 'eye-bitten' livestock:

> they thinke there bee some that bewitch their horses with looking upon them; and then they use the helpe of some old hagges, who saying a few prayers with a lowde voice, make them well againe.[98]

He further explained that these magical practitioners also diagnosed, and presumably cured, individuals who suspected they had been attacked by fairies, first by visiting the location of the original attack and saying a few prayers and incantations out loud, and then by whispering prayers into the ear of the victim.[99] Fr. Goode also provided a rare indication of the type of verbal charms used by cunning-folk in Co. Limerick in the treatment of cattle ailments:

> there is a certain small worme, breeding in their horses feete ... [and] against this worme, they send for a wise woman, who is brought, to the horse on two severall Mon-daies, and one Thursday. She breatheth upon the place where the worme lieth; and after shee hath rehearsed a charme, the horse recoverth. This charme they teach many for a piece of money, making them to sweare, that they will not revealst to anybody.[100]

In early modern England, written charms were often laid out on specially produced parchment and had a variety of magical purposes, but were principally designed to protect or to cure those humans and livestock from the effects of witchcraft. Those designed for humans were not to be read or flaunted openly by the user and were often required to be kept close to the body. Most written charms had a strong religious element to them, containing Catholic exorcisms or passages from the Bible, and were usually supplied by cunning-folk.[101] Written protective charms used by Irish Catholics, however, were designed to be read aloud and/or worn close to the body. Francis Bernard, Church of Ireland dean of Ardagh, described that in the aftermath of the siege of Drogheda in 1642 it was widely reported that Irish soldiers were rendered impervious to the deadly effects of both bullet and sword due to the protective 'paper charmes' they carried with them.[102] He also copied verbatim a number of written charms found on Irish soldiers captured at Dundalk.[103] One charm, for example, read:

> This is the measure of the wound of the side of our Lord Jesus Christ which was brought from Constantinople unto the Emperour Charles within a chest of Gold as a Relique most precious to that effect, that no envie might him take, and it hath such vertue that he or shee that shall read it, or heare it read, or will beare it about them, that neither fire, water, tempest, knife, launce, sword, neither yet the Devill shall hurt them. And also any woman with child, the day that she seeth the said measure of the wound of our Lord, shee shall not die any sudden death, in the time of her burthen, but shall be delivered with lesse paine, and whatsoever they be that desire this about them in the way of devotion, they shall not die any sudden death, and by the sight of meditation on this wound, they shall gaine victory over their enemies; and further, care shall not damage them, and moreover, the day that he or shee shall read it, or heare it read, they shall not die an evill death.[104]

A staunch Protestant, and virulently anti-Catholic, Bernard regarded charms as 'delusions' born of a superstitious religion.[105] Not all Protestants were so opposed to written charms. In the seventeenth-century stock-book of the Protestant Penrose-Fitzgerald estate, the following was found by Raymond Gillespie: 'ABRACADABRA, these words will cure the shaking ague by writing of it in a piece of paper and put about the sick party's neck'.[106] And as we have seen the mother of Mary Dunbar, a member of the (small) Presbyterian gentry, had no qualms in using one procured from a priest. In the mid-eighteenth century, a shorter protective charm was found on the body of a 'poor Irish soldier, who was killed in the late war' and which contained the following words, '*Tres Reges Sancti* Melchior, Gaspar, and Baltasar, *orate pro nobis nunc and in hora mortis nostrae*', followed by the words 'these tickets ... are for travellers, against misfortunes in their travels, against the Headache, falling-sickness, fevers, witchcraft, and all other misfortunes, and sudden death'.[107] Both curative and protective written charms, often supplied by cunning-folk, continued to be worn in Ireland up until the twentieth century.[108]

As we have seen, Protestant commentators delved deep into the stock of well-worn anti-Catholic rhetoric that Catholic priests encouraged, facilitated, and on occasion supplied magical aid to the flocks. There seems to have been at least some element of truth in this. In early modern Ireland, Catholic priests were often regarded by their flocks as a conduit for the Holy, the harnessing of which was perceived as essential for the avoidance of eternal damnation and torment, to secure victory in war, and as a way to deal with disease, illness, and crop failure.[109] Bernard Gray, a late sixteenth-century Franciscan, cured cattle with holy water, an activity he ironically claimed to have undertaken to prevent his parishioners from resorting to the charms and spells of cunning-folk.[110] In Callen, Co. Kildare in 1609, Anastasia Sobechan, having been bewitched by 'magical spells' which caused her to vomit 'small pieces of cloth and wood', was cured by Rev. Lord Abbot Bernard, who tied 'a girdle round her body that had touched the holy relic' at the monastery at Holy Cross in Tipperary.[111] Similarly 'a St. Francis girdle', designed to protect the wearer from harm, was found on the body of a fallen Irish soldier during the siege of Drogheda in 1642.[112] It was a common belief among early modern Irish Catholics that God's healing power could be accessed by channelling the power of Saints by visiting a place associated with them, such as a Holy Well, or by touching holy relics linked to their lives.[113] In the early seventeenth century, a reportedly 'ignorant man' from King's County (Offaly) healed cattle using the Book of Durrow (associated with St. Columcille) that had been soaked in water.[114]

The participation of Catholic clergy in the purveyance of magical protection was condemned as superstitious across early modern Europe by clerical hierarchies eager to impose Tridentine reforms on laity and clergy alike.[115] The situation, it seems, was no different in Ireland. An early seventeenth-century, Irish-Franciscan catechism condemned the use of counter-charms because they were demonic in origin,[116] and as Raymond Gillespie points out, 'the decrees of the various Catholic synods in seventeenth-century Ireland required priests to hide sheela-na-gigs, prohibit invocations of the devil, prevent the gathering of 'magical' herbs, and stop the preparation of virility potions ... holy wells and other sites of devotion were also to be controlled'.[117] In February 1612, the Counter-Reformation-influenced Ulster Synod stated that 'another abuse we wish to correct is, that of laymen, who bring with them some pretended relics of saints, dip them in water, and then, with various religious exorcisms, sprinkle men and beasts – for this is clearly an act of superstition, not of piety'.[118] The Synods of Armagh in 1614 and 1618 condemned the use of dishonourable spells and charms at funeral feasts,[119] while that of Tuam in 1632 directed priests to 'teach their sheep often to rout superstitious remedies to illnesses' and wounds and trust those sanctioned by the Church instead.[120] In the 1640s, Irish Synods became concerned once more with the apparent increase in lay invocation of evil spirits, witchcraft, and magical healing using holy relics and blessing.[121] In Restoration Ireland, in 1661, the Synod of Cashel ruled that the diocesan bishop was responsible for reforming the 'superstitious veneration of places, of wells and of other matters',[122] and urged parish priests to stamp out fortune-telling and the wearing of protective charms around necks and hands.[123] The Synod of Ossory in 1672 condemned cunning-folk, magical healers, and fortune-tellers as superstitious and dangerous, while that of Meath in 1686 became the last 'to devote considerable attention to superstition'.[124] However, the mid-eighteenth century saw a few notable reforming clerics, in an era of *de facto* religious toleration at the tail end of the Penal Era, renew the Catholic Church's attack on popular magic and cunning-folk, of which more will be said in Chapter 7.

Conclusion

It has been argued in this chapter that cunning-folk operated in both Catholic and Protestant Ireland in the early modern period, and encompassed both genders. In Gaelic, Catholic Ireland, at a parish level at least, priests may have occasionally acted as *de facto* cunning-folk, or at the very least facilitated the use of magic. We have been left little information on the social status of cunning-folk, but they seem to have been from the same social order as their clients: the lower orders; and in only one case do we have evidence of fees being received. Irish cunning-folk specialised in three main areas: firstly, finding lost or stolen goods or treasure; secondly, the diagnosis, detection, and curing of witchcraft; and thirdly, in Gaelic-Irish and Catholic areas, protection against, and curing of, fairy attack on livestock and humans. Written protective charms were also used in Catholic communities, and it is likely these originated, as they did elsewhere, from cunning-folk. If the practice of popular magic was, from the late sixteenth century onwards, essentially illegal, there is no evidence of any concerted effort by the civil authorities to stamp it out. Clerical (and some lay) elites, of the three main religious denominations, however, regarded it as religiously and socially dangerous up until the eighteenth century, with the Presbyterian Church doling out light punishments to individual practitioners. Whatever the denomination, opposition to cunning-folk was articulated in the much same way as it was by demonologists in Europe and England, with Protestant witchcraft writers eager to link them to perceived theological inadequacies of Catholicism. This fed into a larger concern of all Churches, to impose on the laity 'right religion', which of course meant in each case their own brand of Christianity.

4
Witchcraft Accusations in Early Modern Ireland

When the last witchcraft trial was held at Leicester, England, in 1717,[1] around 500 people, mainly women, had been executed during the previous 150 years. This figure represents just over 1% of the estimated 40,000 people put to death for witchcraft in Europe between 1400 and 1800, a period when England held 5% of the total European population.[2] Taking into consideration that early modern Scotland held roughly a quarter of the population of England, Scottish witch-hunting was 12 times more intense: of the 3,837 people tried for witchcraft, around two-thirds were convicted and executed.[3] Put another way, and if we take historian Julian Goodare's slightly higher figure of 2,500 executions, Scottish witch-hunting was five times more intense than the European average.[4] Recent academic studies suggest that prosecution and execution rates in Ireland failed to reach double figures.[5]

Lack of Witch-hunting in Ireland

The two main historians to consider this issue of the absence of a sustained Irish witch-hunt, Raymond Gillespie and Elwyn Lapoint, suggest that the answer cannot be found in the witchcraft beliefs of Irish people, as both Catholic natives and Protestant settlers shared in the witchcraft beliefs characteristic of other European cultures.[6] It is further contended that the conundrum of Ireland's immunity to witchcraft is not to be solved by reference to its laws and legal infra-structure because they were almost identical to England after the Elizabethan conquest.[7] If lack of belief or of appropriate legal machinery cannot been held accountable for the paucity of Irish witch-hunting, the unwillingness of the majority Catholic, Gaelic-Irish population to levy formal witchcraft accusations has been regarded as a more convincing explanation. Lapoint argues that this community, rather than involve secular authorities and lodge formal accusations, preferred to fight witchcraft attacks using informal magical and/or religious means, a decision rooted in resentment of the Elizabethan imposition of English rule and legal machinery on their country. Implicit in this model is the contention that formal accusations were rare in Protestant Ireland, leading to few prosecutions, trials, and convictions.[8] Gillespie on the other hand argues that this is an 'unlikely' explanation because, 'on the basis of surviving Irish court records, it is clear that the native Irish were deeply involved in the workings of the common law system by the 1640s ... [and] eagerly prosecuted theft, assault, and murder through these courts'.[9] Accusations of witchcraft, he suggests, were rare in both Catholic and Protestant Ireland because witch-hunting was not state-directed as it was in England: the main threat to social and political order was not the witch but the Gaelic-Irish. He maintains that disputes which often led to witchcraft accusations were resolved locally in cohesive Irish communities, precluding the need for recourse to outside, secular authorities. More importantly, the social, economic, and demographic shifts which created the village tensions that underlay witchcraft accusations in England, according to the Keith Thomas/Alan Macfarlane charity-refused model, were absent in Ireland.[10] Jonathan Barry has summarised the Thomas-Macfarlane model as 'the hypothesis that most accusations of witchcraft arose from situations where the accused was refused some charity by the accuser, who then felt guilt and attributed subsequent misfortune to the malice of the person refused'.[11]

These interpretations, however, are problematic. As we have seen, the mass of the population in early modern Ireland, the Catholic Gaelic-Irish, did not make formal witchcraft accusations (whereby keeping prosecution rates low) because of their culturally-distinct witchcraft beliefs. In Gaelic-Irish culture, the activities of butter-stealing witches were restricted to the periodic interruption of dairy production and were easily countered by religious, magical, or ritualistic means, and consequently they posed a minimal economic and social threat to their communities. There was thus less need for recourse to the law to have those believed responsible prosecuted, incarcerated, or executed in order to prevent future witchcraft attacks, cease present ones, or provide the victim or their relatives with closure or retribution. In any case, they had they already had strong explanatory supernatural mechanisms for misfortune in the form of fairy belief and, to a lesser extent, the evil-eye. Furthermore, although their political and religious leaders in the medieval and early modern period were more influenced by continental conceptions of witchcraft and sorcery, these accusations primarily involved the political elite.[12]

Secondly, Ireland's legal comparability to England, although incontrovertible, has been slightly overplayed in Irish witchcraft historiography, as it is arguable that it only possessed the legal infrastructure to enforce the 1586 statute by the early seventeenth century, and after 1604 England possessed a markedly different witchcraft statute.[13] Thirdly, the charity-refused model has been challenged as the primary explanatory model for witchcraft accusation in early modern England. In contrast to the findings of Thomas and Macfarlane, a significant number of English witches were not powerless, socially isolated, marginal, poor, old, or widowed, and around 20% were male.[14] Research into those accused of witchcraft in early modern Wales, which from the mid-sixteenth century shared legal and administrative machinery with England, has revealed a similar pattern.[15] Reputation,[16] age,[17] and gender[18] are now regarded as determining the accuser/accused relationship, and it is difficult to maintain that witchcraft accusation in England was a top-down process, as most accusations originated among the lower orders, with the judiciary handling them in such a way as to keep prosecution and conviction rates low in comparison to the rest of Europe.[19] Even in Scotland, where the late Christina Larner made the connection between witch-hunting and efforts to establish absolutism and build a Godly State,[20] it has been argued that Scottish governments worked to restrain and limit the activities of local witch-hunters.[21] Furthermore, most of those accused of *maleficium* in Scotland were middle-aged females, implicated by their neighbours (usually their social equals) after some sort of inter-personal conflict, followed by an otherwise inexplicable misfortune. Suspects were also named as accomplices by other witches, usually during medium and large hunts which could involve hundreds of people.[22] Both patterns of accusation can be seen to varying degrees in European witch trials, played out against a background of intense social, religious, political, economic, and climatic change.[23]

In this chapter it will be argued that by the mid-seventeenth century, accusations of malefic, demonic witchcraft were being made by, and against, Presbyterian and Church of Ireland settlers.[24] In short, in common with other geographically peripheral European countries, witchcraft accusation and prosecution for malefic witchcraft came late to Ireland, but come they did.[25] It will be further argued that a number of reasons, not least the way these accusations were handled by church and state authorities, ensured only a minority reached court or ended in successful prosecution. These trials will be explored in the next chapter. Together, both chapters provide a greater understanding of the religious, social, and political context in which these accusations were made.

Accusations that failed to reach court

In England, criminal prosecution was expensive and undertaken by the victim of witchcraft, their family, or friends, when other ways to deal with situation at hand had been considered, exhausted, or discounted. This included the stoicism and private prayer approved by mainstream Protestantism, which was most likely to be adopted by those higher up the social ladder. Furthermore, those with the economic means to do so consulted physicians, whilst others opted for direct action against the witch such as scratching, threats, assault, or the use of counter-magic. As a result of this range of ways to deal with bewitchment an unknown number of cases would have ended in neither formal accusation nor prosecution.[26] In Ireland, witchcraft cases also failed to reach court, or even come to the attention of the legal profession, for a variety of reasons. As we saw in the previous chapter, Irish Protestants employed anti-witch measures provided by cunning-folk, and it may have been that victims or their relatives found closure after a suspected witchcraft attack in this way, thus vitiating the need for legal recourse. It is also clear that some accusers died before a suspect could be named, examined, and indicted. Sir James Ware noted that on 4 October 1630, John Cave of Dublin 'suddenly d'parted this life' after four days of 'being possessed with a conceit that he could not drink', stating before he died that 'hee was bewitched by a woman at Powerscourt'.[27] Victims of witchcraft were sometimes at a loss as to who was responsible. In March 1668 Thomas Jervis noted that 'there was never such a loss of cattle for many years, many dying fat and no one knowing their distemper. Tom Corbett's are all dead, cutting two inches of fat upon the brisket, so that no man can persuade him but that his were bewitched'.[28] In Carnmoney, Co. Antrim in 1672, neighbours suspected that Presbyterian minister James Shaw and his wife had been murdered by witches in the parish who were never identified.[29] Similarly, in Islandmagee, Co. Antrim, in early 1711, no-one was prosecuted for the murder of elderly minster's wife, Ann Haltridge, although her neighbours believed her death to be the work of witchcraft.[30]

At other times, accusers were persuaded to drop their charges by the accused, as was the case with Cork woman Barbara Blaugdon, a Quaker, who in the 1650s narrowly escaped being murdered by an angry mob by means of a butcher's knife.[31] Some Irish victims also learnt to live with their bewitchment in common with counterparts in England.[32] A petition lodged by the wife of William Ryan of Castletown Co. Tipperary at the consistory court of Killaloe in 1704 for a maintenance allowance, 'and in due time ... [a] divorce', claimed that Ryan had circumvented (as opposed to remedying) his impotency (which ensured in the six months after their wedding that their stormy marriage was never consummated) by taking 'himself to the whore whom he declared formerly bewitched him'.[33] Ryan's accusation is not unprecedented in early modern witchcraft. It was a widely held belief in seventeenth-century France that witches rendered grooms impotent through incantation and sympathetic magic in the form of knots tied in string.[34]

Accusations were also not acted upon if the accuser, even if of high status, was believed mentally unstable. It was on these grounds that in a letter of November 1668 to Lord Lieutenant James Butler, duke of Ormond, Michael Boyle, Church of Ireland Archbishop of Dublin, dismissed the elderly and rapidly declining Bishop of Ossory, Griffiths Williams' belief 'that he is bewitched, and that Captain [Thomas] Evans hath bin an Instrument in doeing it'. He went on to say, 'so little hath he bin acquainted with sickness that his imaginations worke strongly [and] strangely upon his present condition'.[35] Captain Evans of Kilcreene, Kilkenny was born in Wales and came to Ireland in 1649, probably with Colonel Peter Stubber's second regiment, and served as a JP and a sheriff of Kilkenny in 1656 before being elected to the Irish parliament in 1661.[36] Ormond was also concerned about the damage 'the dotage or frenzy' of an elderly bishop such as Williams was doing to his diocese and the Established Church in general,[37] and wished to replace the troublesome and combative bishop with a younger man, Dean Joseph Teate. Williams outlived Teate, who drowned in a shipwreck off the coast of Arklow in December 1670.[38] Given these circumstances, Ormond, a deeply religious man who gave supernatural matters careful consideration,[39] was in no doubt that Williams' witchcraft accusations were baseless: 'the matter seems to mee so cleare that ... I cannot think the Captaine a Conjurer as the B[isho]p does'.[40]

Summary justice: witchcraft in the 1640s

The 1641 rebellion which engulfed the whole country, plunging it into a decade of almost total war,[41] also witnessed a rise in the prominence of witchcraft and imprisonment and execution without trial.

In Scotland, England (specifically East Anglia), and Wales, the disruption of the normal machinery of authority and justice in the civil war period, combined with a heightened fear of the Devil and his works, heralded a high point in witchcraft accusation and prosecution.[42] The rebellion that started on 22 October 1641 began as a plan by Ulster Catholic gentry, including Sir Phelim O'Neill, to capture key castles, forts, and large houses in south and mid-Ulster as a position from which to negotiate with Dublin and the Crown better terms to ensure security of tenure for their lands and liberty of conscience in religious matters. This planned, 'bloodless revolt' quickly turned into a popular uprising with widespread robbing, killing, and ejection directed against the Protestant and English settler population. During the winter of 1641–2, Ireland descended into war as law and order (in particular the Crown Court System) and the authority of central and local government collapsed.[43]

Among those attacked by Catholic mobs were Presbyterian women, including wives of ministers.[44] Protestant and English women were also accused of witchcraft by the upper reaches of insurgent forces. Anne Dawson claimed that Edmond O'Donnelly of Co. Armagh drowned the wife of James Maxwell (probably during the winter of 1641–2) after Sir Phelim O'Neill 'told him that ... [she] was a witch and that he never had good loocke [luck] after he once kissed her'.[45] Mary McAuliffe has argued that witchcraft accusations in Ireland involving kissing were taken more seriously by male elites because it represented unregulated, 'polluted' female touch and unrestrained, overt female sexuality and as such a potent threat to patriarchy.[46] In Gaelic society women not only had a low and essentially dependant status, womanhood itself was idealised as chaste, pious, silent, hospitable, and charitable; all of which was bolstered by the portrayal of women by male clergy in the Catholic church as inherently lustful and greedy, a source of potential entrapment and temptation.[47] Even if the gender persecution model, which portrays witchcraft accusation and prosecution as essentially women-hunting,[48] is regarded as simplistic, especially in its portrayal of early modern women as passive, subjugated, dependant, and unassertive,[49] those women, such as Maxwell's wife, who displayed behaviour deemed socially unacceptable were nevertheless more susceptible to charges of witchcraft.[50]

In January 1642, Janet Stringer, who was 39 and married, was apprehended along with an English Protestant, Richard Mewdon, near Clonakilty, Cork, by troops of Cormac McCarthy Reagh, commander of the Munster insurgents. She was then bound, taken prisoner and put in a dungeon in Kilbrittain castle. Mewden was later hanged but

Janet was saved from the hangman's noose by Cormac's mother, Ellen, daughter of David Roche, second viscount Fermoy. After working as a servant in the castle for a few days, Janet was taken by Cormac's soldiers to a cabin in the woods near Enniskean, Co. Cork,[51] where she was deprived of food, beaten, and forced to wear the rope that had been used to hang Mewden.[52] She was also 'much threatened by divers of … [Cormac's] souldjers to be kill[e]d, called English whore and told that shee bewitched the English unto them: (which indeed they sawe att that tyme not farr from them)'. Janet was eventually released after Cormac's mother once more 'mediated for her'.[53] The motivation for Ellen's treatment of Dawson is impossible to discern but it is clear that clemency was not always demonstrated by Irish women towards English settlers. As Michael Perceval Maxwell has put it, 'in at least seven different counties it was remarked that the women took a strong role in hurting the British'.[54]

In January 1642, Alasdair (Alexander) MacColla MacDonnell and his Catholic recruits killed between 60 and 90 Protestant soldiers at the crossing of the river Bann at Portnaw, near Kilrea, Co. Antrim, before joining with forces from Co. Londonderry, and (unsuccessfully) besieging Ballintoy House, burning down Dunluce House and marching onto Coleraine.[55] Tragically and ironically, 'Jennett Dilliston als Wilson' had been killed shortly beforehand by a number of men sent by Gilduffe O'Cahan of Dunseverick Co. Antrim, who believed that Wilson was about to use 'her witchcraft' against Irish forces and prevent them from entering her village, Ballintoy.[56] Upon hearing that 90-year-old Wilson, who was his tenant and had been recently staying in his house near Ballintoy, had been killed, John McCart confronted O' Cahan who 'reproved him bitterly, and told him that he would not feed and maintetaine his mother for nothing of that age, and said that the said Jennet was a witch and deserved to be killed'.[57]

As people tried to come to terms with the sudden breakdown of consensus and order, the 1640s saw an upsurge in Ireland in manifestations of the supernatural in the culture of both Catholic and Protestant communities, of ghosts, prophecies, and of seeing respective military successes and failures in providential terms. The hand of God was seen in early Irish victories, which in turn proved to Catholic Irish elites that they were God's chosen people and conversely that settlers were divine enemies. It was not too far a leap from this suggestion to view Protestants in demonic terms and some of their number as witches. Furthermore, since in their view Protestants were already damned and thus beyond the bounds of moral responsibility, it was no sin to kill them.[58]

In this way, Wilson's murder was doubly justified: she was not only a witch but a Protestant, actively engaged against the Irish military campaign. Similarly, the killing by hungry parliamentary forces of a witch after the first battle of Newbury in 1643 was justified in news-sheets as the execution of a Royalist spy.[59] A popular witchcraft pamphlet printed in the same year described the woman as a demonic old hag who controlled the current of a river by magical means and chewed bullets fired at her, and was defeated only when a trooper broke her spell by slashing her across the face with his sword; a feat regarded as providential, proving God was on the side of the parliamentarians and Satan on the side of the King.[60] However, O'Cahan offered a further mitigating factor in the killing of Wilson: her age. Old age and gender is an area of early modern Irish culture and society that awaits detailed research, but there existed a 'powerful cultural current of hatred of elder women in early modern Europe'.[61] By the seventeenth century, the stereotype of the witch as a wizened old woman was fully formed in cheap printed accounts of witchcraft as well as in learned demonological works, which in their turn influenced public perceptions.[62] Taken as a whole, older women (aged around 50 and above) were proportionally over-represented in those formally accused of witchcraft in early modern Europe.[63] This has been explained in a number of ways: by the sometimes lengthy periods of time between the time a reputation for witchcraft was first gained and that of the first formal accusation;[64] by the fact that older women were more likely to demonstrate the aggressive behaviour associated with witches due to biological and psychological changes brought on by the menopause, as well as their often precarious socioeconomic circumstances and the socio-cultural restrictions placed on their behaviour;[65] and because of emotional and psychological factors that caused antagonism between younger women with children, or who had just given birth, or whose children had died, and older women who could no longer have children.[66]

Seventeenth-century Irish Protestants, as well as Catholics, were not above taking the law into their own hands with regards to suspected witches (see below), and Protestant forces in the 1640s also accused their military opponents of using witchcraft to thwart their military campaign. Sir James Turner, who was a major in Lord Sinclair's army, which was dispatched by the Scottish government to fight insurgents and assist Protestant settlers in Ulster, described how in May 1642, when marching through the Mourne mountains in Co. Down on the way to Carrickfergus, Co. Antrim, his troops were beset by a rain- and hailstorm of such severity that his soldiers and their officers attributed

it 'to the devilish skill of some Irish witches'. Turner further remarked
that if the storm was caused by witches, 'then I am sure their master [the
Devil] gave us good proofe he was reallie prince of the air'.[67] Scottish
soldiers came from a culture where belief in malefic, demonic witchcraft was not only strong but witchcraft accusation and prosecution
remained a reality.[68] Furthermore, they arrived in a country in which
Protestant settlers from the Elizabethan period onwards had demonised
Irish women, whom they deemed, as Mary O'Dowd has pointed out, 'to
have all the worst characteristics traditionally associated with women
and none of the redeeming ones', and as such 'represented not only a
threat to male colonial settlers but to the whole civilising influence of
English society in Ireland'.[69] For the members of the elite such as Turner
and his officers, it was easier to believe that the Devil and his agents,
witches, were active in the world in times of crisis when political and
religious certainties were undermined and established order threatened.[70] During the bitter Confederate wars of the 1640s,[71] either accusations made by Protestants against fellow Protestants were dealt with
by church courts, or suspects were committed without trial to county
jail due to the disruption of the Assize court system.[72] In January 1646,
William Beale and Arthur Annesley, based in Belfast, reported that there
was 'no course settled for trial of felons, witches and other malefactors'
by Assize judges that put 'the country to unnecessary charge for prisoners'. Beale and Annesley suggested that if 'justices of the peace were
commanded to keep sessions as formerly, it may suffice till judges be
appointed'.[73]

Judicial scepticism?

If serendipity, informal arbitration, execution, and imprisonment without trial during the 1640s played a role in keeping prosecution rates low
in Protestant Ireland after the passing of the 1586 Act, the activities of
local judiciaries may have played a greater one in the later seventeenth
century. In England, the majority of witchcraft trials took place in twice-
yearly Assize courts before senior, experienced Westminster judges,
who were culturally and socially distanced from the malice and local
tensions usually surrounding witchcraft prosecution. Importantly, they
were aware of what constituted sufficient proof for witchcraft and were
able to direct the male petty jury (in whose hands conviction or acquittal ultimately lay) on these matters when they summed-up proceedings
at the end of the trial. The decisive influence of these men, coupled
with an often expensive trial process, and the fact that JPs and grand

jurymen, being broadly in line with educated opinion, were acutely aware of the evidential problems involved in adequately proving the crime of witchcraft and therefore unlikely to take witchcraft accusations lightly, kept prosecution and indictment rates relatively low in Elizabethan and Stuart England.[74] Despite a spike in witchcraft prosecution in 1645–7 due to the activities of witch-finders Matthew Hopkins and John Stearne,[75] the Restoration era produced judiciaries culturally distanced from victims and accusers, and so cautious and sceptical in their handling of the evidence brought before them that witchcraft prosecution, trials, and convictions fell away to nothing.[76] This scepticism, increased governmental control over trials, along with a number of legal and cultural shifts, saw a similar situation emerge, albeit at different times, in seventeenth- and eighteenth-century Europe.[77] In Scotland, witch-hunting before this time was a local affair, with Kirk Sessions, burgh magistrates, and sheriffs responsible for official identification of witches and initial investigations into the veracity of accusations. Most trials were held in Lowland local courts (under commission after 1597 from the Privy Council in Edinburgh), before an assize or jury of legally untrained local magistrates, parish elders, and lairds. These men struggled with impartiality and objectivity to such an extent that in 90% of the cases that came before them they returned a guilty verdict. Along with the use of extra-legal torture to gain confessions and the absence of a grand jury, the local aspect of Scottish witch-hunting explains its comparative ferocity, as well as how individual trials became mass witch-hunts.[78]

In Ireland, after the collapse of Crown Courts in the 1640s, it was not until 1655 that JPs began operating once more and regular circuits of Assize judges were established.[79] In the latter half of seventeenth century, the Irish judiciary, in common with their English counterparts, became increasingly sceptical of the traditional evidence of witchcraft and consequently reluctant to prosecute on the basis of them. In Islandmagee, Co. Antrim, in 1711, before finally indicting the accused, local constables, clergy, and members of the elite carefully tested the victim's claim that her symptoms of demonic possession worsened on the approach of a suspected witch.[80] Furthermore, at least one Irish JP, in common with English counterparts in the later seventeenth century,[81] was exercising summary jurisdiction as a way to punish people for witchcraft, satiate popular demand for justice, and avoid a trial by jury. In March 1686, Cork merchant Christopher Crofts noted that his 'poor boy Jack to all appearances lay dying' having endured 'a convulsion for eight or nine hours'.[82] Crofts noted that his wife and 'several others' were of 'the opinion that he is bewitched' by 'the old woman, the mother of Nell Welsh', because 'she was reputed a bad woman' and Jack had been 'playing by her that day'.[83] The fact that Jack's symptoms, convulsions, would have been widely recognised at the time as those of demonic possession would not have helped.[84] In insular, close-knit, early modern communities the reputation of both individuals and households was all-important, and when misfortune occurred, past acts of witchcraft were recalled to inform the current situation. In this way, past behaviour or misfortune could be re-cast as suspicious. In practice, this meant those with a reputation for witchcraft, or who belonged to a family of reputed witches, were more likely to face prosecution.[85] This accusation is also notable for the significant involvement of local women in bringing it to the attention of the authorities. James Sharpe has argued that women in early modern England were involved in nearly every aspect of witchcraft prosecution – from accusation, to evidence gathering, to appearing in court – because in a patriarchal society this provided power in their restricted spheres of influence.[86] In Clive Holmes' reading, however, English women were increasingly involved during the seventeenth century in the machinery of prosecution of witches both as witnesses and gatherers of evidence, such as physical proof of a devil's mark on the body of the accused, at the behest of male investigators: in short, patriarchy and misogyny took not a secondary but a primary role in making women accuse each other.[87] In contrast to his wife, Crofts believed his son's illness was caused by 'the hand of God'. Despite misgivings, he had the old woman and her daughter committed to the Cork Bridewell, where the latter was to stay 'some time, because she is with child and therefore cannot be whipped'.[88] The use of such discretionary powers in Ireland was usually limited to religious infractions such as Sabbath-breaking or swearing.[89] Witchcraft, however, qualified as both a secular and an ecclesiastical crime.

Irish grand juries were also not above rejecting indictments drafted by JPs. In Charleville, Co. Cork, in early 1660, Patrick Fitzmaurice, Baron Kerry, petitioned Roger Boyle, first earl of Orrery and Lord President of Munster, and a man with first-hand experience of, and scholarly interest in, witchcraft and the demonic,[90] to issue a special warrant to have a woman recently acquitted of witchcraft by a Grand jury re-arrested and placed in Cork jail for bewitching his wife, Honora. Honora was reported to have 'vomited pins and nails, wood and straw' and was 'every day in most horrid pains and tortures'. Fitzmaurice had accused the woman in question of his wife's bewitchment because her symptoms eased when the suspect was imprisoned but returned immediately upon her release. As soon as Boyle's 'warrant was executed and the woman [placed] in custody', Honora 'was immediately at ease as upon observation of all circumstances they perceiv'd'.[91] It was widely believed that imprisonment cured, or at least alleviated the symptoms of bewitchment and demonic possession.[92] The fact that it took a special warrant requested by a member of the political elite to have the suspect arrested further attests to the lack of enthusiasm at that time among Ireland's judiciary for prosecuting suspected witches. Although it is impossible to discern the precise nature of the accusation, it would appear that, given Honora's symptoms, this was a demonic possession case. As such, it provided Honora with the ways and means to subvert the strict social rules of behaviour that governed female gentry-life and reassert her central position within her household. The very fact that the suspected witch had been accused of witchcraft in the past indicates that the politics of reputation were at play.[93]

Scepticism even crept into the trial process itself, with one of the judges trying the Islandmagee witches, Anthony Upton, Justice of the Common Pleas, advising the jury not to return a guilty verdict on the strength of the, by then, controversial spectral evidence laid before them.[94] The conviction and passing of the death sentence on Marion Fisher in September 1655 at Co. Antrim Assizes at Carrickfergus, for murdering Alexander Gilbert by means of witchcraft, was quashed in November 1656, after Sir James Barry, first Baron Santry, prompted by a petition of the girl's father, Robert Fisher, re-examined the case. Barry's appeal report stated that Gilbert had died of natural causes and that Marion displayed signs of mental instability both during the trial and after it when imprisoned, presumably throwing doubt on a previously obtained confession.[95] Unfortunately the surviving records provide no indication as to the circumstances in which the original accusation arose.

The role of Protestant church courts

Witchcraft prosecution remained low in Ireland because the Catholic majority did not make formal accusations of malefic witchcraft, and Protestants did so late in the century, when sceptical judiciaries were unwilling to prosecute. It remains to be seen however if the Protestant clergy also helped to keep witchcraft trials to a minimum. Although a lack of institutional records makes it impossible to adequately gauge the Church of Ireland's role, fragmentary evidence suggests that its ecclesiastical courts, in common with those of the early modern Church of England,[96] did not handle many witchcraft cases, or make an effort to punish them.[97] Certainly, Archbishop of Dublin William King's claim that the Church of Ireland's denominationally-specific sacrament of baptism, and its required 'renunciation of the de[vil] [and] all his works', protected its communicants from 'Satan [and] ... his imps', ensuring 'few of this communion are ever hurt by witches or witchcraft', implies that its ecclesiastical courts did not handle witchcraft cases due to a lack of demand.[98] By the early eighteenth century, civil prosecutions for witch-craft were becoming rare in Scotland and Kirk Sessions and presbyteries lost their traditional role in identifying witches and investigating accusa-tions prior to indictment and trial. However, these church courts, which presided over the moral discipline of their congregations, continued to sporadically arbitrate witchcraft accusations and suspicions in the form of defamation, cursing, and counter-witchcraft cases.[99] Working in a different, English-style legal context, the Presbyterian Church in Ireland could not have played such a central role in witch-hunting as it did in Scotland. However, almost from inception its sessions, presbyteries and meetings arbitrated witchcraft accusations and associated slander cases rather than pass them onto civil authorities.[100] Not only did communities in early modern Ireland tend to resolve disputes among themselves,[101] in seventeenth-century Presbyterian Ulster it was 'the custom ... [to] consult with the[ir] ministers' when witchcraft was first suspected.[102] In July 1647, conflict and the suspension of the crown court system ensured that the South Antrim parish of Templepatrick, and afterwards the Presbytery of Antrim, had no option but to handle a witchcraft accusation made against Janet Dilson themselves, eventually resolving the case in favour of the accused.[103] In more settled times, in February 1656, Elizabeth Kennedy of Islandmagee, Co. Antrim complained to the Antrim meeting that 'one Thomas Etkin in the same place ... called her an witch and Said he wold prove the same'. The meeting referred the matter back to the Islandmagee Session to 'try the woman and censure the slanderer, or returne the proven process to the next meeting'.[104] The Antrim Meeting was attended by elders and ministers who formed the core of its leadership at that time, and acted as 'a sort of halfway house, an intermediate body between the local ministers and sessions, and the presbytery that covered all of Ulster', as well as acting as a church court.[105] The facts that the case was not mentioned again in the Antrim minutes, and the Islandmagee Session book is no longer extant, mean it can be assumed that Etkin was found not guilty of witchcraft and the accuser censured for 'slander' instead.[106]

By the early eighteenth century, when the Presbyterian Church was more organised and highly structured, and the Presbyterian community became increasingly cut off from the Anglican establishment, both at parish and local government level, this impulse to handle its own moral discipline within its own ecclesiastical structure became stronger.[107] Consequently, various sessions and presbyteries in Ulster continued to deliberate over witchcraft cases in a diligent and even-handed manner. In doing so, the Irish ministers and elders who managed these cases may have been taking their lead from religious counterparts in Scotland, and in demanding even stronger evidence of guilt may have been influenced by an increasingly sceptical Irish judiciary. When this proof was not forthcoming they worked to mend relations between both accuser and the accused. In July 1718, Sarah Osburn was brought before the Donaghedy Session in Co. Tyrone, accused by an elder, John Love, of 'charming' to effect 'a very great bodily injury' on him. In the first instance, the Session, followed by the Strabane Presbytery, found 'Love's behaviour towards the woman ... scandalous', and he was duly suspended from office until 'there appear in him visible marks of his repentance'. It was also noted that Osburn refused to pray for the recovery of Love, and at the next meeting of the Presbytery, on 13 August 1718, it was decided that if her conduct raised any more concern the Donaghedy Session was free to ask the Presbytery for advice as to a suitable course of action. The ruling did little to resolve the situation and the conflict rumbled on for a year until the Presbytery decided to absolve both parties of blame to allow Love and Osburn 'to agree and forgive one another'. After considering further accusations and witness statements brought by both parties, it ruled in March 1719 that Osburn was to be declared 'innocent from the pulpit' and Love freed from his current censure.[108] In October 1731, another witchcraft case at Carnmoney Session was dropped because both the accuser and the accused were deemed to have used un-Christian magical practices.[109]

In May 1701, William Lockert complained to the Connor Presbyterian Church Session, Co. Antrim, that 'Agnes Woodburn scandalised him with [an accusation of] witchcraft'. When the Session called Woodburn to appear before them, she denied slander by stating that she had not said 'such things of his name'.[110] At the next Session, a few days later, Lockert appeared before the Session, which 'rebuked both parties and after admonishment they ... parted friends'.[111] This was a rare accusation of a man of witchcraft in Ireland.[112] Another slander case was handled in April 1721 by the Carnmoney Session, at which Margaret Williamson complained that 'Mary Coruth had branded her with witchcraft and that she can prove that she said so'. Aware that the would-be slanderer was of 'good report', the Session agreed to let an elder, John

McMahon, interview her and inform them of his findings at their next meeting.[113] The meeting must have reported in Coruth's favour, for the matter was later dropped by the Session. In November 1723, Sarah Moor lodged a complaint at the Aghadowey Session in Co. Londonderry that Timothy Knox, Mary Asking, and Robert White had 'defam'd her, saying she is a witch'. The Session then ordered Moor to 'bring all her evidences to prove the charges against them next Session', while congregation elder, John Givan, ordered 'the defendants to appear ... before this Session'.[114] Knox, White, and Asking duly appeared at the next Session, in April 1724, 'acknowledging that they were rash in calling Sarah Moor a witch and promised to refrain such reproaches hereafter'. Moor acknowledged this ruling was 'satisfactory and was made friends w[i]th all of them'.[115] In October 1731, James Henderson and his wife were referred by Ardstraw Session in Co. Tyrone to the Strabane Presbytery, held in Strabane, to give 'their evidences in prosecution for of their complaint ag[ain]st James Allen for calling his wife devil witch etc.'. James Allen was then called before the committee which duly considered whether he 'had fully proven his charge of devilry [and] and witchery etc. ag[ain]st Henderson's wife, and it carry'd in the negative' following an unanimous vote. The question was then 'put whether Allen's charg[e]s did not appear to be groundless and scandalous, and it carry'd in the affirmative', again after a unanimous vote. Allen was then 'rebuk'd' by the moderator of the Presbytery, and it was resolved that 'the woman's innocence' should be declared publicly before the congregation at Ardstraw Presbyterian Church.[116]

These slander cases attest to the popular fear of witchcraft attack and the social stigma of being accused, even informally, of being a witch. They also suggest that, just as in England, many of those accused of witchcraft in Ireland defended themselves and their good name, often vigorously.[117] Although it is equally true, as Alison Rowlands has put it, that 'in many regions, women, especially if they were poor, might simply have ... lacked the social, financial and educational resources to mount effective strategies in their own defence'.[118] Furthermore, as Presbyterian records survive in uneven numbers, it is possible that the arbitration of witchcraft disputes in this way by the Church was even more widespread than suggested here, helping to channel accusations away from civil magistrates and discouraging future accusations by finding in favour of those accused and by censuring 'slanderers'. It may have even helped prevent vigilante action in an era when judiciaries were unwilling to prosecute witches. In late seventeenth- and early eighteenth-century England, a lack of ecclesiastical intervention, high judicial scepticism, and official inaction ensured that popular fear of witches frequently exploded in acts of communal justice against suspects. As Scottish kirks continued to investigate witchcraft accusation and suspicion up until the mid-eighteenth century, acts of witchcraft-associated vigilante violence were infrequent.[119] This is not to say that vigilante action did not occasionally take place in early modern Europe when the witch-hunts were at their height in the sixteenth and seventeenth centuries, both as a means to satiate popular demand for justice and to avoid an often expensive prosecution process.[120]

The 1698 Antrim case, when an old woman was murdered for the bewitchment of a young girl, demonstrates that when accusations were not arbitrated by church courts and when clergy encouraged them, and presumably the legal authorities failed to act, Presbyterian communities did take the law into their own hands (of which more will be said below). The Presbyterian minister of Antrim, Rev. William Adair, not only failed to refer this case over to his Session or Presbytery, but also confirmed the girl was a demoniac.[121] He also assisted the condemned party just before she was put to death, 'in her last agony, and at that moment on which depends eternity'. He even asked her to 'dissolve the spell' she had cast on the girl, to which she replied that 'it was not in her power because the Ember-weeks were past since she had bewitched her; adding, that should she undo the villanies she had perpetrated, the child would not so quickly recover, for two other witches ... had also given her mortal infections, from the effects whereof she could not without difficulty, and much time, be delivered'.[122] After the 'witch' was put to death, Adair visited the girl, whose condition worsened, especially when he read passages from the Bible or touched her.[123] As has been suggested, the girl was then taken to a cunning-person in Dublin by her mother, and was only cured by the magical ointment prepared by Higgs.[124] The reasons why Adair went against prevailing clerical protocol with regards to witchcraft cases are impossible to establish due to a lack of evidence. William Adair had transcribed his father Patrick's book on Presbyterianism in Ireland which contained a vivid description of the murder by witches of Presbyterian minister James Shaw and his wife in Co. Antrim in 1672. It could be thus conjectured that the fact the witches believed to have killed the Shaws were never brought to justice may have made him anxious to avoid history repeating itself.[125]

It has long been held that the 1698 Antrim affair was a typical trial for witchcraft carried out under the 1586 Irish Witchcraft Act,[126] but in reality it was an act of communal violence carried out by a 'vigilante' mob. There are several reasons to believe that the Antrim 'witch' in 1698 was murdered by her neighbours, above and beyond the fact that this was the version of events given, up until at least the late nineteenth century, in local folklore accounts.[127] First of all, in his pamphlet, Daniel Higgs rendered anonymous the accused and the two other female witches she named as accomplices, as well as the victim and the 'executioner', in order to protect the identity of the latter and release them from the threat of future prosecution for murder.[128] That Higgs simply did not know their names is untenable, as he was intimately involved with the case for a number of months, housing and nursing the victim himself.[129] The omission of the names of accusers and accused is extremely rare in witchcraft pamphlets, as part of their raison d'être was to relate to an eager reading public the details of trials and those involved.[130] It is also interesting to note that Higgs only appears in the possession narrative after the murder of the suspect, thus preventing him from being an accessory before, if not after, the fact.[131] His possession narrative also demonstrates that the legal formalities of prosecution were not followed during either the witch's apprehension or the attainment of her confession, and no details are given of the trial itself.[132] The fact that the 'witch' was executed in the first place is indicative of extra-legal activity: the suspect did not kill her victim and there is no indication she had more than one conviction for witchcraft; thus under the dictates of the Irish Witchcraft Act she should have been imprisoned for a year and pilloried. The method of execution, in that the Antrim 'witch' was 'strangled and burnt' in common with Scottish witches,[133] also suggests foul play: under common law in Ireland even women who had committed murder were hanged as criminals and not burnt, as this was a fate reserved for heretics and traitors.[134]

Conclusion

Unlike in Gaelic-Irish popular culture, in Protestant, settler Ireland by the mid-seventeenth century there was a high level of belief in malefic and demonic witchcraft, and this, contrary to previous readings, manifested itself in sporadic but significant numbers of formal accusations by Protestants. In common with their counterparts in later seventeenth-century England, in Ireland accusations for witchcraft were made by both men and women and rooted in interpersonal, political, and religious conflict. In Ireland, where gender roles were particularly well defined, it is no surprise that those who did not meet the behavioural norms, or whose physical appearance was that of a stereotypical witch, or had a reputation for witchcraft were more likely to be accused of witchcraft.

That these accusations did not end in prosecution and conviction at the hands of Assize judges was due to the fact that they were levied at a time of high judicial scepticism towards witchcraft in Ireland and most of Europe. As ministers were often approached first when witchcraft was suspected, Presbyterian Church courts in form of sessions and presbyteries were first to deal with accusations. The ministers and elders who managed these bodies were increasingly reluctant, as the seventeenth turned into the eighteenth century, to turn over cases to local agents of law enforcement, preferring to deal with them, in common with other religious and moral offences, within their own, insular communities. In doing so, they may have been also following the example of their 'sister' Church in Scotland. The fact that they scrutinised each accusation in an even-handed manner may have been because they were operating in period when judicial scepticism, but not disbelief, was a growing part of Protestant culture. In doing so, they immunised the north of Ireland, for the most part, from the type of acts of communal justice experienced in England during the era of declining witchcraft prosecutions. The fact these courts also censured witchcraft accusers for slander may have made it less attractive to levy accusations without careful consideration.

5
Witchcraft Trials and Demonic Possession in Early Modern Ireland

Trials for witchcraft in Ireland

If the checks and balances described in the last chapter kept prosecution rates for witchcraft low in Protestant Ireland, while fear of malefic witches remained part of popular culture, there were nonetheless occasions when they failed to operate. Using cases identified by Seymour in *Irish Witchcraft and Demonology* (Dublin, 1913), Elwen Lapoint argued that in early modern Ireland women were prosecuted for witchcraft on nine occasions, which resulted in three executions.[1] These calculations require adjustment, as Seymour actually detailed six trials and five executions in his book: Dame Alice Kyteler and associates, Kilkenny, 1324 (execution of Petronella de Midia); 'two witches', Kilkenny, 1578 (both executed); Anglican minister, John Aston of Mellifont, Co. Louth, 1606; Florence Newton, 1661 (executed); anonymous witch, Antrim, 1698 (executed); and eight women at Islandmagee in 1711.[2] Seymour's calculations, however, also require re-evaluation as he excluded the conviction of Marion Fisher in 1655, and the Kyteler case was a sorcery-cum-treason trial and occurred in the medieval rather than in the early modern period. Similarly, the two Kilkenny witches were tried in 1578 before witchcraft was a secular crime in Ireland, and Aston was prosecuted not for witchcraft but for popular magic.[3] Furthermore, as was established in the previous chapter, the 1698 execution was an instance of popular summary justice rather than a witchcraft trial and, as we shall see in this chapter, the Islandmagee witchcraft case engendered two separate trials. In total then, there were four recorded trials for witchcraft in early modern Ireland, resulting in one execution.[4] As little is known about the conviction of Fisher in 1655 beyond that related in the previous chapter, it is to the more richly documented cases of

Florence Newton (1661) and the Islandmagee witchcraft trial of 1711 we must turn to ascertain why these accusations in particular were played out in open court in front of Assize judges, when others were arbitrated at a local level. As both cases involve a central accuser displaying the symptoms of demonic possession, it is first necessary to discuss this phenomenon in early modern Britain and Ireland.

Demonic possession

Demonic possession had roots in educated Catholic and Protestant culture as well as in the popular mind. Classical Greek and Roman texts demonstrate that possession was part of the mental landscape of Western Europe for centuries, and the Bible, especially the New Testament, contains numerous examples of Jesus Christ casting out devils from human bodies. The symptoms of possession were stereotyped and displayed little change in their essential nature throughout the early modern period. This characteristic, along with its frequency and the publicity that high-profile cases created, meant people in Britain and its colonies knew, by the seventeenth century, what the signs and symptoms of possession were and how to identify a demoniac. These signs were not only variously described in the Bible but debated in witchcraft and demonological tracts and in popular pamphlets about well-known trials. In individual cases, however, not all of the symptoms of possession were manifest and some were more noticeable or marked than others. Demoniacs were particularly prone to bodily convulsions but they also cried, screamed, displayed supernatural strength, and spoke foreign languages without prior knowledge of them. Others symptoms included demonic ventriloquism, where the incumbent demon(s) spoke using the 'host', and clairvoyance, where the demoniac knew about things beyond their years and experience. Demoniacs also encountered strange smells and noises, levitated, felt living things moving beneath their skin, and vomited household objects. They lost the power of speech, went blind, and were paralysed and/or insensitive to pain while entranced. The possessed often refused to eat or drink, blasphemed, and displayed an aversion to anything associated with God or religion, the Bible in particular. As it was common for bewitched people in early modern England to see otherwise invisible spectres of their tormentors, this became a prominent proof in trials in the mid-seventeenth century, especially in those involving possession.[5]

Demonic possession came in two main forms in the early modern period. The first form was direct possession by Satan himself or one of his lesser demons and was found more often on the Continent. In early modern Christian orthodoxy it was associated with sin, as Satan was believed to target the sinful, under licence from God. The second type of possession was more common in Britain and (as we shall see) Ireland. In this reading, witches were believed to have chosen a victim, conjured up evil spirits, and commanded them to enter them. Although contemporaries failed to point out there was no Biblical connection between possession and witchcraft, it was associated with 'victimhood', as a demoniac was regarded as the helpless victim of a witch's malice. These possession/witchcraft accusations were often followed by the prosecution of those deemed responsible.[6]

In both Catholic and Protestant Europe, possession cases reached almost epidemic proportions in the years after the Reformation, in the late sixteenth and early seventeenth centuries.[7] A recent survey of surviving witchcraft literature by Phillip Almond has revealed over 100 cases of possession in England between 1550 and 1700. In this analysis, the vast majority of demoniacs were under the age of 20, with females forming a slight majority.[8] For example, in 1593, the five daughters (ranging from nine years of age to 15) of Huntingdonshire gentleman, Robert Throckmorton, accused elderly Alice Samuel, her husband John, and daughter Agnes of conjuring and commanding evil demons to enter their bodies. For this crime and the murder of Lady Cromwell (second wife of Sir Henry Cromwell of Hinchinbrook), the 'witches of Warboys' were convicted and hanged.[9]

The educated may have believed in possession in early modern Britain but they often had very different views on how to cure it. The medieval Church had provided a means to command evil spirits to leave the human body using the formalised rite of exorcism by priests acting in the name of God.[10] As Keith Thomas described it, 'the ritual of exorcism, with the sign of the cross, symbolic breathing (*insufflatio*), holy water, and the command to the Devil to depart in God's name, was further developed by the Catholic Church of the Counter Reformation in its numerous prescribed manuals of exorcism'.[11] Catholic priests in early modern England often justified their use of the rite of exorcism by reference to Jesus' disciples, who were given the power to rid human bodies of unclean spirits. Between the springs of 1585 and1586, 12 Catholic priests in Denham, Buckinghamshire, drove spirits from six individuals, and during the next century members of their denomination continued to perform exorcisms in secret. Reformation-era Protestantism, however, shunned this rite, seeing it either as straightforward sorcery or as a proselytising tool used by Catholic priests to ensnare the gullible.[12]

Although there was no direct discussion of demonic possession in the English Witchcraft Acts of 1563 and 1604, it was recognised in Canon law by the Church of England in 1604, ecclesiastical legislation which also effectively prohibited the Protestant version of exorcism, de-possession. De-possession was often performed by 'hotter' Protestant ministers, using fasting and prayer as a way to implore God to banish evil spirits back to Hell. The new provisions in the 1604 Canons, however, did not quite reflect the hostility to de-possession ceremonies in certain circles in the Established Church, which continued to be performed in private during the seventeenth century by English nonconformists.[13] In contrast to England and Ireland, possession in Scotland before the end of the seventeenth century was attributed by the educated elite to Satan alone and interpreted as the consequence of sin and moral failure on the part of the victim. This had the effect of making people less willing to expose themselves to ridicule by accusing others of their possession. No doubt influenced by anti-Sadduceeism trends in British demonology, in the 1690s the Godly elite of the Church of Scotland began to recognise the English type of possession and take accusations involving it seriously. To the Scottish Godly elite, possession narratives were a useful weapon in the fight against atheism and bolstered their attempts to explain the Universe in spiritual rather than in new, 'scientific', materialist terms. As a result, between 1696 and 1704, Presbyterian lowland Scotland experienced its first wave of possessions and trials, such as the widely publicised case of 11-year-old Christian Shaw, the Laird of Bargarran's daughter who lived in Erskine, Renfrewshire. In late 1696, Shaw began having fits, was unable to eat, experienced bodily pains, and vomited hot embers, pins, hair, and hay mixed with dung. She was also temporarily unable to speak, hear, or see, and on occasion became stiff and lifeless. After local ministers, neighbours, and family members fasted and prayed for her, and physicians and apothecaries failed to cure her by medical means, seven people were tried, convicted, and executed for her possession.[14]

Demonic possession in early Modern Ireland

If knowledge about demonic possession in early modern Britain and Europe has grown dramatically in the last four decades of the twentieth century, the subject, in particular its relationship with witchcraft in Ireland, remains under-researched.[15] Nevertheless, early seventeenth-century Irish Catholic priests were carrying out exorcisms, including a Jesuit priest in Munster who exorcised a Spanish-speaking demon in

1614.[16] Furthermore, as Raymond Gillespie has established, 'exorcism, for which a standard Catholic form had appeared in 1614 as part of the Roman Ritual of Pope Paul V, was carried out in haphazard way during the seventeenth century' in Ireland, with Catholic clergy using 'whatever manifestation of the power of God was locally accepted and available, adapting their methods to suit local customs'. Some clergy used only the sign of the cross and prayer, others the host or relics, while English rather than Latin was most commonly used.[17] At the end of the century, however, John Dunton pointed out that Fr. Keeren operated in Dublin as a *de facto* cunning-man and exorcist using the standardised Roman ritual.[18] English Protestant Dunton was convinced Keeren's exorcisms were impostures, remarking acerbically that, 'for my part, I think the Devil is in the presumptuous Priest, rather than the melancholy person'.[19]

In common with their counterparts in Britain, non-conforming Irish Protestant ministers performed de-possessions. In his autobiography, Robert Blair described how in Larne, Co. Antrim in 1630 some recent converts to Protestantism began to convulse during his Sunday service. The affected people later claimed their fits were 'the work of the Lord' and were possessed by the spirit of God. Blair noted that as 'daily the number' of converts 'increased ... both pastor and people' began to think their possession was inspired by Satan 'the destroyer', who 'playing the ape' did so in order 'to slander and disgrace the work of the Lord'. The following Sunday, when another demoniac screamed and convulsed, Blair rebuked the 'lying spirit' for daring to disturb 'the worship of God', ordering it 'in the name and authority of Jesus Christ not to disturb that congregation' again. Blair described with satisfaction that from that point on, 'we met with no more of that work' of the Devil.[20]

The Larne de-possession was of course an instance of direct demonic possession but in March of the same year the first case involving witchcraft came before the secular, Protestant authorities. This occurred when an un-named 14-year-old girl, who, after being committed to Dublin Castle, confessed to having only 'pretended to be possessed by the divell'. She further claimed that she had performed 'her feats by his instructions', namely those of Fr. Stephen Browne, who had 'used exorcisms' in an attempt to free her from her demonic tormentor.[21] Browne was born into a well-known Catholic family in Dublin in 1599, completed his studies at the Discalced Carmelite College in Louvain, and established a friary and an extremely popular chapel in Cook Street, Dublin in the mid-1620s.[22] In August 1630, a few months after the girl's accusation, Browne was committed to Dublin Castle, where he remained for a year without trial.[23] Browne's imprisonment had in reality little to do with his role in the girl's exorcism but was used by Lord Justices Adam Loftus, Viscount Loftus of Ely, and Sir Richard Boyle, earl of Cork, as a pretext to arrest him for his perceived role in the Cook Street Riot on 26 December 1629. The riot erupted after Mayor of Dublin, Christopher Forster, and Church of Ireland Archbishop of Dublin, Launcelot Bulkeley, accompanied by soldiers, raided a Franciscan Chapel as part of a wider clamp-down by the Irish administration on resurgent Catholicism and a proliferation of friaries, convents, and mass houses.[24] During Browne's incarceration, in March 1631, the girl once again began to show 'many signes of (either) being bewitched (or possessed by the divell)'. However, this time she 'accused Browne's mother to have bewitched her by crossing her in the street' as she made her way home from Sir William Ryvers house after being examined by the sheriff of the city.[25] Browne's mother, along with his aunt and sister, was imprisoned for seven weeks but later released.[26]

Astrologer Allan Makcouldy predicted in his Dublin-published almanac for the year 1632 that 'witches and Sorcerers shall abound this season' and that judges should therefore try all suspects and execute the guilty.[27] By this time, however, Browne was free, having been released from prison; a situation which Lord Deputy Wentworth, who arrived in Dublin in 1633, sought to reverse to make a very public statement about what he considered the recent, unacceptable growth of religious orders in the country.[28] During the next two years, Browne was brought twice before Lord Wentworth and the Privy Council which, on the second occasion, included chief baron of the Exchequer, Sir Richard Bolton, who tellingly accused him of using exorcism to lure Protestants away from their religion and allegiance to the King, while making explicit reference to the Cook Street incident.[29] On 11 February 1635, Browne was 'censured in [the] star chamber in £3000 fine to the King and to be pilloried, as an imposter and sorcerer'.[30] The 'Star Chamber' was, in theory, the highest court with criminal jurisdiction in Ireland and although it survived the abolition of the English Star Chamber in 1641, it ceased to operate after the 1640s, despite the fact that its officers continued to be appointed and paid up until 1702.[31] Wentworth justified Browne's arrest and conviction to the King's secretary, John Coke, on the grounds that he had 'vitiated a younge girle' and 'made her an instrument of setting forth a false miracle to abuse the people with all pretending shee was forsooth possesst, and by his prayers, (charmes and spells rather) to be dispossessed'. He went on to state that 'the proofe was in my judgement sufficient if it had been at a King's bench barr to have hanged him, for in truth I am persuaded there was witchcraft in the case'.[32] Wentworth's denunciation of exorcism as a Catholic proselytising tool was, as has been suggested, not uncommon among Protestant commentators, nor indeed was a call to have perpetrators tried under witchcraft legislation in criminal courts such as the King's Bench, which dealt with both civil and criminal cases.[33] In 1664, Church of Ireland Bishop of Down and Connor, Jeremy Taylor, expressed similar sentiments, regarding as a 'horrible impiety ... the infinite superstitions and incantations, or charms us'd by ... [Catholic] priests in their exercising possessed persons',[34] warning 'that if any man amongst us should use such things, he would be in danger of being tried at the next Assizes for a witch or a conjurer'.[35] When Browne was pilloried on 18 February 1635, and forced to wear a sign inscribed with 'imposter and seducer',[36] Wentworth noted with disgust that he took his punishment with 'some confidence as if he had suffered for the corpse of Christ'. Wentworth went on to blame Browne's 'martyrdome' for panicking and 'affrighting' the Catholic crowd that had gathered to watch his ordeal into believing a Catholic rebellion was imminent.[37] Unable to pay the massive fine imposed him, Browne remained in prison until August 1636, when, after the intercession of Henrietta Maria, Catholic wife of Charles I, his fine was remitted and he was released.[38]

There were no demonic possession cases or calls for witchcraft trials in the remaining years of the 1630s, as Archbishop Laud ironically highlighted in a letter to Bishop Bramhall: 'I did not think I should have received any news for Ireland concerning witches but if my Lord fall[s] to conjuring of them I make no doubt but I shall quickly hear more'.[39] Bramhall, as has been noted, would have no need to 'conjure up' witches as Ireland plunged into rebellion and war in the 1640s.[40] Demonic possession was also in abeyance but in the 1650s, Irish gentlemen and healer, Valentine Greatrakes, investigated a demonic obsession at the Charleville home in Co. Cork of his patron, Roger Boyle, earl of Orrery.[41] Demonic obsession was a phenomenon distinct from possession but nevertheless linked to it, and more so in learned demonology than in popular culture. If demonic possession occurred when a demonic spirit entered the human body in order to control it, demonic obsession was when a demon followed an individual and attacked them externally. The obsessing demon however also tempted them in the hope of eventually possessing them, even making them think and do things usually inconceivable. In common with possession, obsession was not necessarily linked to the presence of witchcraft.[42] Another instance of demonic obsession occurred in 1678 when a young niece of

'Alderman Arundel in Dublin' was pursued by 'very terrible noises' in the 'chambers she frequented', becoming 'enfeebled' in both body and mind until the demon was driven away by the prayer and fasting of some local non-conformist ministers.[43] In June 1702, the minister and elder of Carnmoney Presbyterian Session in Co. Antrim investigated a case of demonic obsession in the house of a member of the congregation. The investigations were brought to a halt when the disturbances stopped as suddenly as they had started.[44]

In the late 1650s, Sir Jerome (or Hierome) Sankey, a lay preacher and one of the most prominent Baptists in Ireland, attempted the depossession of a Mr Wadman. A sceptical, mocking account of the case written by Sankey's political enemy, Sir William Petty,[45] inferred that Wadman's 'odd expressions' were misinterpreted by Sankey as demonic possession but were in fact the result of Wadman 'being in a fit of melancholy, reflecting upon the death of his wife'. Petty went onto describe how immediately after this diagnosis Sankey undertook to 'cast out the divel' but soon became 'weary of his vain exorcismes' and informed 'the spectators' that 'Wadman's divel was of that sort which required fasting aswel as prayer to expel it'. As Sankey had 'plentifully ... eaten and tipled that evening', he resolved to come back the next evening.[46] Sankey, whom Petty disparaged as Catholic by referring to him as an 'Exorcist', returned the next day, 'more duely prepared by fasting, and having eaten but three eggs', only to find that 'the Divel departed' as Wadham had 'been let blood in the meantime'.[47] In other words, to Petty's mind, there was nothing supernatural about this episode at all, Wadman's possession was caused by mental illness and its symptoms had been relieved by a method of surgical intervention commonly used in such cases, bloodletting.[48] The early 1660s in Ireland witnessed another possession case in Cork, that of Honora, wife of Baron Fitzmaurice; a case in which Roger Boyle was also involved.[49]

Youghal, Cork 1661

The first well-documented trial for witchcraft involving possession came a year later on 11 September 1661. Although surviving sources remain maddeningly silent on the matter, it is generally assumed that Florence Newton was convicted of murder by means of witchcraft at Cork Assizes and executed shortly afterwards.[50] There is no need to repeat the narrative of the trial in detail as this has been done elsewhere,[51] as has the role of gender in the case[52] and the involvement of Valentine Greatrakes.[53] Joseph Glanvill's *Saducismus Triumphatus* is the main source for the

Youghal case,[54] as it was for Tory Francis Bragge who used it to compare Newton's trial to that of Jane Wenham in Hertfordshire in 1712 in a controversial, pamphlet defence of traditional witchcraft belief.[55] The account in *Saducismus Triumphatus* itself was based on a trial transcript prepared by the judge who presided at the trial, Sir William Aston.[56] Mary Longdon's initial accusation of Newton fits the charity-refused model, with the former refusing to give the latter some of her master John Pyne's beer, provoking her to leave muttering threats. The case soon transformed into an almost textbook English demonic possession, becoming a capital case when Newton was accused of bewitching to death her gaoler, David Jones.[57] The fact that Longdon was a demoniac is an aspect of the trial that has not been discussed in existing historiography, and by exploring it, this chapter will explain why this case was taken so seriously by local elites who controlled the machinery of prosecution.

A week after the initial refusal of charity, Longdon claimed that upon meeting Newton once more she kissed her and uttered the following words interpreted as a threat: 'I bear thee no ill will, and I pray thee do thou bear me none'.[58] A few days after this, she was visited by Newton and the Devil, who in the relatively common guise of 'a little old man in silk cloths' tempted her to become a witch herself.[59] It was relatively common in early modern witchcraft/possession cases for demoniacs, especially those from hotter Protestant backgrounds, to claim they had been tempted by the Devil but by embodying Christian piety had resisted him.[60] Three weeks later Londgon began to experience an impressive array of possession symptoms: from convulsive fits; to vomiting household objects; to Bibles being snatched from her hands by unseen forces; and intermittent spectral visits by Newton, who stuck pins into her flesh. It was further reported that Longdon was transported whilst in a trance-like state, to various parts of her master's house,[61] and just before 'the first beginning of her fits, several (and very many) small stones would fall upon her as she went up and down, and would follow her from place to place, and from one room to another, and would hit her on the head, shoulders and arms, and fall to the ground and vanish away'.[62] Mysterious stone-throwing, which in Greek translates as *lithobolia*, was reported from the early medieval period onwards but in seventeenth-century England and America it was primarily associated with witchcraft and demonic activity rather than with ghosts.[63]

When Newton was imprisoned to await trial, Longdon's symptoms temporarily ceased, but became worse when the suspect was left unbolted in her cell. This provided Newton with the opportunity to resume her spectral attacks once more.[64] As has been suggested, it was widely believed that the death or imprisonment of a suspected witch alleviated or cured the symptoms of bewitchment and possession. Furthermore, as Peter Elmer has pointed out, it was a 'well-established principle that the victims of witchcraft were likely to suffer fits and seizures in the presence of those who caused their affliction'.[65] Consequently Newton's guilt was further established by the fact that Longdon 'was always worse when she was brought unto her and her fits more violent than at another time'.[66]

Even when demonic possession was accepted in principle, particular instances of it were often hotly disputed, as a range of alternative, and occasionally complementary, explanations were available: from deliberate imposture to natural illness or demonically-wrought hallucination or illusion. Physicians and cunning-folk were often called upon to help steer prosecutors along the correct explanatory pathway.[67] In Glanvill's account, Longdon's possession is explained solely in terms of witchcraft, and unlike in another Cork possession case occurring a quarter of century later in 1686, neither 'natural' illness nor divine intervention are referred to as possible, alternative explanatory mechanisms.[68] Given its associations with sin and moral transgression, it is perhaps unsurprising that Longdon chose to explain her possession in terms of witchcraft. Certainly, the idea that the Devil wronged sinners and misfortune befell them as a result was a concept not unknown in seventeenth-century Irish popular literature. In 1673, a Dublin broadsheet told of an un-named female servant of Mr Mount of Dublin, who having committed a small misdemeanour in her master's house tried to cover up her sin, and prove her innocence by stating, in 'that common (but most wicked) way', that 'the devil might burn her alive if she did it'. This disavowal backfired and her master found her that night in the kitchen, with her body burnt black with no indication of the presence of fire near her body or clothes.[69] In the days that followed her body burned with a 'supernatural fire' with local physicians concluding that her injuries were of 'the Lord's doing'.[70] The girl's flesh was slowly consumed by 'fire' as she was displayed in Exchequer Lane in Dublin as 'a publick spectacle to the whole city which almost generally has been to see her'.[71] Much the same warning was served up in a late seventeenth-century novel about a prince serving in King William's army in August 1690 who fell in love and married a girl from Clonmel:

> poor Beelzebub is wrong'd, for he could not do us half the mischiefs we receive, unless we helped him against one another, and of all people I think the envious are his principle agents.[72]

If we are to reject the possibility that Longdon was actually possessed, and preclude retrospective diagnosis,[73] then it becomes a distinct possibility that Longdon, to a greater of lesser extent, faked her possession. As symptoms of possession were stereotyped and could be copied easily, there were unsurprisingly many well-publicised cases of imposture in early modern Britain. In London in 1574 two young girls, Agnes Briggs and Rachel Pinder, simulated their possession before accusing a local woman of their bewitchment.[74] In 1605–6, the scepticism of James I towards the possession of 19-year-old gentlewoman, Anne Gunter was instrumental in her being exposed as a fraud and later prosecuted (along with her father Brian) for making a false witchcraft accusation.[75] In Bilston, Staffordshire in 1620, the 12-year-old son of a tenant farmer, William Perry, under the tutelage of a Catholic priest, counterfeited his possession, which he attributed to the witchcraft of elderly Joan Cocke.[76] In 1698 in Hammersmith, London, Sarah Fowles was tried at the Old Bailey (London's main criminal court) for pretending to be possessed and making a false accusation of witchcraft.[77] In the early eighteenth century, Richard Hathaway, a blacksmith's apprentice from Southwark accused Sarah Morduck or Moredike, the wife of a waterman, of bewitching him by means of demonic possession. Morduck stood trial for witchcraft at Guildford Assizes in summer 1701 and was acquitted. Hathaway was deemed an imposter by the jury and later prosecuted for assault and rioting. He was tried at the Surrey Assizes on 25 March 1702 and given six months hard labour, pilloried, and flogged.[78] Even Scotland was not immune from imposture, as the case of Patrick Morton detailed below attests.

In common with many British demoniacs, faking her possession would have provided Longdon with the attention, concern, and sympathy of the local community, as well as enabling her to move from the margins of adult attention to the centre, from invisibility to notoriety, and from a position of powerlessness to one of empowerment through the use and control of her body. Demoniacs were not accountable for their own actions and were thereby liberated from normal rules of behaviour: they could scream, shout, blaspheme, tear up Bibles, curse, and act in a sexually inappropriate manner without reproach. They were also provided with a means to rebel against the restrictions of a pious upbringing, including the demands of saying prayers and singing psalms.[79] Indeed, as Keith Thomas suggested, 'a conspicuous feature of the cases of possession about which details survive is that they frequently originated in a religious environment ... [and] it could be plausibly urged that the victims were engaging in a hysterical reaction against the religious discipline and repression to which they had been subjected'.[80] Demoniacs were also able to overturn the strict age hierarchy that existed at that time, which expected children and adolescents to respect and obey their elders, by accusing older men and women of their bewitchment.[81] In Marion Gibson's words, 'when both the family and the wider political world were so regulated by hierarchies enforceable by violence, then recourse to the supernatural world offered an opportunity to challenge, invert, mock and subvert those hierarchies'.[82] It has also been suggested that possession provided a covert way for demoniacs to attack those in their community toward whom they, or their neighbours, harboured a grudge.[83]

Peter Elmer has suggested that accusations of witchcraft were more likely to arise and be taken seriously by judges and magistrates in communities where elite fear of the devil's powers was heightened, when 'their sense of religious and political order was currently under threat', or at times of 'actual polarisation and strife'.[84] Religious and political tension was palpable in Restoration Youghal, for which the appearance of a witch provided an explanation and outlet. Many of those involved with Newton's investigation, prosecution, and trial (Pyne, Greatrakes, his henchman Edward Perry, and Mayor of Youghal, Richard Mayre or Myers) were particularly affected by these tensions, as they formed part of a community of Godly families who had allied themselves with the Cromwellian regime. If the re-establishment of the Church of Ireland in 1660 was not bad enough, they lived in fear of 'sectarian subversion' by the town's Baptists, Ranters, and Quakers, as well as of encroachment on their political and economic power by the seemingly ascendant local Catholic population.[85]

There was, beyond that of Longdon herself, little female involvement in the legal process against Newton, either in collecting or giving evidence. Newton's prosecution, in other words, was left in the hands of local male elites.[86] As has been already mentioned, women who displayed behaviour considered socially unacceptable for women were more susceptible to charges of witchcraft.[87] Newton fell into the former category because she bewitched her victims by kissing them: in a patriarchal community frightened by overt, female sexuality this act embodied the social anathema of unregulated touch.[88] Reputation also played a part in convincing local elites of Newton's guilt. When investigating the bewitchment of Longdon, Mayor Richard Mayre stated that 'three aldermen in Youghall' had informed him that Newton had kissed their children and that they had 'died presently after'.[89] Indeed, Mayre believed that Newton had killed his daughter Grace using witchcraft;

a fact he believed was attested to by an autopsy he had ordered to be carried out on her body and which revealed no natural illness or disease present at the time of death.[90] Similarly, before the Antrim 'witch' was murdered by a mob in 1698, she was recorded as not only having 'confest' to the main victim's bewitchment and possession but to other 'like feats'.[91] Personal antagonism felt towards Newton, on account of his daughter's death, may explain why Mayor Mayre was particularly eager in March 1661 to use the controversial 'neo-torture'[92] of the swimming-test on her in the chilly weather conditions of early spring. Mayre however aborted this course of action when Newton gave a full confession, that she had 'done her [Longdon] wrong with a kiss'.[93] The swimming test was employed throughout the seventeenth century, but was never recognised legally as proof of witchcraft. Nevertheless, juries and judges often accepted it as such, and figures of authority in local communities, such as constables, clergymen, and magistrates, organised, sanctioned, or merely tolerated its use – or at least they did so up until the end of the seventeenth century. Elite opinion, however, may have begun to turn against swimming as early as 1645, when parliament condemned it outright in reaction to the excesses of witch-finders Hopkins and Stearne during the East Anglian witch-hunts.[94]

The Islandmagee witches

Longdon's accusation that Newton had occasioned her demonic possession by means of witchcraft was rooted in interpersonal conflict as well as the social tensions created by the restrictive bonds placed on children and adolescents at that time. The charge was taken seriously by the local elite because it was levied by a believable witness, who ensured the momentum of the accusation was maintained throughout the various legal obstacles it had to negotiate before trial. It occurred at a time of political crisis and heightened fear of the devil, and was levied against a woman who not only had a reputation for witchcraft, but who flouted gender-based cultural and social conventions. A similar mechanism can be used to explain why numerous women were prosecuted and convicted at Carrickfergus Assizes in March 1711 for the possession of Mary Dunbar, an intelligent, good-looking, and educated gentlewoman of 18.[95]

In late February 1711, Ann Haltridge, elderly widow of local Presbyterian minister, Rev. John Haltridge, was staying in the house of her son James, in the small, rural peninsula of Islandmagee, Co. Antrim. At various times during her stay, beds were stripped by unseen hands and bed-clothes rearranged in the shape of a corpse; stones were hurled at windows, household objects disappeared before re-appearing days later, and a demonic apparition in the form of a small boy in black clothes foretold Ann's death. Finally, on 21 February 1711, Ann died of inexplicable stabbing pains in her back. Almost immediately, the local community, which contained around 300 Presbyterians of Scottish heritage, began to suspect that the root of Ann's demonic obsession was witchcraft, albeit of an undetermined source: not least because in her final sickness she was reported to have been heard speaking to the spectres of her otherwise invisible attackers.[96]

After her funeral, on 27 February 1711, Ann's daughter, along with her niece Mary Dunbar, arrived from nearby Castlereagh, Co. Down. Upon Mary's arrival the demonic disturbances began to shake the household once more, from household objects and clothes apparently moving of their own volition and an increase in instances of *lithobolia*. More importantly, Dunbar began to display, over the course of a few weeks, an increasing range of possession symptoms, from fitting and catatonic seizures, to vomiting of household objects, levitation, seemingly impossible bodily contortions, an aversion to the Bible and prayers, and the appearance of strong sulphurous smell in the house. She was also visited, in spectral form, by eight Presbyterian women from Islandmagee and neighbouring towns and villages. Dunbar was able to identify these women by their appearance and the names they used to address one another.[97] On 31 March 1711 at Carrickfergus Assizes, in a particularly lengthy trial that took just under eight hours, all eight women pleaded not guilty but were nevertheless convicted of witchcraft (for a first offence where the victim had survived) under the dictates of the 1586 Act, and sentenced to one year imprisonment and four stints in the pillory on market-day.[98]

From the sixteenth century onwards, it was customary for English demoniacs to be examined by doctors in the early stages of their possession. These medical professionals, as well as lawmen and clergy were well aware of the range of possible explanations for the physical and mental symptoms displayed by possessed patients, from divine to demonic intervention to natural illness. A diagnosis of witchcraft was thus usually the last resort for most English physicians, but in the sixteenth and seventeenth centuries many made this diagnosis, and some even testified at witchcraft cases. Thomas Browne, for example, appeared at Lowestoft Assizes in March 1662 to give evidence supporting the claim that two young female victims were genuinely possessed. Physicians were occasionally put under pressure by relatives or friends of the afflicted to attribute illness to witchcraft or possession as a solution to a mysterious illness explicable in human terms and which placed no responsibility, moral or otherwise, on the victim or their family. Towards the end of the seventeenth century, English physicians from mainstream, Church of England backgrounds became increasingly reluctant to use possession as a means to explain illness. The picture in dissenting, nonconformist communities in England was somewhat different, where witchcraft accusation continued to be made, of which a few ended up in court. More importantly, dissenting physicians played a leading role in establishing diabolism as the root cause of their patients' maladies.[99]

There is no evidence, however, that Mary Dunbar was examined by a physician or any other type of medical practitioner, such as an apothecary or surgeon. This may be partly explained by the limited access to medical care available in eighteenth-century, provincial Ireland. Many of the characteristics of modern medical structures, such as increased state intervention, institutionalisation, and professionalization emerged during the course of the late seventeenth and eighteenth centuries. There was no legal barrier to Presbyterians pursuing a medical career, and many did so in Ulster in the early eighteenth century, but trained professionals tended to be found in Dublin or larger towns. This left the provinces with a meagre supply of trained practitioners and the mass of population with little access to professional medical care. In common with the rest of the British Isles, members of Protestant gentry, such as Dunbar, would not have considered it socially acceptable to enter a provincial or metropolitan hospital or infirmary. In any case, these were not founded in any great number in provincial Ireland until the late eighteenth century, and even then they catered for a very small number of the curable, 'deserving' poor. Licensed, university-trained physicians did not come cheap and although Dunbar may have been afforded the status of 'gentlewoman', she may have had little by the way of a personal fortune. Although a guest in the Haltridge house, hospitality and charity then, as now, had a limit and it may have been beyond the family's means to bring a physician from Belfast or Antrim.[100]

Unlike that of the medical profession, there was, however, high clerical involvement in the case from the beginning. Rev. Robert Sinclair, Presbyterian minister of Islandmagee from May 1704 until his death in January 1731, visited Ann Haltridge during her final illness to pray and fast for her divine deliverance from the demonic entity that plagued her.[101] Sinclair and other local grandees organised the first tests of the first three women (Janet Carson, Janet Liston, née Sellor, and her daughter Elizabeth) who Dunbar accused of attacking her in spectral form and orchestrating her possession. These tests were of the type that were relatively common in investigations and prosecutions for witch-craft in England, especially those involving demonic possession: the ability to recite the Lord's Prayer, a task deemed impossible for witches to undertake as agents of the Devil; and the reaction of the victim to the approach or touch of the accused, a test made more stringent by ensuring their approach was a 'blind' one, or by bringing them before the suspect as part of a crude identity parade.[102] As an 'absolute stran-ger' to Islandmagee, who had not been within 'fifteen miles of the place',[103] Dunbar deposed to have never met the accused (physically, in person) before they were brought before her.[104] So convinced was Sinclair, along with members of the Haltridge household and leading members of the local community, by the outcome of these tests that he forewent any involvement of his clerical hierarchies or his Church court and immediately passed the case to civil authorities.[105] From this point on, Whig Mayor of Carrickfergus, Edward Clements, in his ex-officio role as JP, and helped by local constables, watchmen and Islandmagee grandees, took depositions, tracked down, tested (in the same way as Carson, Liston, and Sellors, sometimes repeatedly) and imprisoned five more Presbyterian women from Islandmagee and its environs. It could be argued that these investigations were to some extent informed by instructions given in Bolton's manual for JPs, in particular their search in the suspects' houses for image magic in the form of pictures or charms.[106]

In lieu of any contemporary medical evidence for Dunbar's condi-tion, it could be concluded that she faked her possession and for much the same reasons as Mary Longdon. Dunbar, however, lived under even stricter religious and social hierarchies that those of Longdon, as she was an unmarried, 18-year-old female and part of the wider circle of a respected Presbyterian, clerical family.[107] It is also highly possible that she was, along with other Presbyterians in Islandmagee, aware that other communities in the British Calvinist network had recently been affected by outbreaks of witchcraft involving demonic possession, from the widely publicised cases in Presbyterian central Scotland between 1696 and 1704, to the severe witch-hunting in Congregationalist New England in 1692. Knowledge of such cases could have been transferred to the north of Ireland by the medium of print through the large num-bers of books imported both legally and illegally into Derry, Belfast, and Coleraine from England and, more importantly, Scotland. Cultural transmission could have been engendered orally by Scottish economic refugees pouring into Ulster in increasing numbers in the 1690s. It is even conceivable that the educated Dunbar could have learned the 'part' of demoniac by reading published accounts of the Scottish or American trials, or indeed the 1661 Youghal or 1698 Antrim cases. Early modern impostors after all, often learnt the script of possession in this manner. In 1597 in Nottingham, William Sommers began to display the signs of possession after he had taken bread and butter from an old woman and read an account of the possession of the Throckmorton children who, five years earlier, had accused Agnes Samuel and her family of their bewitchment. In 1616, a young man named Henrie Smith had nine women executed at Leicester for sending their familiars to attack him. Smith had faked his symptoms after reading about the Throckmorton children and, in common with Anne Gunter a few years earlier, was eventually exposed as a fraud by King James I and the Archbishop of Canterbury, George Abbott. In Paisley, Scotland, in 1699, the published account of the possession of Christian Shaw had a hand in shaping accusations made by Margaret Murdoch and Margaret Laird against more than 20 people. In 1705, in the fishing village of Pittenweem, Scotland, Janet Cornfoot was badly beaten and crushed to death by a mob after her prosecution for the bewitchment of the 16-year-old son of a blacksmith, Patrick Morton, failed. Morton faked his possession after the local minister, Patrick Cowper, read him a published account of the Christian Shaw case.[108]

Dunbar arguably selected the women in question because they were believable 'witches', in that they variously had reputations for witchcraft, failed to meet accepted standards of female appearance, or were publicly acknowledged to have transgressed accepted moral and behavioural norms for females at that time. This partly explains why local male clerical and legal elites rallied behind Dunbar's accusation and played a prominent role in the pre-trial process. It also explains why so many (mainly Presbyterian) men from Islandmagee and the surrounding area gave sworn depositions to Mayor Clements affirming Dunbar's claims or testified in open court on the day of the trial to the same effect.[109] A contemporary, unpublished pamphlet account states that one of the accused, Janet Liston, 'had been for a great many years under the repute of witch, and her daughter [Elizabeth Sellor] for some time'.[110] Politician and astronomer Samuel Molyneux informed his guardian and uncle Dr Thomas Molyneux that the 'accused persons' made 'frequent vaunts and threats of their own revenge and power'.[111] William Tisdall, high Church Tory vicar of Belfast and trial attendee, stated that 'the supposed witches were eight in number, six of them with ... [a] variety of ill looks' and 'diabolical appearances'.[112] Of the accused, Catherine McCalmond 'a lame woman' from Islandmagee was commonly regarded as 'ignorant, irreligious, [and] of an ill fame', and

Janet Main from Broadisland as 'an ignorant woman of a malicious temper'. Janet Millar from Carrickfergus was said to be a 'little woman' with 'dark brown hair', 'one eye sunk in her head', with 'the side of her face drawn together and fingers ... crooked at the ends, having been all occasioned by falling in the fire'. James Blythe, from Larne, Co. Antrim, claimed that Millar was 'smoking a pipe of tobacco' and 'fell into a great rage, and cursed and swore horribly' when he informed her that a warrant had been issued to 'parade' her before Dunbar. In her deposition, Dunbar stated that Elizabeth Sellor was small and 'lame of leg'.[113]

In any case, if we accept the premise that communities were more likely to believe witchcraft accusation at times of religious and political crisis, then Presbyterian Ulster during the reign of Queen Anne was a prime candidate for an outbreak of witch-hunting. Protestant dissenters there felt threatened on one side from Catholic insurgency and Jacobite invasion, and on the other from some members of the Protestant Ascendancy determined to impose an Anglican 'confessional state' on Ireland; an aim they believed was embodied in the Sacramental Test clause of the 1704 Irish Popery Act. Furthermore, all of this occurred against a backdrop of almost 'total' war with Louis XIV's France, and intense party-political struggle. High Church Tory polemicists, among whom William Tisdall figured prominently, argued in print that Presbyterians were inherently republican and rebellious and thus posed a serious threat to the Established Church and state in Ireland. These high-church arguments struck a chord with an Anglican elite who felt threatened by the growing strength of Ulster Presbyterianism, in terms both of population and of the extent, cohesion and sophistication of the Presbyterian ecclesiastical structure. Whigs, on the other hand, called for Protestant unity in the face of the common enemy, and questioned the commitment of their Tory rivals to the defence of the Revolution of 1688. The political situation not only made this particular instance of witchcraft more plausible, but the accusation and trial also provided party-political factions, who were at each other's throats in the part of north Antrim where Islandmagee lay, with an oppositional platform.[114] By explaining away Dunbar's symptoms in sceptical terms of direct demonic intervention and hallucination, while being careful to uphold theological orthodoxies such as belief in witchcraft, Tisdall could attack head-on the Antrim Presbyterian elite who supported the accusation, in particular the Presbyterian-friendly Whig faction that dominated Carrickfergus borough corporation, headed by the dissenting Mayor Clements.[115] Crucially for Tisdall, his position was shared by one of the two presiding judges in the trial, Tory Justice

Anthony Upton. When summing up the evidence, Upton advised the jury to bring in a not-guilty verdict, informing them that the accused should not be convicted on 'the sole testimony of the afflicted person's visionary images'.[116] This scepticism regarding the validity of spectral evidence was famously displayed by Sir Mathew Hale's assistant lawyer during the trial of Amy Deny or Duny and Rose Cullender in Bury St. Edmunds, Suffolk in 1662.[117] The other presiding judge, Whig Justice of the Queen's Bench, James MacCartney, instructed the Carrickfergus jury to find the defendants guilty. MacCartney, who in common with Upton, was a native of Co. Antrim, was not only wary of Upton's high-church Tory motivations, but betrayed an implicit trust of the testimony of the (mainly) Presbyterian deponents of his home county.[118] As we know, the 12 members of the Jury took MacCartney's advice.

William Sellor

After the trial, William Tisdall interviewed Mary Dunbar, who stated that two women and a man whom she did not know had appeared to her in court, struck her dumb and threatened to 'put pen knives down her throat'. At five o'clock that evening, Dunbar set out on horseback to her mother's house in Castlereagh. In common with many demoniacs, she relapsed a day after the trial, experiencing 'several fainting fits'. She also vomited pins and feathers she claimed had been 'put into her mouth by her tormentors'. During the succeeding week, Dunbar fitted regularly and vomited pins and feathers and on 8 April 1711, she complained that a man of medium height, with light brown, curly hair and who wore a brown bonnet and shabby clothes, appeared to her and had threatened to kill her if she informed on him to the authorities. The man was subsequently identified as William Sellor, husband and father respectively to convicted witches, Janet Liston and Elizabeth Sellor.[119] A warrant was issued for Sellor's arrest on 10 April, but as it was being served he fled from his Islandmagee home only to be captured shortly afterwards, four miles away. Sellor was then brought before the girl, who it was reported, 'did not accuse him for fear of his threatening; so he was let go', presumably by a local constable. Two days later, however, Dunbar told of how Sellor, in spectral form, threatened to kill her with a butcher's knife, 'the blade of which was broken and welded together', before stabbing her just below the right shoulder, the wound of which was clearly visible to onlookers. The next day Dunbar's 'friends in … Island[magee]' were informed (possibly by the girl's mother) of her torments and an un-named constable arrested Sellor, during which his guard, John Brown, was assaulted with a 'drinking horn'. Sellor was finally arrested, imprisoned, and tried at the Assizes, presumably in Carrickfergus, where he was found guilty of bewitching Mary Dunbar.[120] Unfortunately this is all we know about Sellor's arrest and trial: there are no surviving depositions, letters, or any other record produced by the court which would corroborate what is related in the unpublished, contemporary pamphlet account. Even the barest genealogical data on Sellor is impossible to find; there is no will, death, baptism, or marriage record, or even a gravestone inscription. This lack of primary material is particularly frustrating given that he was the only male formally prosecuted for witchcraft in Ireland. Furthermore, although men were certainly brought before Protestant church courts for magical offences, malefic or demonic, witchcraft is rarely mentioned. This raises the question as to what was so different about William Sellor that made him a target for Mary Dunbar's accusation in the first place and, more importantly, to make it stick. To find any type of answer to this question it is best to consider briefly male witches in early modern Europe, who made up around a fifth of all those tried for witchcraft.

Until recently male witches have been sidelined in witchcraft historiography as collateral damage: men who found themselves caught up in large-scale trials (especially on the continent) when the witch stereotype of an older female began to disintegrate; or were accused because of their association with suspected women, in particular sons and husbands of witches. This association often brought with it an anti-social feminisation, where male witches took on supposedly female characteristics such as spite, envy, wantonness, and intellectual fragility or weak-mindedness. In recent years, this interpretation has been developed, and occasionally challenged, through regional analysis and case studies of individual trials. Research has shown that accusers and witch-hunters in Tuscany and in some of the German states used witchcraft prosecution to target opponents and rivals for political, social, and financial reasons. In Scotland, the number of men prosecuted for witchcraft actually declined during large witch-hunts but those believed to have dabbled in elite magic or sorcery for political ends, or were practising cunning-folk, were particularly susceptible to accusation. In the Catholic Duchy of Carinthia in Austria, young, male, wandering, vagrants prone to begging were vulnerable to charges of witchcraft.[121] Robert Walinski-Kiehl has argued that in early modern Germany men accused of witchcraft had often 'violated expectations of masculinity embodied in the ideal of the honest, reliable, married, household head ... and they tended to display the following negative social and moral characteristics: bringing the family into debt, involvement in questionable business practices, theft, drunkenness, gambling, bigamy, and adultery'.[122] While Malcolm Gaskill has pointed out that many English male witches had no known association with female counterparts and often failed to meet contemporary standards of masculinity, where 'self-restraint and recourse to law ... were elevated as the highest ideas across the social order'.[123]

William Sellor had a bad temper, drank alcohol (from a 'horn'), tried to evade local agents of law enforcement, was unkempt, and had allowed his wife and daughter, who were his moral and legal responsibilities, to stray into the clutches of the Devil.[124] He was thus very far from the ideal of head of a household, which may have made it easier for his neighbours to believe he was a man capable of the diabolical deeds attributed to him by Dunbar. The very fact he was the husband of a convicted witch would have made him guilty by association in many people's eyes. Necessity may also have been the mother of invention here, as Dunbar needed, whether consciously or sub-consciously, to prolong her possession and William Sellor was the perfect candidate. She may have been able to describe him to prosecutors because she may have met him earlier during the interrogation or testing of his wife, although there is no mention of any meeting between the two in surviving records.

As Philip Almond has put it, 'the drama' of demonic possession 'ended only when the demoniac, delivered from the Devil and returned to normality, was integrated back into the human community'.[125] The consequence of this is that many of them, including Mary Dunbar, disappear from the historical record and no more can be discovered about them or their later lives. It is assumed that her possession ended with the imprisonment of William Sellor on 13 April, the date at which the demonic disturbances at Knowehead house finally came to an end.[126]

Irish Witches in other countries

Witches of Irish birth were also prosecuted in other parts of early modern Europe and America. Irish-born Marioun Colington of Haddington, East Lothian, Scotland, was caught up in the North Berwick witch hunt of 1590–1, when she was implicated by another suspected witch of meeting with the devil and conspiring to use witchcraft to sink the Royal ship bringing James VI and his bride, Princess Anne, back from Denmark.[127] The great, great grandmother of Sir Patrick Dun,[128] Aberdeen-born Irish physician and president of the King and Queen's College of Physicians in Ireland in the late seventeenth and early eighteenth century, was caught up in another large-scale Scottish witch-hunt in Aberdeenshire in 1597. Christen Michell, widow of Aberdeen official and Lister (or Dyer) Charles Dun, was implicated by the confessions of other witches and possessed a long reputation for witchcraft in her local area. As with most suspects in the later stages of the Aberdeenshire witch-hunt, Mitchell's interrogators used to torture to extort a confession from her, as well as the names of accomplices. Mitchell was tried on 9 March 1597 in a local court convened at Aberdeen Tollbooth, before temporary, untrained Judges Leslie and Rutherford, and chancellor of Assize (or jury), James Stewart. She was found guilty and immediately put to death after the Scottish method of execution: strangulation and burning.[129] In February 1678, Bessie Weir was strangled and burned at Gallows Green in Paisley, Scotland, after being found guilty (along with five 'accomplices') at a local trial, albeit one which included central representation sent from Edinburgh, for the attempted murder of landlord Sir George Maxwell of Pollock. It was reputed that she had been tried and convicted in Ireland before her trial in Scotland but had escaped, with the help of the Devil, before she could be executed. There is however no documentary evidence of Weir being tried for witchcraft in Ireland.[130]

In 1688, Mary Glover, an impoverished, elderly, widowed, Irish-Catholic servant, with a long reputation for witchcraft, was accused of bewitching the four children of mason John Goodwin in Boston, Massachusetts. Soon after an altercation with Glover, the Goodwin children began experiencing fits, convulsions, various bodily contortions and the inability to hear, speak, or see. Local physician, Dr Thomas Oakes was unable to find any natural causes for their illness and so concluded it was the work of witches. As their symptoms worsened, neighbours offered the family a number of charms procured from cunning-folk but they refused to use them, judging prayer as the only remedy available to good Christians. The Goodwin children recovered temporarily when Glover was jailed by local magistrates. A native Irish speaker (whom Cotton Mather visited in jail before chronicling the case in a long pamphlet account), Glover spoke through an interpreter in court due to claims a spell had been laid on her. She finally confessed when poppets found in her house were produced and which caused her victims to fit when Glover touched them. Glover was then examined by five or six physicians who reported that she was mentally fit enough to have the death sentence passed. During their examination it was found that she could recite most of her *Pater Noster* in Latin but could not recite the Lord's Prayer. While awaiting execution, she was further accused by a woman called Hughes of killing her neighbour six years previously, as well as attacking her son in spirit form in the shape of a black person with a blue cap. She also confessed, again in Irish through an interpreter, to these accusations and to attending a witches' Sabbat. Just before Glover was hanged on 16 November 1688, she stated that the Goodwin children would not have any relief by her death because other witches were involved. This indeed proved to be the case and the children were only cured by repeated fasting, and prayer carried out by Rev. Mather.[131]

Conclusion

There were only a handful of witchcraft trials in early modern Ireland, with only a small proportion of the total population of Ireland making formal accusations. Most accusations, however, did not reach court due to a number of reasons, including arbitration (either on an informal basis or overseen by Church courts), magical intervention, the exercise of extra-legal summary justice, and the rise of judicial scepticism towards witchcraft. For these checks and balances to fail and a witchcraft trial to occur, a specific set of circumstances had to present themselves: an accusation of demonic possession, a believable young accuser, socially suspect 'witches', wider social and political strife, and a general heightened fear of the devil and his works. As we shall see in the next chapter, even by the early eighteenth century, Protestant elites still saw the Universe in largely magical and moral terms, and still believed in witchcraft, despite any scepticism some of their number might have had towards proving specific instances of it. As it did for Protestants trying to bolster belief in a universe permeated by spiritual forces, demonic possession provided them with verifiable evidence of witchcraft in the form of a main accuser, the demoniac. The possessed party could also be relied upon to keep the pressure on legal authorities to ensure that an investigation was seen through to its logical conclusion, a trial.

Irish women were also prosecuted for witchcraft abroad – in Scotland during large witch-hunts, and in America in a possession case that bore striking similarities to both the 1698 and 1711 Antrim cases. More work, however, needs to be done on witchcraft in Irish diaspora communities before we can establish more fully the reasons for this.

6
Witchcraft in Modern Ireland: After the Trials

This chapter will examine popular belief in witchcraft in Protestant and Catholic communities in Ireland after the witch trials, from the early eighteenth century onwards. Through the lens of public discourse, parliamentary and court records, and folklore sources, the decline in educated belief will also be explored, along with the attitude of legal authorities to cases involving witchcraft before and after the repeal of the Irish Witchcraft Act in 1821. Before doing so, it is necessary to consider decline, decriminalisation, and repeal in other countries in the British Isles and elsewhere.

Decline in trials

The decline in numbers of witchcraft trials, an end to mass panics, a rise in acquittal rates and a drop in the number of executions began in most territories across Europe in the mid-to-late seventeenth century, albeit at different times and at different rates. Judicial prosecution and execution of witches eventually shuddered to a stop in the mid-to-late eighteenth century, amid a smattering of late, exceptional cases in Sweden, Switzerland, and Poland. The initial decline in witchcraft trials is not generally considered the consequence of disbelief in witchcraft in educated culture but rather due to higher evidentiary standards employed by judiciaries, a reduction in the use of judicial torture, increased state control of local trials and more provision of legal representation for suspects. This judicial scepticism was followed in some areas by statutory decriminalisation. The 1563 and 1604 English Witchcraft Acts, along with the 1563 Scottish Witchcraft Act, were repealed in 1736. As has been suggested, long before the Repeal Act decriminalised witchcraft, trials had been in decline in England. In Scotland, the last sentence of execution was passed by the central criminal courts in 1706, and the last successful prosecution occurred in 1709 in Dumfries; although a woman was reputedly found guilty of witchcraft by a sheriff's court in Dornoch in 1727.[1]

Decline in belief

The view that the English elite had rejected witchcraft in the late seventeenth century primarily because they subscribed to a 'scientific' view of the Universe that left little room for of immaterial forces, including witchcraft and magic, enjoyed a central place in the historiography of decline until relatively recently.[2] It is now generally agreed that decline occurred in some countries (France, England, and Spain) before the new mechanical philosophy was fully developed and that there were no direct attacks on witchcraft by its leading exponents, with some, such as Robert Boyle and Joseph Glanvill, actively defending it. The Royal Society, as a matter of corporate policy, avoided discussion of witchcraft and magic altogether. Rationality and empiricism long associated with 'Scientific Revolution' and the Enlightenment are no longer regarded as intrinsically inimical to demonology, and the extent to which both developments altered the mental world of the educated has been problematised.[3] Nevertheless, Michael Wasser has argued that the Cartesian natural philosophy disseminated in Scottish Universities and by moderate clergyman during the later seventeenth century gradually chipped away at committed witchcraft belief in Scotland.[4] Brian Levack has suggested that intellectual changes 'in the upper levels of European society', namely 'the growth of Cartesian doubt, the spread of the mechanical philosophy and the conviction that there were natural causes of supernatural phenomena', caused doubt, if not disbelief, about the reality of witchcraft, perhaps even among those who controlled the machinery of prosecution.[5] Although acknowledging that there was no straightforward victory for rationalists, armed with the weapons of the new science over spiritual and occult forces, James Sharpe has highlighted other intellectual changes, enhanced by social and cultural polarisation across plebeian and patrician lines, that affected the overall credibility of witchcraft belief in educated culture:

> there was a slow process taking place in which old ways of categorizing and compartmentalising knowledge (this was essentially the polymathic age) were changing. The old system (perhaps demonstrated at its clearest in neoplatonism) of correspondences, of the interplay

between the microcosm and the macrocosm, of sympathetic actions and hence sympathetic magic, was becoming less tenable. Newly located and more definite wedges were being driven between the scientific and the occult, between the natural and the spiritual, and hence magic and witchcraft were becoming marginalized.[6]

Accompanying these intellectual shifts was change in religious sensibilities and mentalities demonstrated by the fact that mainstream religion in Europe was becoming less zealous and 'enthusiastic', if not necessarily religiously tolerant, from the later seventeenth century onward.[7] In England certainly, albeit as a drawn-out, far from hegemonic development, religion became more 'reasonable', in that religious truth to a greater or lesser extent increasingly had to be conformable to reason as well as revelation. This was accompanied by a naturalisation of outlook marked by a gradual move away from the idea that divine providence directly and frequently interfered in everyday human affairs towards one that accepted the reality of God's ability to direct human affairs but was unwilling to see his hand in apparently miraculous occurrences, natural disasters, monstrous births, or apparitions. A belief that Satan or demons constantly interfered in the workings of the temporal world also lost much of its cultural currency, and the notion that Hell was a physical place of eternal torment was increasingly challenged. Astrology, a quasi-scientific, 'occult' belief inhabiting the same mental landscape as witchcraft and magic, was increasingly rejected on the grounds it was vulgar and enthusiastic and as such more suited to the lower orders.[8] In a similar vein, Peter Maxwell-Stuart suggests that although popular witchcraft and magic continued in Scotland among the mass of the population, the gentry and professional classes pulled away from such beliefs during the course of the eighteenth century in a wider process of social and cultural distancing.[9] Michael Knights has associated this naturalisation of outlook among the English elite specifically with Whig circles during the reign of Queen Anne; a naturalisation which, along with other political and intellectual factors identifiable with the intense Whig and Tory party conflict of that period and the early phase of the English enlightenment, helped to marginalise witchcraft belief:

> The Wenham trial has to be seen in the context of the High Church enthusiasm that followed Sacheverell's trial and of a conviction that belief in the supernatural needed bolstering in order to support belief in God and the Church of England. Similarly the attack on witchcraft has to be seen as part of a politicized campaign against 'priestcraft'

and reflected a demand for higher scientific and eventual standards of proof. Here, then, was another strand of a contested enlightenment that operated at the very local level.[10]

This idea that politicisation of witchcraft lead to its demise in educated culture was made most forcibly by Ian Bostridge, who argued that decline occurred at the end of the second decade of the eighteenth century because it was no longer needed, or able, to perform its original ideological function of forging Christian unity by bolstering the ideal of a confessional state: firstly it was revealing itself to be more capable of fostering disunity and discord rather than forging religious and political concord; and secondly, as an idea it was increasingly being regarded as either unattainable or intellectually unattractive, especially after the Wenham trial, which saw credulity and incredulity in witchcraft belief become polarised across party lines.[11] By the time the Whig party had achieved political ascendancy in the 1720s, 'having then become associated with the losers [non-jurors and high-flying Tories] in the political struggle, belief in witchcraft came to be seen as fit matter for ridicule'.[12] The party-politicisation model of decline has been challenged by Michael Hunter, who argues that moderate scepticism once associated with irreligion and free-thinking became orthodox in both Whig and Tory circles in the early eighteenth century because outright belief was deemed even more intellectually unattractive due to its associations with disruptive religious enthusiasm.[13]

Owen Davies has argued that by the mid-eighteenth century 'the bulk of orthodox Anglican intellectual opinion did not reject the concept of witchcraft – just that witches ceased to exist in enlightened Britain'.[14] Put another way by the same historian, while many educated English people 'continued to believe that witchcraft had existed and could exist, but ceased to believe that it continued in their own times',[15] others were more forthright and considered 'witchcraft to be a vulgar notion bred of ignorance and credulity'.[16] Moreover, a minority of Church of England and Protestant non-conformist clergy, along with Wesleyan and early Primitive Methodists continued to believe in demonic, malefic witchcraft as part of their adherence to Biblical authority.[17] While Francis Young has demonstrated that English Catholic laity and clergy (although they did not actively promote it) continued to believe in witchcraft well into the nineteenth century in much the same way as they had in the early modern period,[18] Malcolm Gaskill has eschewed the idea of educated decline altogether, arguing that 'witchcraft was still very much alive as a subject in the eighteenth century, but that its meaning could vary according to context',[19] and 'to characterise the history of witchcraft in terms of simple models – whether of the dynamics of accusation, or the decline in beliefs – is to overlook the variety, subtlety and contingency of how attitudes, ideas, perceptions and behaviour were deployed in practice and changed over time', and that 'even sensitive attempts to identify distinctions between popular culture and the culture of the elite tend to narrow the issues at stake'.[20]

The historiography of decline is thus a complex and evolving one, but collectively it suggests that in Britain, in the early to mid-eighteenth century, an active belief in witches had been marginalised, if not altogether extinguished, in mainstream educated culture for a mixture of intellectual, social, political, and cultural reasons. However, for the vast majority of those placed lower down the social ladder, especially those living in small, close-knit rural areas, the existence of the malefic witch continued to be regarded as a threat to their property and persons in the eighteenth and nineteenth centuries.[21] The same holds true for North America[22] and for Wales, where from the eighteenth up until the mid-nineteenth century there was continuing popular belief in both butter-stealing and malefic witches (who were occasionally associated with diabolism), even if they were rarely identified or punished in acts of communal justice.[23] Although there was some scepticism in popular as well as educated culture towards witchcraft in England, it was for this reason that the 1736 Witchcraft Repeal Act, which replaced the crime of witchcraft with that of pretended witchcraft punishable by a maximum of one year's imprisonment, would have not received support from the country as a whole.[24] Nevertheless for about 150 years after its enactment, recourse was made to local authority figures to deal with witchcraft, and failing this, mobs illegally swum, scratched, and weighed (against the Church Bible) suspected witches.[25] This is not to say that the Repeal Bill passed into law during the 1735/6 session of parliament with little opposition or public debate, as was believed to be the case until recently.[26] It was in fact an articulation of Whig intent to secularise the state in lieu of more contentious legislation to remove or relax legal restrictions on Catholics and non-conformists, as well as a way to restrict or control the activities of cunning-folk and fortune-tellers. The facts that Scottish witchcraft legislation was added in as an amendment by the House of Lords and Ireland was bypassed altogether have been taken as indication of the disinterest of the House of Commons towards Scottish and Irish affairs. Opposition to repeal came from Protestant non-conformists (and possibly Catholics), High Church Anglicans – who were usually, but not always, Tory in political outlook, and Scottish, Calvinist 'high-flying' opponents of Sir Robert Walpole and his government, such as James Erskine, Lord Grange.[27]

Witchcraft in Ireland after the Witch trials

Research into witchcraft in Ireland after the Islandmagee trial of 1711 is still in its infancy and what has been done is almost solely concerned with the beliefs of the majority of the Irish population, the Catholic native Irish. Before examining Catholic witchcraft, however, it is necessary to first consider eighteenth- and early nineteenth-century Catholicism. As has been touched upon in earlier chapters, religious uniformity, gained through the imposition of religious practices and standards based on Tridentine directives and guided by the local Catholic hierarchy, was impossible to impose in seventeenth- and early eighteenth-century Ireland, in a religious atmosphere of conflict, crisis, intolerance, and restriction.[28] By the 1720s, Irish Catholics were able to practise their religion and the Penal Laws which related specifically to religious worship (in contrast to those relating to ownership of land and political activity) were enforced only at times of acute political crisis, in particular during Jacobite invasions and rebellion scares.[29] A decade later, all but the most zealous of the Protestant Ascendancy had given up converting Catholics to the brand of Protestantism offered by the Church of Ireland. More importantly, the ecclesiastical and paro-chial structure of the Catholic Church began to recover, and Catholics were able practise their faith and the persecution of priests had all but ceased. Meanwhile, the Catholic population was growing steadily and in Dublin an Irish literary, devotional, and intellectual scene flourished. Some penal legislation, however, was enforced periodically, again at times of crisis, such as that forbidding Catholics to carry arms, which remained on the statute book until 1793.[30]

In the early to mid-eighteenth century, the extent of formal religious practice remained uneven, and popular Catholicism blended official, orthodox ritual and doctrine with calendar customs, charms, divina-tion, prophecies, and a belief in fairies and other supernatural beings. Orthodox Catholic ritual was reinterpreted magically at a local level: prayers to Saints (particularly on specific 'pattern' days) for example were used alongside protective rites at Holy Wells believed to be imbued with curative or healing properties.[31] The late eighteenth century saw the passing of Catholic Relief Acts (of 1772, 1778, and 1782) which removed some of the legal restrictions on Catholic land ownership and religious activity. It also witnessed the beginning of a process of internal reform of Church structures, clerical discipline, and performance spear-headed by a cadre of committed clergy and reforming bishops. Despite this effort by clerical reformers, the religious practices of the laity in the late eighteenth and early nineteenth centuries, particularly in remote, Gaelic regions, often fell below the standards of Canon law. In common with the earlier period, the doctrine and rituals of official Catholicism were intermixed with a gamut of supernatural beliefs and practices. Although some rank and file Catholic clergy continued to variously ignore, encourage, and, more rarely, facilitate non-Christian, supernatural observances, ritual, customs, and counter-magical prac-tices, this was far more common in the 1770s than it was in the 1830s. The post-famine period witnessed a strengthened Catholic church, marked by a continued rise in mass attendance and an increase in the number of priests, who were more closely controlled and monitored by clerical superiors.[32] As Sean Connolly has pointed out it, 'this revital-ised Church was able to impose its discipline effectively on a smaller and more affluent laity, laying the foundations for the almost universal popular piety' in generations to come.[33]

Historians specifically concerned with the non-Christian supernatu-ral have demonstrated that belief in fairies, the evil-eye, harmful but essentially non-demonic witchcraft, and beneficial magic continued in Catholic Ireland at a popular level beyond the eighteenth century, deep into late nineteenth century and beyond (albeit in a more localised, weaker form), as a way to deal with uncertainty in a predominantly agricultural and rural economy where existence, especially at subsist-ence level, was often precarious.[34] Fairy belief in the modern period has been shown to have often centred on the effects of elf-bolts and fairy blast on cattle and changeling abduction of healthy infants and young women of child-bearing age who had been replaced by sickly or irritable substitutes.[35] Suspected changelings were variously held over fires, beaten, abandoned, and branded with hot pokers in a bid to expel the possessing fairy or force the return of the healthy woman or child.[36] The case of Bridget Cleary, a suspected changeling murdered by her husband and others in 1895 in Co. Tipperary, is the case study on which discussions of changeling killing usually centre,[37] but it is clear the crime was far more widespread,[38] extending as far north as Ulster.[39] Richard Jenkins has argued that witchcraft in Catholic Gaelic-Irish culture symbolised deviance from behavioural norms and, centring on disputes between families, it was firmly associated with older women. Witchcraft came in two main forms: the use of the intentional evil-eye to cause malfunctions in agricultural equipment, or illness or death in livestock or humans (usually male adults and adolescents); and butter-stealing witches who stole (particularly on May Eve) milk from cows in the form of a hare, or who appropriated the 'profit' from butter, making it impossible to churn, using a variety of magical methods.[40] This description of eighteenth- and nineteenth-century Gaelic-Irish witchcraft belief as two-pronged, however, underestimates the strength of belief in the butter-stealing witch figure in that culture.[41] Moreover, the picture becomes more complex when one considers the fact that the intentional evil-eye was not only a supernatural phenomenon in its own right but also used by butter-stealing witches.[42]

For example, a travelogue of Britain and Ireland published in 1787 in Italian by an anonymous, Venetian writer provided a classic description of the Gaelic-Irish butter-witch:

> If a woman asks for fire on the first day of May, they send her away swearing, thinking her a witch who will use that fire in the summer to make enchantments and rob them of all their butter.[43]

Thomas Crofton Croker, a Protestant from a well-connected background in Cork city, noted in his *Researches in the South of Ireland* ... (1824), with an undertone of revulsion, that 'vulgar Irish' continued to believe in witchcraft.[44] The witchcraft he described was malefic magic directed both towards humans and milk and butter production. He recounted the folklore surrounding 'Nanny Steer, whose malign glance produced madness',[45] and 'the vulgar superstition regarding witches' that they change into the shape of a hare 'suck the teats of cows, and thus either deprive them of their milk or communicate an injurious effect to it'.[46] He also related folk-tales of farmers shooting and wounding hares that they then tracked to cabins where they found 'an old woman smeared with blood and gasping for breath, extended almost lifeless on the floor, having, it is presumed, recovered her natural shape'.[47] A review in *The Dublin Penny Journal* in 1834 of a later re-issue of a compendium volume of Croker's work argued that by detailing popular 'superstitions' he inadvertently strengthened belief in them.[48] The *Ordnance Survey Memoirs of Ireland* (OSMI),[49] which date from the 1830s, confirm widespread belief in butter-stealing witches. In 1835, OSMI collector J. Stokes noted of the parish of Clandermot in Co. Londonderry:

> So prone indeed are the people to superstition that they believe themselves honoured, not only by the residence of cunning women among them, but even of reputed witches ... an old woman of

Ardlough ... was believed to have the power of transforming herself into any shape, and her neighbours would sooner forfeit a sum of money than incur her displeasure, being persuaded that she had similar power over themselves and their cattle.[50]

While in July 1836, C.W. Ligar wrote in relation to the parish of Termoneeny, Co. Londonderry:

the Presbyterians, the descendants of the Scotch settlers, and the Roman Catholics, the descendants of the native Irish, are equally superstitious, respecting the existence and mischievous propensities of the fairies ... and also that there are certain men and women who by merely looking at a cow or horse can deprive the one of milk and kill the other.[51]

Newspapers also provide a glimpse into the shadowy world of butter-witches.[52] In July 1844, the Cork Examiner detailed, for the amusement of its readers, an affidavit sworn before a JP in Co. Kilkenny by, in their view, a credulous member of the public. Ellen Stapleton of Muckalee, Co. Kilkenny, deposed that she had been 'accused by James McCann and his family, of injuring them by taking away the butter of their five cows, and adding it to her own, by ... witchcraft, necromancy, incantations, and certain charms'. Ellen went onto deny the accusations or having used any 'charms'.[53]

The belief in butter-witches continued into the second half of the nineteenth century. Sir William Wilde in *Irish Popular Superstitions* (1852) described the counter-charms and measures employed, especially in Catholic South and West of Ireland, to protect cattle on May Eve and May Day from the attacks of butter-stealing witches. These witches were described as employing a variety of magical means to carry out their nefarious deeds. They stole milk directly in the form of a hare but also employed sympathetic magic by removing food, fire, or other every-day objects from targeted households, or by drawing water from wells or skimming dew from grass or fields on May Eve or May Morning.[54] In October 1864, the *Nenagh Guardian* noted that 'poor dupes in the rural district', especially 'Irishmen' of the 'Celtic race', continued 'to believe in witches', stating that this was to be 'expected from the illiterate and ignorant'.[55] Around the same time, William Smith O'Brien, Irish Nationalist and founder of the Young Ireland movement, in an unpublished paper on the 'traditions of the Irish peasantry', noted the existence of beliefs in butter-stealing witches in Co. Monaghan and the

rituals undertaken to protect cows from their influence.[56] An anonymous letter to the editor of the *Irish Times* published on 7 July 1894
informed that:

> I have repeatedly been told by most respectable and intelligent farm-
> ers that some old women have the art of taking their neighbours'
> butter by some mysterious process, and that there is no part of the
> year that they can use their art to greater advantage than on the 1st
> of May.[57]

In the same year, folklorist Leland L. Duncan recounted oral traditions
involving witches who stole the profit from milk by gathering dew from
long grass, removing thatch from the roofs of neighbouring houses or,
more ominously, by dipping severed hands of the newly deceased into
butter-churns.[58] In July 1908, at Belturbet Petty Sessions in Co. Cavan,
James McCaffrey complained that Mary McCaffrey had committed
a breach of the peace by using 'abusive and threatening language'
towards him, in particular by accusing him of 'practising witchcraft'
and his wife Alice 'of being a witch and turning herself into a hare and
taking butter'.[59] The case was dismissed when McCaffrey withdrew the
complaint.[60] In 1911, folklorist Thomas Johnson Westropp argued that
it was now only older people in Co. Clare who held committed belief
'in the charming away, or taking, of milk and butter', with young people, in public at least 'usually denying 'that they held this belief'.[61] The
Irish folklore Commission records collected in the 1920s and 1930s and
housed in University College, Dublin, provide rich examples of oral
traditions relating to butter-stealing witches who used the evil-eye or
sympathetic magic, or turned into hares.[62]

Ongoing research will uncover the Catholic clergy's attitude, in the
later eighteenth and nineteenth century,[63] to the wider non-Christian
supernatural and to witchcraft in particular. At present, anecdotal
evidence suggests that by the late eighteenth century, high-ranking
Catholics, as they did in England, still believed in malefic, demonic
witchcraft. Reforming Roman Catholic bishop of Kerry, Dr Nicholas
Madgett, in a Latin treatise of moral philosophy, *Constitutio Ecclesiastica*
(written around 1764), which tackled the pastoral problems of his
diocese, condemned the superstitious magical beliefs of his lower class
parishioners;[64] nevertheless he believed in witches himself and that
they harmed 'milk and butter ... by sorcery'.[65] Unlike his parishioners,
he saw butter-stealing witches in elite, demonic terms, as agents of 'the
Devil', with whom he had made 'a pact' and 'through whom he worked

his sorcery'.[66] In 1829, a Catholic cunning-woman named Connors from near Ballymurran, Co. Wexford was suspected of stealing the productiveness from her neighbours' butter and transferring it to her own using the evil-eye. As penance, she was made to stand in chapel on a Sunday dressed in a white sheet, which, the Protestant *Belfast Newsletter* (BNL) delighted in reporting, made 'the unfortunate creature look more like a ghost than a witch'.[67]

Witchcraft in Protestant Ireland

In contrast to Catholic Ireland, little research has been done on witchcraft and magic in Protestant communities in the eighteenth and early nineteenth centuries.[68] In an era of slowly increasing literacy rates, especially among the male population, and in the context of an expanding print culture and printing industry, especially in Dublin where the book trade catered primarily for an English-speaking, Protestant population,[69] public discourse, from newspapers to periodicals to pamphlets, along with folklore and other sources, belie a gradual decline in educated Protestant belief in the eighteenth century, along with continuing, popular belief up until the twentieth century. Although it is admitted that public discourse relating to witchcraft may not necessarily reflect private belief (even if it was able to shape it), with expressions of credulity commonly regarded as more suited to the home or the tavern, they provide an indication of the Ascendancy 'party-line' on matters of witchcraft.[70] What also emerges from this discussion is that witchcraft is much more of an issue after 1750 in metropolitan and leading provincial newspapers and periodicals, written by and for Irish Protestants, and almost universally regarded as an irrational, outmoded belief system, incompatible with enlightened, polite society.

Stymied scepticism? c.1711–1740

As we saw in earlier chapters, by the time witchcraft accusations were being made by Protestant settlers in the later seventeenth century, judicial scepticism helped to keep prosecution rates for witchcraft low. In Ireland, as elsewhere, this does not necessarily equate to disbelief. During the prosecution and trial of the 'Islandmagee witches' in 1711, scepticism was restricted to disputing the case for the prosecution solely on evidentiary grounds, in particular the validity of spectral evidence. Although the trial provided a public, oppositional platform for prominent Whigs and Tories from Co. Antrim, the party politicisation of witchcraft in Ireland should not be overstated. The fact that Mayor Edward Clements was a Whig and friendly to Presbyterians no doubt made it easier for him to take Dunbar's accusations seriously enough to warrant a full investigation into them; a decision which would prove pivotal in turning her accusations into prosecutions and ultimately criminal convictions. However, witchcraft only became a party issue in Ireland on the day of the trial and was never part of the ideological armoury of Irish Whigs and Tories.[71] More importantly, during the trial, incredulity did not become associated with Whiggish social and cultural ideology, nor with a questioning of a moral view of the universe. Raymond Gillespie, who has done most to chart this part of the mental world of early modern Ireland, has summed up the situation thus:

the inhabitants of early modern Ireland saw themselves living in a world propagated not only by benign presences which drew on the powers of God but also by maleficent ones, drawing on the power of the devil. Heaven and Hell were powerful realities in this world.[72]

Early eighteenth-century Irish Protestant polite society was far from tolerant of those who flirted with the demonic, even if only for shock value. In 1729, Vincent Fitzgerald and John Jackman 'were tried at Dublin on a charge of having been in the habit of drinking healths to the Devil and his Angels'.[73] The *Dublin Hellfire Club* (linked to, or perhaps co-terminus with, *The Blasters* club led by painter Peter Lens), founded in 1737 and comprising nobility and high-ranking members of the Protestant gentry, dabbled in a variety of debaucheries, blasphemies, anti-Christian mockery, and pseudo-Satanic worship. In March 1738, these activities provoked the House of Lords' Standing Committee for Religion to prosecute Lens.[74] This being said, astrology in Ireland by the start of the eighteenth century was beginning to lose credibility in elite, Protestant circles, where it was increasingly identified with political and religious unorthodoxy. As a result, Irish almanacs, in common with English counterparts, began to place more emphasis on amusement rather than astrological content.[75] Early modern Irish Catholicism may have had little theological difficulty in absorbing 'wonders' into its wider concepts of the miraculous, but modern miracles, questionable prophets, and certain aspects of angelology were challenged as a matter of Irish Protestant orthodoxy, just as they were in England.[76] At Drogheda Assizes in April 1712, educated gentleman, Thomas Riggs, and his companion John Woods, Irish converts to the controversial millenarian group, The French Prophets, were found guilty of perverting 'several of her Majesty's good subjects from the pure religion as by Law Establish'd' by claiming they were prophets 'sent immediately from God' through whom He 'speaks secret things'. In common with their English and French co-religionists, Woods and Riggs were portrayed during the trial as false prophets praying on the gullibility of the ignorant masses, and their fits, convulsions, speaking in tongues, and prophesies were attributed to either deliberate deception or demonic possession.[77]

If the concept of witchcraft and the magical, moral universe was far from marginal in early eighteenth-century, educated, Irish Protestant culture, what was the position in the century or so that followed? As the only eighteenth-century English witchcraft sceptic living in Ireland in the 1720s and 1730s,[78] Bishop Francis Hutchinson is in a prime position to throw some light on the mid-eighteenth century. As I have suggested elsewhere, most of Hutchinson's time in Ireland was concerned with social and economic improvement, achieved through various projects and also the mass-conversion of the Gaelic-speaking, Catholic population to Protestantism, an end he believed would also secure their political pacification.[79] Although by 1723 Hutchinson was using witchcraft as an economic improvement metaphor – 'trade is witchcraft and works wonders'[80] – he had not abandoned his scholarly interest in it. Along with practitioners of popular magic, he kept a track in his commonplace book of incidents in his diocese of witchcraft involving butter-stealing witches and demonic possession. He noted that Protestant dissenters, a 'Mr Smith' and a 'Mr Higgison', claimed to have vomited, respectively, 'straw' and a 'pin', and that an unnamed man in his diocese 'swore that taking aim at a hare an old wo[ma]n rose up'.[81] Hutchinson was immensely proud of his 'old writings', including the *Historical Essay*, and took them with him to Dublin in 1726 to 'shew' to associates there along with his more recent literary output.[82] It would have pleased him that both first and second editions of his witchcraft book,[83] along with those of other luminaries of the sceptical canon, Thomas Ady and Reginald Scot, found their way into the libraries of prominent Irish Protestant physicians and higher clergy up until the early nineteenth century.[84] In the late eighteenth century, even Irish Catholics owned Hutchinson's *Historical Essay*: Gaelic scribe Muiris Ó Gormáin's copy was almost certainly bought at the auction of the books of his former Catholic patron, Dr John Fergus.[85] More importantly, in a commonplace book dating from the 1730s, Hutchinson noted that in his library lay 'Mr Boulton's answer to my *Historical Essay* and my reply to that with a sermon concerning the right use of Scriptures in readiness but not yet printed'.[86] Hutchinson probably penned this reply (which is no longer extant) to Richard Boulton's *The Possibility or Reality of Magick, Sorcery and Witchcraft, Demonology. Or a Vindication of a Compleat History of Magick Sorcery and Witchcraft. In Answer to Dr Hutchinson's Historical Essay* (London, 1722) immediately after its publication.

Hutchinson may have also written a short, anonymous essay on witchcraft for the *Dublin Weekly Journal (DWJ)* in 1725.[87] Belfast-born Presbyterian essayist and poet, James Arbuckle, whose politico-religious sympathies were those of a Latitudinarian-Whig, was the main contributor and editor of the Dublin-based *DWJ*, a periodical modelled closely on Joseph Addison and Richard Steele's *Spectator*. Arbuckle formed part of the Molesworth Circle that shared enlightenment values, including a reverence for theories of politeness and sociability, and met regularly in Dublin the 1720s. As it was comprised of such philosophical luminaries as Lord Robert Molesworth, Francis Hutcheson, and John Toland, it played a central role in shaping Irish philosophy during the early eighteenth century.[88] As has been suggested, Bishop Hutchinson was also an enlightened, Latitudinarian-Whig taken with the blossoming culture of politeness, and a fierce critic of its anti-type, religious enthusiasm. We also know that by 1726 he was in contact with Francis Hutcheson (who also contributed to the *DWJ*), with whom he discussed religious matters.[89] Internal evidence also links the *DWJ* article to Hutchinson's *Historical Essay* and his particular brand of moderate witchcraft scepticism: he did not deny outright that witchcraft existed, affirmed the importance to orthodox Christianity of belief in Angels and Demons, and avoided any discussion of repeal of the English Witchcraft Acts. Instead he designed a book that would ensure a gradual tailing off of formal accusations by encouraging a continuance of judicial scepticism and by influencing popular witchcraft beliefs.[90] Hutchinson stated in *DWJ*: that 'there are both good and bad spirits, is, I think very plain both from reason and argument'. The 'multitudes of ignorant people' – the 'vulgar' – he continued, were 'extremely addicted to superstition, and terrifying themselves with very common and ordinary occurrences, as the immediate effects of a Divine interposition, or the operations of certain inferior spirits, who, either out of good-will or malice, but for the most part the latter, were supposed to interest themselves, and have a great hand in all human affairs'. He went onto say that 'the most popular and prevailing spirit of superstition among us is the wise and pious doctrine of witches and apparitions, which has been so industriously propagated for many ages among the common people', and that as a result 'many an old woman has suffered ... whose only crime was old-age and ugliness, accompanied perhaps with a little ill-nature'.[91] In terms that could have come straight from the *Historical Essay*,[92] he also argued that, 'if a young girl happened to turn splenetick for want of a husband, instantly she was bewitched, and never left vomiting hay, buttons and crooked pins, till all the old women in the neighbourhood were either cruelly butchered, or their lives made miserable thro the odium of those wicked arts imputed to them'. His *Historical Essay* is even name-checked in the *DWJ* essay as a good starting place for anyone who seeks 'a great number of unquestionable facts' to prove 'how easy it may be for cunning and malicious people to play a vast number of extraordinary pranks, without the assistance of the Devil, or any other evil spirit but their own'.[93] Hutchinson was not above self-recommendation and had on previous occasions paraded his publications before clerical superiors to secure career advancement.[94]

Even Hutchinson's relatively moderate scepticism was too much for some clerical colleagues. Archbishop William King's credulity in matters of witchcraft has already been discussed, and this in conjunction with anti-English sentiment explains why he treated Hutchinson to such a hostile reception when he was elevated to the bishopric of Down and Connor in late 1720. In December 1720, Anglican Bishop of Kilmore, Timothy Godwin, informed Archbishop of Canterbury, William Wake, that Hutchinson's *Historical Essay* had angered Archbishop King:

> I know Dr Hutchinson a little, and I think he has always maintained a good character, but he must expect to be attacked by his Grace of St Sepultures [Archbishop William King] for his book about witchcraft, but I suppose he will keep as much he can out of his way.[95]

Hutchinson's witchcraft book (and perhaps even his *DWJ* article) was mocked in an anonymous ballad published in early 1726:

> Least witches and spirits our children should fright,
> He [Hutchinson] on that occasion did learnedly write,
> And at tea told her Grace [his wife] t'was no breach of the law,
> Tho' men should spew pins and old women spit straws.[96]

Although early to mid-eighteenth century Presbyterian elders and ministers who presided over Sessions and Presbyteries took popular magic more seriously than instances of witchcraft, censuring those involved in the former and arbitrating accusation involving the latter, there is no indication that their scepticism was underpinned by disbelief.[97] The words 'witch' and 'witchcraft' continued to be included in spelling manuals and dictionaries published in Dublin and presented in a way that assumed credulity in the reader,[98] with an edition of Bolton's handbook for JPs appearing in 1750, complete with a section on witchcraft.[99] The fact that the Irish parliament remained silent on witchcraft during the 1735–6 session of parliament, as the Repeal Act passed through Westminster, is further indication that most leading members of the Irish Protestant Ascendancy, whose interest parliament ultimately represented, had no real political or ideological objection to traditional witchcraft belief. In any case, MPs and peers in the Irish Commons and Lords in the relatively muted 1735–6 session were more concerned with the issue of Agistment (tithes on pasturage grazed by barren or dry cattle) and the furtherance of social and economic improvement schemes and projects by legislative means.[100]

Protestant elite attitudes to Witchcraft, c. 1740–1821

The social, cultural, and intellectual shifts associated with the Enlightenment and espoused by Whigs such as Arbuckle and Hutchinson took increasing hold of mainstream, Irish Protestant educated culture during the course of the eighteenth century, especially from the mid-1700s onwards: from the necessity of placing religion on a reasonable as well as a revelatory basis; to stymied religious toleration and ecumenicalism; to the further expansion of print and literacy, and the deepening attraction of the cultures of sociability, politeness, and improvement.[101] Whether these cultural and religious shifts, along with the influence of the work of both continental and home-grown intellectuals on Irish political ideals, the arts and sciences, constituted a specifically Irish Enlightenment is an issue that cannot be resolved here.[102] What is clear is that from the mid-eighteenth century onwards, Protestant public discourse began to condemn traditional witchcraft belief (along with notions of an interventionist Satan) as incompatible with its own self-image as an enlightened, polite Ascendancy; an image often at odds with the grimmer realities of widespread poverty, agrarian unrest, popular sectarianism, and religious conflict. In the immediate aftermath of the 1798 rebellion, anti-Catholicism began to be voiced by Irish Protestant elites, with any co-operation or toleration they might have had for Catholics (and vice versa) evaporating in the 1820s, amid heightened religious revival and militancy and the rise of popular politics surrounding the campaign for Catholic Emancipation.[103] In much the same manner as counterparts in Britain, the Netherlands, and America,[104] Irish Protestant writers condemned witchcraft by largely ignoring continuing popular belief in their own country and portraying witchcraft as a problem of an unenlightened, irrational past, or one peculiar to other countries, especially those deemed backward or ignorant. Both European and non-European territories which continued to prosecute witches after 1740 were particular targets, with some Protestant writers unable to resist the temptation to equate witchcraft to perceived superstitious Catholicism.

In an article entitled 'Of Witchcraft' on the front page of the June 1750 issue of the Limerick-based *Munster Journal*, begun in 1739 (as *The Limerick Journal*) and printed until 1777,[105] Andrew Welsh stated that one of the 'most unthankful offices in the world, [was] to go about to expose the mistaken notions of witchcraft and spirits'. In the past, he continued, this undertaking 'would have been both dangerous and impious', with sceptics who went against prevailing opinion meeting 'with rough treatment and ill language ... and seldom escaped the imputation of atheism'. To Welsh, the Devil existed but it was nevertheless 'deluded' to think 'that there was an actual society and communion between human creatures and spiritual demons'. He ridiculed the 'supposed contract with the devil' and the 'common marks and symptoms by which witches ... [were] discovered', such as the swimming-test, as well as the belief that witches owned familiars, attended Sabbats, and flew on broomsticks. He went on to argue that in the early modern period witches were in reality 'prodigious ugly' old women, often with 'eyes hollow and red' and 'face shrivelled', who 'lived on alms' and were unable, through senility or fear to defend themselves against witchcraft accusation. In a description of witchcraft accusation patterns that anticipated the charity-refused model, and was redolent of an infamous passage in Scot's *Discoverie of Witchcraft*,[106] Welsh stated when an old woman was refused a 'dish of broth, or the heel of a loaf' and went 'away muttering' she was subsequently accused of otherwise inexplicable 'feats'. Using a well-worn sceptical argument, he argued that witches were 'very poor' despite the fact that they had been promised wealth by 'her master Satan' who has 'mines and hidden treasures in his gift'.[107]

Welsh's sentiments, and to a lesser extent those of Bishop Hutchinson, were echoed just over a decade later in 1762 by Dublin-based actor and playwright George Stayley, who no longer saw witchcraft as a relevant or cogent part of the mental world of the enlightened and educated:

> Witchcraft is a belief grown very much out of fashion of late; not because witches may be more scarce than they were formerly; but because the world is more enlightened by philosophy, and, able from

experimental discoveries, to assign natural causes for a thousand surprising accidents and effects, which in the darker ages of time mere custom, for the sake of ease and expedition, had attributed to witchcraft.[108]

In a similar vein, two years later, *A Colloquial Essay on the Liberal Education, and Other Interesting Subjects,* spoke of how in 'former ages ... all ranks have often embraced notions, that were hurtful to mankind', chief among which was mistaking 'dotage for witchcraft' and making 'senility a capital crime' by rendering the 'most piteous object in the whole parish', usually an old woman, 'the most wretched and detested creature in it'.[109] An article in the *BNL* in November 1767 declared that 'witchcraft ... is much exploded',[110] while a Dublin edition of Richard Mead's *Medica Sacra* (1767) regarded witchcraft belief as a vulgar error and possession the result of severe mental illness or incurable natural disease.[111] In November 1787, Robert Marchbank, master printer and a prominent lottery office keeper in Dame Street, Dublin, stated in the *Freeman's Journal* (FJ) that the then popular practice of using talismans and lucky numbers to procure 'a partial enjoyment of fortune's most valuable favours' was a 'glaring absurdity' in 'the present period, when the antiquated notions of witchcraft, necromancy, second sight and calculation are universally exploded'.[112] In August 1788, an article in the same newspaper quipped that those responsible for a story in an unnamed 'evening paper' which preyed into the 'most secret plans' of John Hely-Hutchinson, second earl of Donoughmore, and discovered he was going to England to seek preferment in 'more superstitious times ... would certainly have been hanged, or drowned for witchcraft'.[113] A Dublin-printed, English translation of the German, Protestant, *Catechism of Health for the Use of Schools and for Domestic Instruction ...* (Dublin, 1794) dismissed any notion that medical practitioners could, or should, attribute disease or illness to supernatural causes:

> Q[uestion]. 298. Can maladies originate in Supernatural causes, such as witchcraft or sorcery?:
> A[nswer]. No; it were nonsensical and foolish to believe it. Nature operates universally; and all diseases spring from natural causes.[114]

Demonic possession

The way in which an actual possession case arising in Carrickfergus was treated in contemporary newspapers further demonstrates how far educated opinion had shifted in the four decades after the Islandmagee trial. In November 1763, the children (one after another) of labourer John Ross of Carrickfergus began to experience distended stomachs and regular fits and violent convulsions, during which it took several men to hold them down. In 1711 in Carrickfergus these symptoms were regarded as proof of witchcraft by local elites but by the 1760s no such attribution was made.[115] Four months later, in April 1764, the Ross children were reported to be in the 'same melancholy surprising state and condition' as before, and as a result the family had been 'rendered real objects of charity' by the borough council.[116] Protestants further down the social ladder in Carrickfergus remained convinced of the power of the Devil and the reality of witchcraft. Lieutenant G.H. Mallock, a collector for the OSMI, noted that in Carrickfergus, 'the lower class are very superstitious', there being an implicit belief in witchcraft ... many will swear that they have seen the Devil: he usually appears here in the form of a black dog and on very dark nights'.[117] Furthermore, a rare exorcism performed in 1824 by Fr. John Carroll on a three-year-old demoniac, at the behest of her parents, in Killinick, Co. Wexford attests to continuing popular Catholic belief in possession. A lowly curate, Carroll's actions were not Episcopally sanctioned and his highly irregular exorcism ceremony ended in the death of the infant. He was later tried for murder and acquitted after an insanity plea was accepted.[118] In eighteenth- and nineteenth-century England, possession continued to enthral educated men and women, while many Anglican clergy remained convinced of the temporal power of the devil. Unlike their parishioners, however, they were loath to link possession to witchcraft and distanced themselves from the de-possessions and exorcisms associated with Methodists and Catholics.[119] In eighteenth-century Spain, Catholic clergy attacked specific aspects of popular belief in demonic possession but did not deny its existence.[120] In enlightenment southern Germany, the activities of Catholic Priest, exorcist, and healer Johann Joseph Gassner sparked an intense, local religious revival, as well as inviting severe criticism from sceptics.[121]

Representing historic witchcraft and sorcery

In November 1781, the *Hibernian Magazine* went back to Ireland's own past to discredit witchcraft, describing the Kilkenny sorcery case of 1324–5, involving the wealthy Dame Alice Kyteler, as 'a frightful picture of the effects of superstition and ecclesiastical tyranny'.[122] A rare discussion of early modern Irish witchcraft appeared in the *Belfast Monthly*

Magazine in August 1809, written by local historian and antiquarian Samuel McSkimmin. McSkimmin contended that the early modern period was 'the reign of superstition' and that 'even so late as 1711, eight women were tried at Carrickfergus for witchcraft'.[123] Two years later, in the first edition of his celebrated history of Carrickfergus, McSkimmin published a detailed narrative account of the Islandmagee witchcraft trial.[124] An account of the trial also appeared in the as yet unpublished OSMI, but this discussion was based on local folklore accounts collected by James Boyle in April 1840. Boyle, one of the most active, and often acerbic, OSMI collectors, stated that the Presbyterian inhabitants of Islandmagee, who were almost all of Scottish descent, believed 'in witchcraft, fairies, brownies and enchantments', and that there were 'few who are not perfectly convinced of the guilt of the unfortunate individuals convicted of witchcraft alleged to have been committed here in 1711'. He went onto describe how 'the house in which the witchcraft alluded to was enacted (situated in Kilcoanmore) is still considered as haunted, and though inhabited, many, even men, will not pass it alone at night'.[125]

Discussions of the age of the great European witch-hunts also provided Irish discourse with an opportunity to contrast their own age and culture with a more barbarous one. In February 1762, the *BNL* printed an 'account of the imposture of the Boy of Bilson' in seventeenth-century England, 'whose extraordinary fits, agitations, and ... surprising distempers' convinced his neighbours that he was 'possessed of a devil and bewitched'.[126] In the 1790s, *Walker's Hibernian Magazine* remembered the countless 'poor wretches' in 'both England and Scotland' put to death for witchcraft. It went onto suggest that their accusers received 'fancied sanction from the Scripture story of the Witch of Endor', and that 'almost all vulgar opinions and tales prevalent among Christians, have, doubtless, originated from hints thrown out in the holy Scriptures'.[127] The same publication, from August 1791, stated that across Europe, from the twelfth to the sixteenth centuries, people of all sex, rank and age were put to death for 'impossible' crimes associated with witchcraft. It went onto argue that the early modern, cultural stereotype of the witch as an old, widowed, wizened woman explains why this demographic was accused of witchcraft and 'committed to jail by an ignorant magistrate, and condemned by as ignorant a judge'.[128] An article in the *Belfast Monthly Magazine*, from December 1791, entitled 'our ancestors', was even more forthright in attributing the witch-hunts to judicial ignorance and credulity: 'the most learned of their judges believed, that one man might have the power by witchcraft, of abusing the faculties of another'.[129] In 1813, the trial of Bury St. Edmunds witches before Sir Mathew Hale in 1662 was regarded by the *Belfast Monthly Magazine* as a shameful episode in Britain's past; of which it noted (erroneously) there was no comparable example in early modern Ireland.[130] In June 1814, the *FJ* provided a sceptical and misogynistic view of why the majority of Scottish witches were older women:

> James the first, it is well known, was a believer in witchcraft, and many a poor old woman was persecuted in his reign. He one day asked Sir John Harrington 'why the Devil did work more with ancient woman than others'. Sir John replied, 'we are taught hereof in Scripture, where it is said, that the Devil walketh in dry places'.[131]

While in October 1827 the *Southern Reporter and Cork Courier*, described how the 'famous' seventeenth-century 'witch-hunter' Matthew Hopkins swam suspected witches to prove their guilt. It went onto claim that Hopkins was eventually forced to undertake the swimming-test himself, which he duly failed.[132]

Witchcraft in other countries

If early modern witch-hunts provided ideological ammunition for an enlightened assault on the follies of belief in witchcraft and magic, so did contemporary instances of witchcraft occurring in other countries, including England. In December 1754, the *BNL* stated that, 'we have had many instances of amazing deceptions being carried on for a time, but time has seldom failed to discover them', before suggesting that the case of a demonically possessed (by means of witchcraft) 19-year-old prostitute, Sarah Gastrell, in London would in time be discovered as such.[133] In March 1759, the neighbours of elderly Susanna Hannokes, from Wingrave, Aylesbury, were scorned for accusing her of bewitching a spinning-wheel and consequently stripping her to her under-clothes and weighing her 'against the Bible', which she 'out-weighed', freeing her from suspicion. The report went onto link this case with that of Ruth Osborne who, in Tring, Hertfordshire in 1751, drowned while undergoing a swimming-test organised by, among others, Thomas Colley, who was subsequently hanged for murder.[134] In December 1769, the *BNL* once more cast a sceptical, mocking eye on continuing popular witchcraft belief in England:

> A poor woman, at Thatchworth, near Wantage in Berkshire, who has been long charged with witchcraft, has at length confessed that she

is a witch, to the great terror of her ignorant neighbours, and to the no small diversion of the more rational.[135]

In November 1808, the *FJ* stated that 'we did imagine that all belief in witchcraft had long been exploded', before detailing how in May 1808 an elderly woman, Ann Izzard, of Great Paxton in Cambridgeshire, was accused by her neighbours of bewitching three young women. The neighbours scratched her skin, stripped her naked, and beat her severely, before trying to swim her; the latter action being thwarted by the local clergyman, Issac Nicholson.[136] Six men and four women were later convicted of Izzard's assault at Huntingdon Assizes and sentenced to between one and two months imprisonment in order to highlight the 'importance of bringing the subject before the public in this way, in order to deter others from such foolish prejudices', namely 'the foolish credulity of the poor people'.[137] In April 1809, the *BNL* reported that Mary Bateman, a reputed witch, was indicted for murder for poisoning Rebecca Perigo.[138] Bateman was a small-time career criminal, swindler, and sometime cunning-person from Leeds who was found guilty of Perigo's murder at York Assizes in March 1809 and executed shortly afterwards.[139] In November of the same year, the *Belfast Monthly Magazine* mocked the credulity of country people in Shropshire and Staffordshire who attributed witchcraft to the success and ease by which a 17-year-old schoolmaster reorganised his local school system.[140]

Particularly harsh words were reserved for Catholic countries on the continent, as well as those that continued to prosecute witches. In December 1775, the *BNL* reported an instance of folly in Poland in 'the palatinate of Kalisch' where 'a gentleman had caused nine old women to be burnt' for bewitching and rendering 'unfruitful the lands in a canton where they inhabited the last summer'.[141] While a letter to the editor of the *BNL* in February 1787 suggested that there were 'few witches or wizards in Spain, the Devil being afraid to contract with a Spaniard, lest he should be cheated'.[142] The matter of Spanish witchcraft was taken more seriously in an article in the *FJ* in April 1789, which argued that 'while the rest of Europe seems daily improving in knowledge, Spain seems still enveloped in Gothic darkness ... a poor woman was burned at Seville [in 1780], by order of the inquisition on a charge of witchcraft'.[143] The *BNL*, in October of the same year, proclaimed that 'new scenes of horror, and unheard of iniquitous practices of despotic ministers, are daily brought to light from the black register of the Bastille ... a young girl, not eight years old, suspected of witchcraft, has been detained in that infernal fortress a full twelve month'.[144] In 1815, in an article entitled

'Superstition and Cruelty', the *BNL* reported the murder and torture of a French Sheppard in Blois, on the banks of the Loire in France, by his neighbours who accused him of bewitching a young child.[145]

In much the same way as newly-enlightened America distanced itself from the Salem witch-hunts by repositioning witchcraft as a non-European phenomenon,[146] Irish Protestants distanced themselves from the perceived irrationality of witchcraft by associating it with non-European cultures. In August 1806, 'a surprising instance of the effects of superstition among the Indian tribes' was reprinted in the *BNL* from a unnamed New York periodical which detailed how 'miserable wretches' accused of witchcraft in America were 'instantly seized, and committed alive to the flames'.[147] In December 1818, it reported that the 'Barbadoes Papers inform us that the penalty of death has been enacted against those who profess and practice the Obeah system of witchcraft, as the only means of checking its enormities, until the slow progress of education and religion shall supersede, in the yet untaught minds of the negroes'.[148] Irish Protestants, such as Sir William Power of Arnnaghmakerrig, Co. Monaghan, who had first-hand experience of non-European witchcraft beliefs discussed them in private in much the same way as public discourse:

> the negroes in Jamaica were disposed and more ignorant than in any of the other islands ... they believed in Obeah, worshipped fetishes and idols and all of them were strong believers in sorcery and witchcraft.[149]

The repeal of the 1586 Witchcraft Act

The amendment of Poynings' Law in 1782 took away the power of the British and Irish privy councils to amend or suppress legislation initiated in the Irish parliament,[150] which was itself abolished by the Act of Union of 1801.[151] A detailed examination of the Irish Witchcraft Repeal Act of 1821 reveals that it passed through both houses of the Westminster parliament quickly and un-controversially, with little interest being shown in it either by the Irish Press or educated elite; an indifference that further attests to the marginalisation of witchcraft belief within Irish educated culture. It is thus hard to disagree with Ian Bostridge's assertion that 'this repeal was, without doubt, a measure of administrative reform pure and simple.'[152] On 7 March 1821, Thomas Spring-Rice, Whig MP for Limerick, made a motion in the House of Commons to bring in criminal reform legislation for Ireland, specifically 'for the repeal of the capital punishments attached to the commission of certain offences in Ireland', including witchcraft, female abduction, concealment of assets by bankrupts, and shoplifting, in order to make them 'as conformable as possible to public opinion'. This was deemed 'particularly necessary' in Ireland 'where there existed such a disposition to prosecute for many capital offences'.[153] Spring-Rice also hoped this new legislation would bring about the further 'assimilation of the laws of the two countries' of Ireland and England. After Spring-Rice's speech, the Tory Chancellor of the Exchequer, Nicholas Vansittart, noted that he 'hoped that the inference would not be drawn, from the thin attendance of the House, that the Gentlemen of England were indifferent to the interests of Ireland', attributing the 'small number then present to the opinion that there can be no opposition to these bills'.[154] Spring-Rice, Charles Grant (Tory Irish Chief Secretary and supporter of Catholic emancipation), James Mackintosh (Scottish Whig and MP for Knaresborough), and Thomas Fowell Buxton (MP for Weymouth and specialist on criminal law) were then charged with preparing the bills and laying them before parliament.[155] Two days later, on 9 March 1821, Spring-Rice presented one of these bills, the Irish Witchcraft Repeal Bill, to the House of Commons, which was read a first time and ordered to be read a second time and printed.[156] The printed *Bill to Repeal an Act, Made in the Parliament of Ireland, in the 28th year of the Reign of Queen Elizabeth, against Witchcraft and Sorcery*, dated 9 March 1821, was perfunctory, stating only that it was 'expedient that the said act should be repealed'.[157] The bill was read a second time on 21 March 1821, and put into a Committee of the Whole House,[158] which reported two days later.[159] On 26 March, it was read a third time and ordered to be taken by Spring-Rice to the House of Lords.[160] Immediately after this order was given, Robert Stewart, Lord Castlereagh, provoked laughter in Commons by remarking 'that the witching hour of night was a very suitable time to give the last sanction of that House to a Witchcraft Repeal Bill'.[161] The bill was read a first time in the House of Lords on 28 March, read a second time on 30 March and ordered to be put before a Committee of the Whole House, which reported on 2 April 1821 that it should be passed without amendment. After a third reading the following day, it was returned to the House of Commons who concurred with the Lords' decision.[162] The Royal Assent was given by commission to the un-amended bill on 6 April 1821 and it passed into law as '1&2 Geo. IV c.18, 1821, An Act to Repeal an Act, made in the Parliament of Ireland in the Twenty Eighth Year of the Reign of Queen Elizabeth, against Witchcraft and Sorcery'.[163]

No discussion of witchcraft belief appeared in Irish newspapers at that time, apart from articles detailing the Repeal Bill's rather uneventful passage through parliament, and a solitary literary response, written by an anonymous, English Anglican: *Antipas; a Solemn Appeal to the Right Reverend the Archbishops and Bishops of the United Churches of England and Ireland: With Reference to Several Bills ... Especially that Concerning Witchcraft and Sorcery* (London, 1821). This pamphlet presented a defence of traditional witchcraft belief married to an intense anti-Catholic, anti-emancipator, and anti-Trinitarian stance. *Antipas* was addressed to the spiritual peers of the House of Lords and had been written on 2 April 1821 during the Repeal Bill's passage through parliament before being printed in London 10 days later.[164] Along with 'Popery and Infidelity', *Antipas* condemned 'sorcery or witchcraft' as the enemy of the 'Church of Christ',[165] stating that the only piece of legislation passed in that session of parliament that would be as detrimental to established, Protestant religion in Britain and Ireland as the Witchcraft Repeal Bill was that for 'Removing such Disabilities, and Granting such an Emancipation to Papists'. This Catholic Relief Bill was thrown out by the House of Lords after its third reading in the Commons on 2 April.[166] If the author's attitude to Catholics, emancipation, and relaxation of restrictions on Protestant dissenters was not clear enough, the author stated: 'conciliation of Dissenters has opened the mouth of blasphemers – concession to Catholics may yet "give place to the devil"'.[167] By linking Catholicism, dissent, and witchcraft, the author was following an Anglican tradition that arose after the 1736 Act effectively silenced public debate on witchcraft, in that the topic was discussed thereafter only as part of wider political debates concerning the relaxation of restrictions on Protestant non-conformists and Catholics.[168] It also reflected the backlash of some Anglican clergy in the early nineteenth century against popular witchcraft and magical beliefs, which they equated with vulgarity and ignorance, and which if not combated would drag the populace into atheism and idolatry.[169] In the pamphlet, witchcraft was defined solely in demonic terms as: 'all kind of influence produced by collusion with Satan; all persons who have dealings with Satan, if not actually entered into formal compact'.[170] That these 'persons are among men', the author declared, is 'abundantly plain from Scripture', citing (chiefly) as evidence of this the stalwart biblical justification of the early modern period, 'Thou Shalt Not Suffer a Witch to Live (Exodus xxii, 18)'.[171] He went on to argue that governments that allowed witchcraft to grow would be visited upon by 'national judgements' from God.[172] He also lamented near the end of his discourse that his view on witchcraft and Satan had 'become very unfashionable',[173] and hoped that the House of Lords would see sense and reject the Witchcraft Repeal Bill.[174] Reproducing Lord Castlereagh's comments in the Commons, as they appeared in *The Times* of 27 March 1821, about the witching hour being an appropriate time for a debate on a Witchcraft Repeal Bill,[175] he stated that he hoped that when the Bill came before the House of Lords, this 'midnight merriment' would be avoided and it would 'be met ... with the solemnity which its peculiar nature demands; and with due consideration to its practical results'.[176] This inflammatory, rather odd, pamphlet did not go unnoticed and was remarked upon during the Catholic Emancipation Bill debate on 16 April 1821 in the House of Commons by pro-Emancipation Tory MP Dudley Ryder, Earl of Harrowby. Ryder ridiculed 'the analogy which the writer had drawn between popery and witchcraft', suggesting that to draw such a comparison was nonsensical because when 'the laws against witchcraft' in England were 'repealed, witchcraft itself altogether ceased' and thus what did 'this profound writer expect from the total repeal of the laws against popery?'[177]

Witchcraft and the law

If there was continuing popular belief in witchcraft in the nineteenth, and to a lesser extent the twentieth century, and the issue was increasingly marginalised in educated culture during the second decade of the eighteenth century, this raises the question as to how Irish legal authorities dealt with witchcraft accusations both before and after the passing of the 1821 Repeal Act. Scant surviving Irish legal sources, which are predisposed toward Assize court records, contain no reference to prosecution for witchcraft.[178] The absence of eighteenth-century witchcraft cases could of course be a distortion caused by loss of records. It is not until the early nineteenth century that we get any real indication of how the law dealt with witchcraft. The handful of cases that involved, at some level, witchcraft accusation, and were brought before one or more magistrates in informal, summary proceedings and later in petty sessions and police and crown courts, suggest they were only taken seriously after 1830 when made as part of an assault allegation.[179] Regular petty sessions were introduced in Ireland between 1823 and 1825 and its magistrates adjudicated lesser offences such as trespass, common assault (after 1830), and larceny, while conducting initial investigations into more serious crimes. Up until the early twentieth century, they were usually held in sparsely furnished, hired rooms, with proceedings tending toward the haphazard and boisterous. By drastically reducing the cost of litigation, petty sessions, along with the establishment in the 1830s of the Irish Constabulary, which policed all of Ireland except the cities of Belfast, Derry, and Dublin, which had their own forces, enabled people, especially in rural areas, to lodge complaints.[180]

In Co. Antrim in 1801, Sally Coulter, widowed, elderly, confused, and possibly suffering from dementia, was accused by her neighbours of causing a recent drought and subsequent crop failure. She was swum as a witch and although this resulted in her death, no charges were brought against the perpetrators, and no coroner's inquest was held. A similar case from around the same time involved a 'thoroughly ill-favoured woman, named Nellie Dunwoody', who not only resembled the stereotype of a witch, a wizened old hag, but laid claim to the supernatural power to harm cattle and humans; a power which reportedly deserted her after she was swum as a witch.[181] In Co. Antrim in 1809, when cunning-woman Mary Butters' counter-charms caused the death of a number of people resulting in her prosecution for murder, no mention was made of the 1586 Witchcraft Act, under whose provisions her criminal actions also fell. This tragedy further demonstrates that popular witchcraft belief by that time had become less polarised, with Presbyterians along with the Catholic Gaelic-Irish attributing the loss of butter and milk to butter-stealing witches.[182] In Union Hall, Co. Cork, in September 1812, 'a man of decent appearance applied to the sitting Magistrate, under symptoms of great distress of mind, for redress of various injuries inflicted upon him, by a person who he said, had long held him in subjection by the power of witchcraft'. The man complained that after he had incurred the 'displeasure' of his neighbour, who was in league 'with the powers of Darkness', he 'destroyed his clothes, tainted his provisions, prevented the smoke ascending the chimneys, soured the liquor in his cellar, and on various occasions ... had so fascinated the powers of vision, that on his return home, all his efforts to discover his own door had prov'd ineffectual'. He then 'entreated the magistrate' to prosecute the accused in order to remove the effects of his bewitchment. The magistrate promised 'to comply with his request, and advised him in the meantime to go home, and rest satisfied that no effort in his power should be wanting to prevent the evil spirit troubling him in future'. This obvious patronisation and placation went unnoticed by the man, who 'declared himself perfectly satisfied, and said, he felt that in consequence of his having thrown himself on the protection of the Bench, the pains with which he had for so long a time been afflicted were very much abated!'[183] Similarly, in August 1815, in Charles Street, Dublin, 'a young man of rather decent appearance', who claimed friends in high places in England, but was labouring under a 'deranged state of mind', appeared before Dublin police magistrates, Sir William Stamer (erstwhile Mayor of Dublin and subsequent Alderman) and Dr Turner, having been arrested by local peace-officers who caught him damaging an upstairs room of a public house that he had entered uninvited. He informed Stamer and Turner that the owners of the public house 'had him under witchcraft for seven years' and that the only way he would be released from their spell was to pull down their house in order to 'lay spirits and put down the devil'. According to the *FJ*, both magistrates endeavoured to placate the man but he told them he would not rest until the people concerned were prosecuted for witchcraft and their house, along with several others in the city, was levelled, as this was the only way to 'put a stop to that damnable thing – witchcraft'. Turner and Stamer then promised him they would prosecute the people he had accused of witchcraft and release him from custody if he did not return to Charles Street. As a safeguard, the magistrates sent peace-officers to guard the premises.[184] In the first three decades of the nineteenth century, Dublin was policed by a parish watch and a number of constables supervised by peace-officers.[185]

In Co. Wexford Petty Sessions in September 1830, a schoolmaster, Donnelly, and his family were accused by 40-year-old tailor, Knox, of keeping a witch in a shape of a weasel in their home which he claimed could read his thoughts. Knox considered this ability particularly dangerous as he was a freemason and conversant with the secrets of his order.[186] Spectators laughed when Knox gave evidence and when Donnelly stated he considered the allegations laid against him a legal affront. JP Charles Arthur Walker, Liberal MP for Co. Wexford and member of Royal Dublin Society, however, explained to Donnelly that men of his office 'were bound by their commission to inquire into all cases of witchcraft', even if he could not prosecute anyone for it because 'the Act of parliament relative to witchcraft has been abolished'. Walker then moved to have the case dismissed, advising Knox that if he wished to pursue the matter farther he would need to engage the services of an attorney, to which Knox replied that if witchcraft were abolished 'then why not abolish witches also?'. Walker's co-magistrate, Cooper, betrayed none of his counterpart's patience, stating that the entire case was 'deplorable' and advised Knox to 'get a few pet rats, and let them loose in the room where the weasel is, and when the weasel comes out knock him down with a goose'.[187]

There is no evidence that Irish courts handled witchcraft 'slander' cases of the type seen in eighteenth- and nineteenth-century England,

and as the 1736 Witchcraft Repeal Act was not introduced into Ireland, the crime of pretended witchcraft did not exist.[188] Assault cases involving witchcraft accusation, however, were brought before judiciaries. For example, suspected witches, or their families, were accused of assaulting their accusers. In March 1837, Catherine (Kitty) McKenna was found guilty, along with six other men, at Co. Antrim Assizes for brutally assaulting brothers John and Oliver McConnell at Ballynahatty fair, Omagh, Co. Tyrone, the previous July after they called her son, Pat, a 'witch'.[189] At Cahir Petty Sessions in Co. Tipperary in October 1895, Thomas Meehan, a farmer from Kilcoran, charged William Burke 'with striking him with a reaping hook' the previous month, after Meehan accused Burke's wife of appropriating the butter from his cows.[190] Burke was found guilty and ordered to keep the peace for 12 months and pay 'sureties' of £20.[191] Accusers were also prosecuted for assaulting suspected witches. In June 1870, James Jamieson was summoned to appear before Belfast Police Court by Alice Hunter for assault and stealing her shawl. Jamieson had been advised by a local 'cow-doctor', or cunning-man, that Hunter had bewitched his cows and that the only way to restore their milk supply was to burn an item of her clothing under the noses of afflicted livestock. Regional Magistrate, E. Orme, bemused by the credulity of both complainant and defendant, fined Jamieson 20 shillings and ordered him to replace Hunter's shawl.[192] In 1892, at New Pallas Petty Sessions in Co. Limerick, Mrs Bowles was prosecuted for breaking Mrs Breen's arm after the latter was discovered trespassing in a perceived attempt to 'steal away her butter'.[193]

Conclusion

In Ireland, belief in witchcraft continued at a popular level, in both Protestant and Catholic communities into the twentieth century, by which time denominational polarisation of witchcraft beliefs along butter-stealing and malefic/demonic lines had diminished: more so in Protestant than in Catholic culture. Furthermore, beliefs surrounding how milk and butter was stolen or appropriated by witches had developed beyond transmogrification into hares and the use of the evil-eye to include a range of artifices based on sympathetic magic. Although the Catholic clerical elite, in the eighteenth century at least, condemned many popular folk beliefs considered superstitious, traditional malefic, demonic witchcraft was still regarded as orthodox, along with various forms of the miraculous. Before the mid-eighteenth century, limited witchcraft scepticism in public discourse was voiced by a small number of enlightened Irish Protestant Whigs. It was only after 1750 that it became increasingly mainstream and acceptable to condemn witchcraft, along with notions of an interventionist Satan, as irrational and vulgar, which in the modern world (as opposed to the early modern one) were only believed in by the lower orders in other parts of Britain, by benighted Catholics and civilisations considered backward or primitive. To have admitted that witchcraft was alive and well in Ireland would have shattered the illusion that, under the guidance of a polite, rational, and enlightened Irish Protestant Ascendancy, eighteenth-century Ireland had made a complete break from the irrational beliefs that drove early modern European witch-hunting.

Cases involving witchcraft occasionally came before magistrates in the early nineteenth century. In common with England,[194] this was at least partly a result of the establishment of regional and metropolitan police forces, police courts, and the extension of petty sessions, which made it easier for complaints to be brought before legal authorities, especially in rural areas. Witchcraft complaints were usually brushed aside by magistrates until the 1830s, when they became linked to assault allegations, which now came under the summary jurisdiction of petty sessions. These cases were reported by an expanding newspaper industry presented with an opportunity to entertain readers with stories of credulous lower orders and deranged accusers: witchcraft belief was by that time considered by the educated to be so self-evidently irrational and ridiculous that there was less need for the educated to distance themselves from it. This marginalisation within educated culture is further attested to by the way the Irish Witchcraft Act slipped quietly from the statute book in 1821.

7
Cunning-folk in Modern Ireland

The aim of this chapter is to establish that cunning-folk, identified as part of popular culture in the early modern period, continued to serve both Catholic and Protestant communities in Ireland up until the twentieth century. Case studies of individual magical practitioners, contemporary clerical attitudes and campaigns, and newspaper reports will be explored to build up a fuller picture of what cunning-folk did, who availed of their services, and how the authorities dealt with them if they fell foul of the law.[1] Cunning-folk were not the only identifiable magical practitioners in Ireland; fortune-tellers and magical healers worked largely in rural areas. In order to demonstrate that these practitioners were distinct from cunning-folk, it is necessary to briefly consider their activities and treatment by the legal authorities.

Magical healers

Recent research has demonstrated that non-commercial magical healers were operating in Catholic and Protestant communities in Ireland from the mid- to the late twentieth century.[2] Magical healers used 'charms' to cure specific ailments and conditions, in particular those affecting the skin, while others also cured animal illness, such as cases of haemorrhage/babesiosis in cattle. They had either been born with the 'gift' of healing or had inherited it from another specialist.[3] It will be suggested below that these practitioners were also present in nineteenth- and early twentieth-century Ireland. However, in order to locate them within the medical marketplace of the period,[4] and provide an indication of their numbers, gender, and class make-up, and geographical spread, a longer, more detailed study is required.

Irish newspapers suggest that from the mid-nineteenth century onwards disgruntled clients of magical healers were lodging complaints with petty sessions and police courts.[5] In August 1856, elderly and poverty-stricken magical healer Margaret Giffen summoned husband and wife, Thomas and Mary Ann Cushley, before Belfast Police Court. She accused them of false imprisonment and forcing her to drink a strange liquid, possibly furnished by a cunning-person. The Cushleys had paid Giffen to cure their sick child but claimed instead that she bewitched him.[6] In January 1897, dealer and part-time magical healer William McIlhattan was summoned to Belfast Recorder's Court to attend the inquest of a 12-month-old infant, John James Stewart. Stewart had died after McIlhattan tried to cure his whooping-cough by a combination of incantation and passing him under a donkey. The jury ruled that the deceased had died from bronchitis and no blame was attributed to McIhatton.[7] The mother of the child, Maggie Stewart, informed presiding coroner, E.S. Finnigan, that 'McIhatton never asked her for money, nor did she give him any at any time'.[8] In 1905, at Galway Petty Sessions, Edward Halloran, a 'small farmer', was 'returned for trial at the Quarter Sessions' for 'selling charms and taking money for doing so'. It was alleged that Halloran had diagnosed John Concannon with tuberculosis and a liver complaint and that after the 'charm' he provided as a cure proved ineffective Concannon 'drowned himself'. Halloran 'admitted giving the charms, but said he did not know it was any harm, and that he took no money for it'.[9]

We also get glimpses of magical healers in non-litigious contexts. It was reported in the *BNL* in September 1853 that James Loughlin, of Gort, Co. Tyrone, had written to the Belfast Board of Guardians, who oversaw the running of the workhouse, to inform them that:

> he was in possession of a certain and effectual remedy for the cure of cholera, and ... as there appeared some likelihood that that epidemic would visit Belfast, he requested the Guardians would make an order to place some patients under his treatment.

The Board of Guardians unsurprisingly rejected Loughlin's proposition.[10] In 1906, folklorist Joseph Meehan described that in rural Co. Leitrim lived elderly Lackey Gallagher who specialised in 'the cure of the ringworm' and whose curative powers were conferred on him at birth, being 'the seventh son of a seventh son'.[11] In 1912, Thomas Johnson Westropp told of how in Co. Clare, 'Denis Curtis near Corofin cures liver complaints, bleeding, and cows that have swallowed raw potatoes'. He went on to state that he 'puts his human patients on their backs on his anvil, and pretends to strike them with a sledge hammer ... on three occasions, on two Mondays and a Thursday'.[12] John Aylward, a labourer aged 84 in 1939, from Co. Wexford, related to a collector of the Irish Folklore Commission that he knew a woman who 'had a prayer for stopping the blood', which she had inherited from another magical healer on their death and which could be used only 'when there was great need for it'.[13]

Fortune-tellers

Although very little research has been carried out into Irish Fortune-tellers in the modern period, it is clear that they were a distinct type of magical practitioner who served both Catholic and Protestant communities. Andrew Holmes has demonstrated that in late eighteenth-century Presbyterian Ulster, 'spaemen and spaewomen were employed to tell the future and provide advice when making decisions'.[14] Around the same time, Presbyterian small farmer and weaver, James Orr, in his poem, 'The Spae-wife', warned of the dangers of fortune-telling and advised his Ulster-Scots audience to trust instead in the wisdom contained in the Bible.[15] Fortune-tellers were also ubiquitous enough in late eighteenth-century Dublin for Protestant readers of the *Hibernian Journal*, founded in 1771, to voice their concern about their corrupting influence on the lower orders and the sharp practices they employed to take money from unwitting clients.[16] In 1820, in Ballingarry, Co. Tipperary, an unnamed Catholic woman was brought before her Archbishop to publicly apologise for telling fortunes and to promise to live a pious life in the future.[17] While in April 1840, OSMI collector James Boyle noted that in Islandmagee, Co. Antrim, 'many old women practise card-cutting and cup-tossing, telling fortunes and interpreting dreams', and that 'Mary Haddock of Carnspindle townland is remarkable for her ability and dexterity in these acquirements'.[18] An article published in the *BNL* in September 1876 raised many of the same issues as the *Hibernian Journal* a century before. It complained that male and female fortune-tellers, who gathered in large towns all over Ireland, tricked servant girls 'out of their wages' by telling them fanciful stories about their marriage prospects.[19]

Apart from an isolated prosecution of an eighteenth-century fortune-teller,[20] it was from the mid-nineteenth century onwards that they were, in common with magical healers, increasingly prosecuted by clients, either for theft, assault, or obtaining money under false pretences.[21]

In September 1844, fortune-teller Esther Ann Johnston was brought before Belfast magistrates for obtaining money under false pretences from Robert McClelland, whom she told she could locate money stolen from him in a robbery.[22] While at Youghal Petty Sessions, Co. Cork, in July 1849, fortune-teller Mary Callaghan pleaded guilty to obtaining money under false pretences from Mary Collins, who had employed her to 'cut the cards' to find the whereabouts of a missing shawl. Magistrate Walter Berwick sentenced Callaghan to nine months' imprisonment.[23] In June 1860, at Saintfield Petty Sessions in Co. Down, Constable Hamilton summoned Eliza Jane Ransom for pretending to tell fortunes.[24] At Armagh Petty Sessions in April 1863, Daniel McGahan (described as 'a simple rustic' in a contemporary newspaper report) initiated proceedings against 'professional spaeman' Owen Magill. Magill had charged McGahan five shillings for informing him that money had been sent to him from America and was awaiting collection at Benburb Post Office in Dungannon, Co. Tyrone. When this information turned out to be false, McGahan went to the police. The petty sessions magistrate dismissed McGahan's complaint, stating sardonically, that he 'did not think the charge could be sustained, as the letter might yet come'.[25] In Co. Cork, in early 1867, Patrick O'Ganagan, an 'itinerant fortune-teller', was fined a shilling for pretending to be 'dumb' and telling the fortunes of 'a crowd of small boys'.[26] Hearing and speech impairment were connected with prescience in popular culture and some fortune-tellers feigned one or both disabilities to enhance their credibility with potential clients. In July 1869, 90-year-old Jane Milligan was brought before Belfast Police Court for obtaining three pounds under false pretences from John McClenaghan and his wife. Jane had been employed by the couple to find their missing son but on failing to do so did not return their fee. It was reported in court that Milligan made a good living from fortune-telling, having 'plenty of money in the bank', which allowed her to go free upon 'entering into her own recognisances in the sum of £5'.[27]

Fortune-tellers were also prosecuted for assault and theft. In November 1853, Ellen Leahy was brought before Kanturk Petty Sessions, Co. Cork, for pick-pocketing Mary Bresnihan, who had consulted her to find out if her son, who had enlisted in the army, was alive or dead. After ruling that they case against Leahy was proved, Kanturk Petty Sessions magistrates passed it to Mallow Quarter Sessions, where in January 1854 she was sentenced to four years' imprisonment.[28] Later the same year, elderly Protestant 'wandering cup-tosser', Janet Carson, was jailed for 14 days by magistrates at Belfast Police Court for stealing a shilling from Rachel Finnock. The theft occurred after Finnock had refused to engage

Carson's services, believing it impious to have anything to do with 'a person ... who had manifestly communion with spirits'.[29] In June 1856, at Ballymena Petty Sessions, Co. Antrim, vagrant William Robinson was given two months imprisonment for assault and obtaining money under false pretences from the servants of Sheppard Thompson. Robinson's *modus operandi* was to pretend to be 'deaf' and 'dumb' and at the time of arrest his travelling companions were two female fortune-tellers who had recently been accused of extorting money from a woman in the Ballymena area.[30] In October 1857, at Dublin Police Court, travelling fortune-teller Mary Stewart was accused by Margaret Purcell and Catherine Daly of stealing a number of items, including a pair of gold earrings. Stewart had told the women she needed to borrow the earrings in order to read their fortunes. She also pretended to 'be both deaf and dumb', a subterfuge revealed to a magistrate 'by a sharp boy, who accompanied her on her travels'. Stewart was also reported to have 'suddenly recovered both speech and hearing' in order to defend herself in court; a task she completed in a 'singularly shrill voice ... popularly ascribed to the effect of whiskey drinking'.[31] In May 1860, elderly, itinerant fortune-teller Jane Stewart from Co. Cavan was imprisoned for verbally abusing and assaulting a client who refused to pay her fee.[32]

Irish fortune-tellers can be seen to have been roughly comparable to practitioners in England and Wales. English and Welsh fortune-tellers were usually women from lower socio-economic groups and advised clients on finance, matters of the heart, gambling, and the whereabouts of lost or stolen goods. Fortune-tellers also employed a range of techniques, from palmistry to reading cards and tea leaves. Along with this more settled, established practitioner, itinerant fortune-tellers attracted clients by going from door to door or by mingling at markets and fairs. In essence roaming beggars, they were occasionally convicted by petty sessions and police courts for vagrancy, theft, or obtaining money under false pretences. By the latter half of the nineteenth century, fortune-telling was becoming more professional, profitable, urban, and respectable. This new respectability was characterised by the avoidance of legal censure, a higher class of clientele, and the self-adoption of names such as 'clairvoyant' and 'medium'.[33] More research is needed to confirm whether this new type of fortune-teller had also set up business in Ireland. It also remains to be established whether the professional judicial astrologers who cast horoscopes and answered hoary questions in late seventeenth-century Irish towns were still operating in the modern period.[34] The origins of modern Irish fortune-tellers also requires exploration if only to confirm my initial impression that they (along with magical healers, if not cunning-folk) were not an established part of early-modern popular culture.

Cunning-folk in modern Ireland

Historians, folklorists, and sociologists have noted the presence in late eighteenth- to mid-twentieth-century Catholic Ireland of professional and semi-professional magical practitioners. These practitioners provided diagnostic services and cures for illness believed to have both natural and supernatural causes. However, they often specialised in the treatment of cattle or humans believed to have been injured by witches, the evil-eye (unintentional and intentional), or fairies. The methodology they employed varied from practitioner to practitioner. Suspected elf-shot cattle were, for example, measured a number of times and if they were found to be shorter at each measurement an affirmative diagnosis was made. As has been mentioned in a previous chapter, diagnosis of fairy attack in humans was far more brutal and often involved heating suspected changelings over a fire. Witches on the other hand were detected by heating pans of milk imbued with pins (of which more will be said below) or by looking into bowls of water. Herbal remedies, written charms, and water imbued with curative amulets were also used to cure witch-afflicted cattle.[35] As Richard Jenkins has pointed out, these practitioners were known in Ireland by variety of names in English: '"wise men" or "wise women" ... "fairy men" or "fairy women" ... "fairy doctors" or "elf doctors" ... "cow charmers" or "cow doctors"'. In Irish, they were referred to 'as lucht pisreóg or "enchanters", doctú irí na síofraí or "fairy doctors", leá (lianna) sí or "fairy healers", bean chumhachtach or "woman with supernatural powers", and mná feasa or "wise women", bean feasa in the singular'.[36] Jenkins further suggests that 'in nineteenth-century Ireland, with national and local newspapers and a road and communications network that was adequate for the purposes of trade and government, some of these practitioners developed reputations such that they could attract patients and cases from across a wide area'.[37] Gearóid Ó Crualaoich has argued that in the early to mid-twentieth-century, traditional Irish oral narratives devoted to tales of mná feasa functioned 'as a communal, psychotherapeutic device that operated so as to enable its hearers to cope with their individual misfortunes and afflictions'.[38]

Due to a lack of comparative work between popular magic in Ireland and elsewhere, this historiography implies that these professional magical practitioners were peculiar to Catholic Ireland.[39] It will be argued below, however, that they were in fact cunning-folk serving Catholic and Protestant communities. In nineteenth- and early twentieth-century England and Wales people continued to resort to cunning-folk as a way to cope with 'the misfortunes, vagaries and stress of life in ... an uncertain world'.[40] Male cunning-folk, who were in the majority, usually had a secondary occupation, such as farmer, artisan, or tradesman, while their female counterparts worked mostly on a full-time basis. Modern cunning-folk provided much the same services, in much the same ways, for similar fees, as their early modern predecessors.[41] Legal action against them became more frequent after 1850 as a result of increased police provision in rural areas, which made it easier for unhappy clients to lodge complaints and for these complaints to be investigated and acted upon. Furthermore, after 1824, magistrates were far happier to prosecute cunning-folk because they could now do so under amended vagrancy laws rather than having to rely on the 1736 Repeal Act, which made overt, distasteful, and embarrassing reference to witchcraft and magic.[42]

Cunning-folk and the Churches

Although we know little of the Church of Ireland's response to popular magic due to a lack of surviving records, in the late eighteenth and early nineteenth centuries, Andrew Holmes has argued that Ulster Presbyterians held a range of 'alternative beliefs to those expounded by preachers and taught through catechisms', which 'provided the means by which lay Presbyterians could deal with the uncertainties of life'.[43] This included belief in the evil-eye, witchcraft, and malevolent fairies. In order to protect themselves from these supernatural agencies, Presbyterians frequented Holy wells, used herbal remedies, protective charms, and amulets, and consulted what Holmes refers to as 'white witches'.[44] However, after the mid-eighteenth century, in common with their counterparts in Scotland,[45] Irish Presbyterian sessions and presbyteries rarely disciplined those engaged in these 'superstitious' practices.[46] There is also no record, at any juncture during the course of the eighteenth century, of the Presbyterian Synod of Ulster displaying concern with the activities of magical practitioners.[47] This does not mean that individual ministers were not worried about traditional popular customs and the perceived 'superstitious beliefs attached to them'. The use of magical amulets and charms was condemned by Presbyterian clergymen as late as 1832, and at Cahan Sessions in the mid-eighteenth century elders were instructed to ask people in their district if they frequented fortune-tellers.[48]

As was suggested in the last chapter, from the late eighteenth century onwards, the higher ranks of the Catholic clergy, helped by reforming priests and followed in time by rank and file subalterns, railed against popular, non-Christian supernatural beliefs, customs, and observances. This included the activities of cunning-folk. In July 1752, Limerick-born Roman Catholic Archbishop of Cashel, James Butler, described how during a visitation of the parish of 'Killinnal' (Killenaule) a case was reported to him of 'a man that goes about cureing people with his botle of witchcrafts'.[49] In July 1759, he noted (with relief) in his visitation book that in Cashel 'nothing belonging to religion has been abused, no negromancers, no faery men or women, or superstitious actions'.[50] Another mid-eighteenth-century, reforming Catholic bishop, John O'Brien of Cloyne and Ross, recommended that only Church-sanctioned defences, such as preaching, were to be used as protection against butter-stealing witches on May Eve and May Day.[51] In the early 1760s, Bishop Madgett, proved a vehement opponent of magical practitioners, regarding them in much the same way as his early modern predecessors, as a demonically-inspired barrier to right religion. Madgett condemned the common sort as backward and ignorant, referring to them as the *'plebei'*, *'idiotae'* and *'ruricolae'*[52] because of their addiction to, among other things, 'vain, superstitious and sinful' customs which they could 'scarcely ever be deterred from'.[53] He was particularly disdainful of divination: 'if something is missing, they think that by turning a sieve the thief can be infallibly detected', in the process, by means of this 'disgraceful action', 'they destroy the good character of honest men and women'.[54] In his opinion, 'superstitious and vain observances' such as these had no 'natural or supernatural connection with the effect or result that is feared or hoped ... their outcome depends entirely on chance if it happens once and thousand times, the women here pay more attention to this chance happening'.[55] Bishop Madgett recommended that those who suspected they had been harmed by witches or fairies 'should have recourse to the exorcisms, prayers and sacrifices of the Church and not to some other magical rites'.[56] Above all, he advised, 'people should never appeal to the devil himself to undo his previous works', because he would 'never do this unless those appealing to him entered into a more firm pact with him than those through whom he worked his sorcery'.[57] Madgett went on to advise priests in his diocese only to absolve cunning-people that came before them 'on the first occasion, provided they promise to abandon' such practices in future.[58] In 1771, in regulations for his diocese of Ferns, Bishop Nicholas Sweetman warned his priests against dabbling in popular magic themselves:

> no pastor, priest or ecclesiastick whatsoever, in the Diocess of Ferns, must presume, sub peona suspensionis et Privationis Beneficii to read Exorcisms, or Gospels, over the already too ignorant, and by such ecclesiasticks too much delude people, or act the fairy doctor in any shape, without express leave in writing, from the Bishop of the Diocess. Under the foregoing article I comprehend all those who bless water to sprinkle sick persons, cattle, fields, etc.[59]

Furthermore, a late eighteenth-century, corrected edition of a work by seventeenth-century Bendictine Monk, Thomas Vincent, stated that it was contrary to the first commandment to 'make use of magic, spells, witchcraft, enchantments, or to consult such persons, or give credit to their sciences or sayings'.[60] In 1819, Archbishop Patrick Everard voiced concern over the 'superstitious' practices of a congregation in Ballingarry, Co. Tipperary.[61] Although Catholic priests during the cholera outbreak in the spring to summer of 1832 uniformly denied any role in providing the Catholic poor with protective charms designed to ward off the disease,[62] there is evidence that priests occasionally provided the laity with supernatural assistance. For example, when cholera spread to Kilkishen, Co. Clare, Fr. Darby Tuohy gave his parishioners holy water for use in protective rituals.[63]

By the mid-nineteenth century, however, parish priests were more likely to censure magical practice and practitioners than to encourage them, to which the careers of two infamous Irish cunning-women, Biddy Early and Moll Anthony, attest. In Feakle, Co. Clare, Biddy Early told fortunes and found lost or stolen cattle and goods by looking into a mirror. She also treated minor ailments using incantation, herbs, and a strange liquid contained in a black bottle. Early also cured 'fairy stricken' children and people afflicted by the evil-eye, and detected and countered butter-stealing witches. She seldom took money for her services, preferring instead payment in kind (gifts of whiskey were particularly welcome) to avoid the possibility of criminal prosecution for obtaining money under false pretences. Successive priests of Feakle, Fr. James Dore (1849–60) and Fr. Andrew Connellan (1860–74), objected to her activities on the grounds they were superstitious and possibly demonic. Early was condemned from the pulpit and local people were encouraged, for their own spiritual well-being, not to avail of her services. This probably explains why she did not attend Sunday Mass, even though she was nominally Catholic throughout her life. Folklore accounts state that on her deathbed in 1874, Early asked for last rites to be administered by Fr. Connellan, and that after her death he threw her magic bottle into a local lake.[64] Moll Anthony (real name Mary Lesson) died in 1878 in Co. Kilkenny and was refused a Christian burial by local priests. In life she had told fortunes, provided cures for minor ailments, healed humans and animals attacked by fairies, and resolved changeling abduction cases. Ironically, and in common with Biddy Early, she was reputed to have received her own magical 'gifts' from the fairies. Anthony's magical methods varied, from the use of herbs, to prayers and incantation. Accounts differ as to how she was paid by clients for her services, whether in cash or with gifts of goods. In common with Biddy Early, Anthony was also rewarded with the coin of social respect and community leadership.[65]

Mary Butters

Mary Butters was an early nineteenth-century cunning-woman made in much the same mould as Biddy Early or Moll Anthony, with one difference: she was Presbyterian. The case of the 'Carnmoney Witch' is an extremely well-documented but as yet under-researched case which provides insight into what Protestant cunning-folk did and how they did it. It also shows how cunning-folk were treated by the contemporary press and legal authorities. The Presbyterian hamlet of Carnmoney, in the parish of Carnmoney, Co. Antrim, in the early nineteenth century contained around 130 people who were mostly tradespeople, 'petty' dealers, farmers, and agricultural labourers, who, although fairly poor, were not poverty-stricken. Carnmoney contained a market-house, a shop, and both day and Sunday schools. In the summer of 1807, Alexander Montgomery, a tailor, who lived near to First Carnmoney, Presbyterian meeting house, became worried when milk from his only cow could not be churned into butter.[66] In Carnmoney, as in other rural areas in Ireland at that time, milk cows were extremely important, as dairy products, especially buttermilk and butter, were cornerstones of the daily diet. More importantly, these commodities were a very important source of cash revenue for smallholders, who sold them to Belfast markets nearby.[67] In a society that operated a strict, gender-based division of labour, women were responsible for 'milking the cows [and] churning [the] butter'.[68] It was therefore unsurprising that it was Montgomery's wife, Elizabeth, who first noticed the problem with the milk and attributed it to the cow having been 'overlooked or bewitched'. Her suspicions were confirmed by 'the concurring testimony of every old woman in the parish, each of whom contributed her story of what she had seen and known in former times'.[69] The first counter-measure employed by Elizabeth to discover 'the witch', or at the very least 'destroy her power over the cow', was to organise a ceremony in which 12 local women blessed the cow 'in a solemn manner'.[70] Branches of the magical Rowan tree and mountain ash were then tied to the cow's tail, witch-stones were hung up in the cow house, and horse-shoes nailed above the byre door and cow stand. The ancient herbal remedy and detoxifier, vervain, was collected and administered to the cow.[71] When these operations failed to bring about any discernable improvement in the cow's condition, Elizabeth decided in early August 1807 to consult Mary Butters.[72] The use of all-embracing protections and semi-skilled counter actions,[73] before a cunning-person was consulted, seems to have been common practice in nineteenth-century Ulster. OSMI collector, J. Stokes, noted in 1835 that the 'application to a cunning woman was the last resort' if a 'business fails' and 'recourse is had to some preternatural observances'. He went on to state:

> The first step is to search about the hob for crickets to which, if found, the evil is attributed. The harmless insects are then usually scalded to death, after which the hob and fire are removed to the other end of the room at whatever expense or inconvenience. Should this prove insufficient, one of the room doors is altered.[74]

Mary Butters lived a few miles away from Carnmoney in Carrickfergus and for a small fee cured bewitched cattle.[75] She also made a living from telling fortunes and some newspaper accounts provided her with the moniker, the 'astrologer'.[76] In a contemporary poem, printed in the *BNL*, Butters is referred to as 'the fellest fortune-teller e'er was seen, A witch, that for sma price, Cou'd cast cantrips [spells], and gie them advice'.[77] Butters' first attempt at un-bewitching the Montgomery cow involved taking some of its milk and churning it 'for some time, observing some ceremony of charm'.[78] She then muttered over the churn, drew a circle around it, and washed it 'in south-running water'.[79] Elizabeth Montgomery, however, was still unable to churn butter, which prompted Butters to announce 'that after nightfall she would try another spell, which could not fail'.[80] At 10 o'clock that night she instructed Alexander Montgomery, and a younger, local man named Carnaghan, to turn their waistcoats inside out and stand by the head of the bewitched cow. They were instructed to remain there until Butters came back after midnight, at which time they were to draw a small amount of blood from her forehead. The rationale behind this ritual, which was surely related to the practice of 'scratching', was that the cut would force a witch assuming Butters' form to reveal her true self.[81] In the meantime, Butters 'caused the door to be shut, the chimney to be stopped [with green turf], and every crevice that could admit air to be carefully closed up'.[82] Accompanying Butters in the newly airtight house was Elizabeth, her son David, and Margaret Lee, an elderly basket-weaver and lodger.[83]

Having remained with the cow all night, at daybreak the men became anxious and Carnaghan returned to the house where he found Elizabeth and David dead and both Lee and Butters unconscious. Carnaghan brought out the dead bodies, but when he returned to rescue Butters and Lee he nearly succumbed himself to the 'sulphurous vapour which filled the house'. The two women were rescued later by some of Montgomery's neighbours.[84] Lee died a few hours later, while Butters recovered fully and quickly. An unsubstantiated twentieth-century report claimed that Butters' recovery was brought about by Montgomery's neighbours throwing her onto a dung heap and giving her 'a few hearty kicks'.[85] Another story circulating closer to the time suggested that villagers took Butters to the edge of a quarry and threatened to throw her in if she would not restore life to Lee and David and Elizabeth Montgomery. Butters was said to have placated the mob, and ultimately saved her life, by insisting that she could only bring the deceased back to life if she were allowed to return to the house the next evening and repeat the rite.[86] When the Montgomery house was later searched a large pot was found on the fire containing milk, needles, large pins, and some crooked nails. The *Belfast Newsletter* reported that although, 'it is not known what strategems she [Butters] employed to work her pretended enchantments', there can be 'little doubt ... that she had been also been burning sulphur, and that the vapour from it had proved fatal to the sufferers'.[87] Mary Butters' anti-bewitchment method was widely used by magical practitioners in Ulster in their efforts to cure bewitched humans and animals.[88]

An inquest into the deaths was held on 19 August 1807, presided over by coroner James Stewart and before '12 respectable jurors'.[89] Alexander Montgomery swore under oath that his cow had been 'bewitched' and that his wife had employed Butters to cure it, while his neighbours attested to the sulphurous smell in the house. The inquest ruled that Elizabeth and David Montgomery and Margaret Lee had died 'from suffocation, occasioned by a woman named Mary Butters, in her making use of some noxious ingredients, in the manner of a charm, to recover a cow, the property of Alexander Montgomery, husband to the deceased'.[90] Butters was arrested by local constables and remanded in custody at Co. Antrim Gaol in Carrickfergus until her trial for murder a few months later, in spring 1808, in the adjoining courtroom of Co. Antrim Assizes.[91] Butters was 'acquitted for want of evidence, as to the manner of the death of the three victims',[92] and on 15 April 1808, the *BNL* reported that, 'Mary Butters, the witch of Carnmoney, was discharged by proclamation'.[93]

The Carnmoney case demonstrates that by the nineteenth century, supernatural belief in popular culture had become less polarised across religious lines, with both Catholic and Protestants believing in profit-stealing witches and malevolent fairies.[94] In 1809, historian Samuel McSkimmin noted that as 'much as reason has triumphed over superstition ... the whole is far from being eradicated, and in nought is it more visible than in the belief concerning witchcraft, and cows losing their milk, or butter, by charms and incantations'.[95] In April 1832, OSMI collector, Lieutenant G.H. Mallock wrote that the inhabitants of Carrickfergus generally 'believed that cows are deprived of their milk either by being "elf-shot" by the fairies or by being blinked. The "evil eye" is confidently believed in here'.[96] In 1836, a colleague, Thomas Fagan, reported that in the parish of Tamlaght O'Crilly, Co. Londonderry, a Presbyterian woman was accused of stealing butter from her neighbours cows by means of an elaborate spell that involved the placement of a 'cross of wood', to which was attached a 'long hair, supposed to have been taken from the tails of the [bewitched] cows', on 'crocks of milk'. Her 'husband, from the shame of his wife being accused and found guilty of so horrible a crime' was 'found dead the same night', having committed suicide. The milk and butter was eventually 'restored by taking a quantity of straw from the eave of the house of the person found guilty and burning under the nostrils of the cow or cows blinked'.[97] In June 1838, James Boyle stated of the parish of Drummond, Co. Antrim, that the belief cows were magically deprived of their milk was 'not confined to any particular sect or denomination'.[98]

The Carnmoney tragedy also precipitated public condemnation by educated Protestants of popular credulity. In 1807, an anonymous account of the case written stated: 'these people were all Presbyterians, and a more gross absurdity was never known among the most unenlightened people on the face of the earth'.[99] Other commentators provided more human explanations for the Carnmomey case. In an unpublished, mid-nineteenth-century memoir, W.O. McGaw, who was born in Carnmoney in 1798 and died at the age of 90 in Carrickfergus, claimed Butters had deliberately poisoned David and Elizabeth Montgomery because they had given evidence to secure the conviction of her relative, David Porter, who was executed in Carrickfergus in 1803 for posting seditious notices. In this reading, Butters had used the opportunity presented by Elizabeth's invitation to exact her revenge and commit premeditated murder. This is why Butters dissuaded Carnaghan from staying in the house on the night of the tragedy and unsuccessfully tried to get Margaret Lee to leave. Lee's devotion to Elizabeth Montgomery, and her subsequent decision to remain in the house, left Butters with only one option, to kill her and thereby silence a potential witness. This hypothesis, McGaw continues, is lent further credence by the fact that Butters had insisted that for her spell to work, David, who was around 20 years of age, married, and living some distance away, had to be brought to Carnmoney to join his mother.[100] McGaw's claims, however plausible, cannot be verified and nothing of this nature was mentioned at the inquest or at Butters' trial. If we exclude the possibility that Butters was a murderer, then we must accept that the reason she was in Carnmoney that night was to cure Montgomery's bewitched cow for money: a stock part of her trade as a cunning-woman.

Cunning-folk in print

Nineteenth-century folklore sources, periodicals, and newspapers provide further evidence that Anthony, Butters, and Early were exceptional examples of a widespread practice. In September 1833, *The Dublin Penny Journal* found 'truly lamentable to behold what a firm footing old superstitions and absurd customs have obtained in the minds of our Irish Peasantry'. Chief among which was the fact that 'every district has its witch, fairy-man, fortune-teller, or prophet, and in parts every village is supplied with its own wise man, or knowing woman, and in these ignorant, though cunning wretches, the most implicit faith is placed by the misguided and deluded people'.[101] In December of the same year, the *BNL* justified its coverage of the case of a cunning-man in Saintfield Co. Down, who almost suffocated trying to counter a bewitched cow, by stating that it was of public benefit to warn of the dangers of popular magic:

> We have stated simple facts which have been authenticated to us by most respectable authority and our object in giving them publicity is that they may illustrate a portion of the spirit of the age and

may serve as a warning to witch-finders in general, if there be any other lurking remnants of such characters in 'that there County' of Down.[102]

While off the coast of Connaught, Catholic 'wise woman, Biddy Garvior' was said to have cured cattle in the 1840s by spitting 'three times on an animal's neck, whisk[ing] the skirt of her dress over the spot in pain and mutter[ing] a secret charm'. Similarly, when a school-mistress inadvertently overlooked one of her pupils, Garvior was said to have spat 'thrice on him with a bless at each act'.[103] Three years later, the *Northern Whig* reported that a tailor from Carrickbeg, Co. Tipperary, who had been paralysed and reduced to 'a feeble ... skeleton', was diag-nosed and cured of 'fairy-blast' by a local 'fairy man'.[104] J.B. Doyle in his *Tours of Ulster ...* (1854) noted that 'when a cow gets sick and loaths her food, she is said to be elf-shot ... [and] immediately, the owners send for the Elf-man or "man of knowledge"' who charged a fee to first discover the wound. This wound, Boyle explained, took skill to find because the 'fairies' had the 'knack of wounding the animal internally without piec-ing the skin'. Once the wound was discovered, the 'elf-man ... proceeds to the cure', which involved prayers and pouring water, into which coins and 'elf-shot' (neo-lithic arrow-heads) had been placed, over the afflicted animal. When not using the 'elf-shot' to cure, the cunning-man hung it in his byre to protect his cows from fairy blast.[105] In 1881, Irish folklorist G.H. Kinahan described how cattle were protected against fairies and butter-witches by 'having them blessed and sprinkled with holy water', or alternatively by procuring 'a charm from some wise woman'.[106] In 1893, Leland L. Duncan related an old story often re-told in contemporary Co. Leitrim of a family in the parish of Fenagh who were unable to churn milk into butter. Having exhausted a number of well-known remedies, the family consulted a travelling cunning-man who 'barred every door and window in the place, and ... in the fire he placed nine irons'. This object of this counter-magic was realised when an old woman arrived at the door in excruciating pain and pleaded to have the irons removed from the fire. The cunning-man informed her that he would not do so until she returned the family's butter; a demand to which she immediately acquiesced.[107] Other cunning-folk had more dubious methodologies. On a visit to the Aran Islands in May 1892, folklorist Nathaniel Colgan noted belief in the 'Cailleach', or an old woman who, with a combination of spells, herbs, and the 'evil-eye' transferred disease from her paying clients to random, unsuspecting members of the public.[108]

Cunning-folk and the courts

Court reports in Irish newspapers suggest that Ireland in the mid-nineteenth century witnessed an upsurge in legal action taken against cunning-folk by disgruntled clients, either for theft or for obtaining money under false pretences.[109] With resonances once more with England, and in common with Irish fortune-tellers and magical healers, complaints against cunning-folk by disgruntled clients increased in line with changes to policing and the court system. In Irish Catholic communities, however, cunning-folk were also tried for murder. This invariably occurred after an inquest revealed their methods of countering changeling abduction had ended in the unlawful killing of a client. Although belief in malevolent fairies was by no means restricted to Catholic communities, it was here that it was traditionally strongest and most sincerely held, particularly in relation to changeling abduction.

In August 1862, elderly Mary Colbert was brought before Cork Police Court for taking money under false pretences from unsuspecting clients by 'pretending' to cure people of 'fairy blast', specifically a young, ill-looking servant, Hannah Sullivan.[110] In late 1864, 40-year-old, Catholic, illiterate Mary Doheny was brought before Carrick-on-Suir Petty Sessions in Co. Tipperary for obtaining money under false pretences from sub-Constable Joseph Reeves. Doheny, who enjoyed a fearful reputation for her magical powers, made a living by diagnosing and curing bewitched cattle, providing love potions to unmarried women, and by contacting the dead on behalf of their relatives. Doheny, however, was employed by Constable Reeves to cure his daughter, who was deathly ill at the time. Doheny's herbal cures, which improved the girl's condition slightly before she died, impressed Constable Reeves so much he provided her with daily meals, food parcels, and gifts of tobacco and money. Doheny further gained Constable Reeves's trust by claiming to have raised the spirit of his son who had died some years before, and by foretelling of the imminent arrival of a large inheritance of land and gold. Reeves's gifts to Doheny were so substantial and regular that he was soon indebted, prompting his sub-Inspector, W.H. Heard, to make the initial complaint against her. Carrick-on-Suir Petty Sessions found the case against Doheny proved and it was referred to Clonmel Quarter Sessions, where in October 1864 a jury found her guilty after a few minutes' deliberation and the judge sentenced her to 12 months' imprisonment with hard labour.[111] Sarah McCann was also found guilty at Co. Down Assizes in July 1870 for taking 15 shillings from Robert Beck to give to a 'wee woman' famed for curing cattle and bewitched children.

Beck, however, became suspicious when the 'wee woman' failed to visit his sick child.[112] In August 1886, Mrs Phelan of Waterford reported to Constable Eustace of the Royal Irish Constabulary that she had been duped out of four shillings by an unnamed cunning-woman who claimed the power to tell the future and to cure her of painful 'stiches in her side'. A description of the cunning-woman was drawn up by the police and a warrant issued for her arrest.[113]

The Irish judiciary it seems had little time for cunning-folk, seeing them at best as con-artists playing on the credulity of the lower classes, whereby perpetuating pernicious, supernatural beliefs. At Limerick Assizes in April 1834, Johanna Sweeney, Bridget Hynes, and Johanna Galvin were given a sentence of transportation for seven years for theft. The Tipperary women, led by Galvin – who was older and 'a daughter of Mrs Jackson ... a celebrated fairy woman and charm-maker', called at John Carthy's house in January 1834 seeking lodging for the night. Once in the house, Galvin took a cup and placed an unnamed herb into it and after careful inspection asked Mrs Carthy 'if anything ailed her daughter'. Mrs Carthy admitted that her daughter suffered from 'a swelling in the neck and throat when she caught cold'. Galvin then prepared a charm that involved boiling herbs and 12 shillings belonging to John Carthy. After this was done, Galvin declared that Carthy's son was in imminent danger from being abducted by fairies if she did not procure a special herb that grew in a local graveyard. Using the opportunity presented by this trip, the women made off with Carthy's money and his coat. After the women had been found guilty by the Jury, presiding Judge, Lord Chief Justice of King's Bench, Charles Kendal Bushe, remarked that 'he lamented the credulity of the prosecutors' and stated sarcastically that he was 'compelled to deprive the country of the medical expertise of the prisoners'.[114] In June 1860, at Saintfield Petty Sessions, magistrate James Crawford commended Constable Hamilton for bringing before him John Mcfarlane, a 'weird-looking old man', for 'obtaining under false pretences, by acting in the capacity of a witch doctor'. When a number of witnesses did not appear for the prosecution, Constable Hamilton informed Crawford that the case 'could go no further' and the case was dismissed. Crawford however stated 'that there was no doubt but that there was a ridiculous idea out about cattle being bewitched, which did great harm; and the constable did quite right in making all the enquiries possible to have it put a stop to'.[115] In January 1861, Magistrate Matthew A. Sankey indicted and placed Anne McAvine in custody for telling Jane Dawson, of Brookeborough, Enniskillen, Co. Fermangh, that she could get her £11,000 from the fairies for a fee paid in instalments and amounting to just under five pounds. For this princely sum, Dawson received a bottle of oil to rub in her eyes and told to board a boat to Scotland, where upon arrival a man would take her to a house to collect her fairy money. Unsurprisingly, neither man nor money materialised. McAvine was tried at Fermanagh Spring Assizes a month later, found guilty by the jury and sentenced to 12 months' imprisonment as warning to others not to take advantage of gullible women like Dawson.[116]

Although not the subject of legal action themselves, cunning-folk were sometimes censured from the bench by magistrates. In August 1871, Elizabeth McKee of Comber, Co. Down, brought Susan Walsh before Newtownards Petty Sessions for throwing a can of water over her. The argument that led to the assault began when Walsh accused McKee of bewitching her daughter, Mrs Gibson. A few days earlier Gibson been informed, 'by a local medical man ... that she was in the last stages of consumption'. Her neighbours, however, convinced her she was bewitched and should consult local cunning-man, Alexander Reading, who lived 'at Whitespots in the neighbourhood of Newtownards'. Reading's 'spells and incantations' were administered to no real effect to Gibson over a three-day period and at a total cost of 30 shillings. It was only when he was informed that McKee had borrowed 'a small quantity of salt' from Gibson a few days before that he informed his client that 'it was Mrs McKee who had bewitched ... [her] and that she was the cause of all their trouble, his power being broken by her superior charms'. Immediately after the assault took place, 'the constable of the Comber district had endeavoured to get up a case against Alexander for receiving money under false pretences'. However, as 'Mrs Gibson, the party through whose hands the money ... had passed, had died shortly after her visits to Alexander, he was unable, with any hope of success to do so'. One of the presiding judges, Regional Magistrate J. Eglinton, informed the court that this was 'third case of pretended witchcraft we have had before us at these Sessions', while JP John Millar commented angrily that if Reading was brought before him he would 'try and take the witchcraft out of him'.[117] Mrs Walsh was fined '3s 6d costs' and Millar reprimanded her 'severely ... saying that it was only on account of her poverty that so small a fine was inflicted'. He ended the proceedings by stating that 'he never recollected hearing of such gross ignorance before'.[118]

The second crime cunning-folk were accused of was the murder of changelings.[119] In September 1851 in Roscrea, Co. Tipperary, six-year-old Maryanne Kelly, who was in the care of a dispensary physician Dr Powell for an 'affection of the brain', died after 'fairy woman' Bridget Peters fed her a variety of herbs prepared in milk (including foxglove, a herb traditionally used as protection against fairies and to cure those afflicted by them), bathed her in water, and placed her naked on a shovel in the open air on three consecutive nights. Peters had convinced Mary Kelly that her daughter, Maryanne, was a changeling and that her rituals were the only way to force the fairies to return her healthy child. At Maryanne's inquest, the coroner ruled that her death had been caused by the actions of Peters and her mother. The jury then returned a verdict of manslaughter and the women were committed to jail to await trial.[120] Peters eventually stood trial at the Tipperary Assizes held at Nenagh on 21 March 1851 and was found guilty.[121] In 1856, in Kilmoganny, Co. Kilkenny, labourer Patrick Kearns became convinced his nine-year-old son, who had been bedridden for weeks, was 'being gradually carried off by the fairies'. On the advice of their neighbour, Patrick Murphy, the Kearns family consulted 'fairy-man' Thomas Donovan, who confirmed the child had been struck by fairy 'blast'. Donovan then dragged the boy out of bed and into the front yard; an ordeal, his inquest heard, that led to his death. Coroner Thomas Izod and the jury further stated that if Donovan could be found, having 'absconded', he should be tried for murder.[122] In the same county, 50 years later, Denis Ganey, a local fairy doctor who had provided Michael Cleary with herbs to cure his changeling wife Bridget was charged not with murder but with assault and ill treatment. He was later released after spending two weeks in Clonmel Gaol.[123]

Despite the fact that cunning-folk often operated on the wrong side of the law, on rare occasions they brought legal action themselves.[124] In January 1871, at Newtownards Quarter Sessions, Co. Down, Hugh Kennedy, from Granshaw, claimed his brother owed him '£14 for wages ... for one year'. Kennedy was a cunning-man employed by his brother when his 'house and lands' were attacked 'by witches' and which as a result had fell 'into a bad condition and his cows into a state of settled melancholy'. Kennedy was renowned locally for his ability of 'putting to flight these unwelcome visitors'. The court eventually awarded 'the plaintiff the sum of 10s' but Kennedy was not satisfied with this amount because he believed 'the services he had rendered, not alone to his brother, but society at large, by the banishment of the "evil ones", was deserving of a more munificent reward'.[125]

Conclusion

A range of magical practitioners served both Catholic and Protestant communities in the modern period. Two main types of commercial fortune-teller can be identified in Ireland: the settled, semi-respectable variety, who served particular areas, and the opportunistic, less scrupulous, itinerant practitioner. For no fee, magical healers provided 'charms' (often involving incantation, prayer, and sympathetic magic) to cure naturally occurring, minor ailments in both cattle and humans. By the mid-nineteenth century, magical healers and fortune-tellers were increasingly prosecuted by disgruntled clients seeking recompense and redress. In common with England, this increase in prosecution was facilitated by the establishment in Ireland of a government-controlled, national police force and the extension of petty sessions; which together made it easier for complaints to made, investigated, and acted upon.

Just as in the early modern period, male and female cunning-folk were a discernable group in Catholic and Protestant Ireland in the eighteenth and nineteenth centuries, perhaps beyond. Their client base was essentially that of other magical practitioners, the rural poor for whom life could be uncertain and conditions extremely harsh. Irish cunning-folk came in two guises: the settled practitioner who served both local clients and those from further afield; and the travelling cunning-person who 'cold-called' clients and was more likely to dabble in unscrupulous practice. This latter practitioner seems to be specific to Ireland. What distinguished cunning-folk from other types of magical practitioner was the range of services they offered, providing a range of the following: they found lost or stolen goods (including cattle); healed natural, minor ailments in cattle and humans; told fortunes; and most importantly diagnosed, protected against, and cured illness believed to have been caused by the evil-eye, fairies, or witches. Most of these attacks centred on livestock but occasionally involved humans, in particular children. Cunning-folk in Ireland were commercial practitioners who were paid for their services with goods or in cash.

It has also been established that by the early nineteenth century, belief in fairies and butter-stealing witches had crossed into Protestant popular culture. It was, however, in Irish Catholic areas where belief in fairies was strongest and where cunning-folk were called upon to resolve cases of suspected changeling abduction. When their highly dangerous methods ended in the death of clients, and subsequent inquests held them responsible, they were prosecuted for murder. From the mid-nineteenth century, legal action was taken against wandering cunning-folk by clients, either for theft or obtaining money under false pretences. This was facilitated by the changes in policing and legal administration described above. On spiritual and religious grounds, Presbyterian and Catholic clerical hierarchies warned their flocks against the use of magical practitioners, just as they had done in the early modern period. Furthermore, by the mid-nineteenth century, Catholic priests were far less likely to indulge cunning-folk than their predecessors, and very few now practised popular magic themselves.

Conclusion

Witchcraft belief in early modern Ireland was divided across cultural and religious as well as social lines. Belief in the female butter-witch, who stole milk in the form of a hare or appropriated its goodness or productiveness by other magical means, was present in Ireland from at least the early medieval era, forming part of a larger corpus of magical beliefs focused on women who used magic to adversely affect fertility or either destroy or engender relationships. In the early modern period, bereft of this wider magical context, easily countered by ritualistic or magical means, and believed to attack food production only at certain times of the year, butter-stealing witches were in Gaelic-Irish culture less threatening than the malefic/demonic witch figure that predominated in most parts of Europe. Again in contrast to existing historiography, it has been argued that older, traditional fairy beliefs, rather than the unintentional evil-eye, inhibited the uptake of the malefic/demonic witchcraft belief in Gaelic-Irish popular culture. Although politically orientated sorcery-cum-treason plots concerned Catholic elites in medieval Ireland, by the early modern period and under the influence of continental demonology, they saw witchcraft accusation in much the same way as their Protestant counterparts, as agents of the devil who harmed and killed using a range of magical means. The English and Scottish Protestant settler population, of all social levels, brought with them strong witchcraft beliefs from their native countries, which, dependant on the social order they belonged to, centred either on *maleficium* or demonic activity.

It has also been confirmed, through the first close scrutiny of its passage through parliament, that the 1586 Irish Witchcraft Act passed quickly and uncontroversially. It was initiated in the Irish House of Commons as part of the rolling-out of the Elizabethan statute book in

Ireland, rather than, as it was in Scotland and England, a reaction by the political and religious elite to concerns of the religious or political threat posed by witchcraft and popular magic. The 1604 English Witchcraft Act was never introduced into Ireland, although largely inconsequential legislative amendments were made to the original Irish Witchcraft Act in the 1630s, when Irish JPs were also furnished with a handbook for identifying and prosecuting witches. A decade before this, in the early seventeenth century, criminal crown courts had been established in Ireland, despite hiatuses in the 1640s and 1689–91 due to war.

In contrast to the Gaelic-Irish, whose more benign, culturally-specific witch figure was not threatening enough to warrant legal proceedings, Irish Protestants made formal accusations to religious and legal authorities from the mid-seventeenth century onwards. In common with England and elsewhere, these initial accusations were, depending on the individual circumstances of each case, rooted in a variety of interpersonal, political, and religious conflict. In Ireland, where gender roles were particularly strong, women (and at least one man) who did not meet behavioural norms or who bore a physical resemblance to the cultural stereotype of witch, or had a reputation for witchcraft, were more likely to be accused of witchcraft. That these accusations did not end in prosecution and conviction at the hands of Assize judges was the result of luck, informal arbitration, pre-trial interventions by magical practitioners (see below), and an increasingly sceptical judiciary of the type found in other parts of late seventeenth- and early eighteenth-century Europe. Importantly, in Ulster, witchcraft cases were arbitrated by Presbyterian church courts who, especially by the early eighteenth century, managed and policed the moral and religious lives of their own insular communities. In doing so, they were following a precedent set by ministers and elders in the Church of Scotland. Sceptical about their ability to establish guilt on the evidences of witchcraft brought before them, but not necessarily harbouring any real doubt about the existence of witches, Irish presbyteries and sessions often sided with the accused and censured the accuser. This may have helped protect against, as it did in Scotland, widespread acts of communal justice (in the early to mid-eighteenth century at least), as it made un-founded allegations a less attractive proposition for would-be accusers.

On occasion, these checks and balances failed, and formal accusations proceed to a witchcraft trial. This was most likely to occur if they were made during periods of heightened religious tension, or in periods of increased general concern over witchcraft, involving possession, and when the accuser was regarded a credible witness and the accused were believable witches in the manner described above. As these trials occurred in a period of general judicial scepticism, demonic possession provided verifiable evidence of witchcraft in the form of a main accuser. It has also been argued that Irish women were prosecuted for witchcraft abroad, in Scotland, during large witch-hunts, and in North America in a witchcraft/possession case that bore striking similarities to both the 1698 and 1711 Antrim outbreaks.

In Catholic and Protestant Ireland, popular witchcraft belief continued into the modern period, with the butter-stealing witch figure predominating in the culture of the former but also spreading to the latter, along with fear of fairies. By the later eighteenth century, even more forcibly than in former times, reforming Catholic clerical elites condemned many popular folk beliefs considered superstitious, while malefic, demonic witchcraft beliefs retained orthodoxy alongside Church-sanctioned manifestations of the miraculous. In the early eighteenth century, in a cultural context of widespread educated belief in an essentially moral, magical universe (although Protestant orthodoxy was turning against astrology and modern miracles), the limited witchcraft scepticism appearing in Protestant public discourse was voiced by a small number of enlightened Whigs. It was only after 1750 that it became mainstream and acceptable to condemn witchcraft outright (along with notions of an interventionist Satan), as irrational and vulgar: either a relic of a bygone, barbarous era or a contemporary 'survival' in the modern world within British lower-class culture, benighted European Catholicism, or civilisations farther afield considered backward or primitive. Continuing popular belief in Ireland was passed over in public discourse as it was considered inimical to the Ascendancy's view of itself as enlightened, rational, and polite, far removed from the enthusiastic, irrational beliefs that had driven drove early modern European witch-hunting. From the early nineteenth century onwards, witchcraft cases were occasionally brought before the judiciary, due to the establishment of regional and metropolitan police forces and police courts and the extension of petty sessions making it easier to do so. Both the way witchcraft accusations were handled by the legal system, in that they were either ignored altogether or dismissed unless they involved allegations of assault, along with the way Irish newspapers now used them to entertain readers with tales of the credulous lower orders, lends more weight to the contention that by the time the Irish Witchcraft Act was removed from the statute book in 1821 witchcraft had been completely marginalised within educated, Protestant culture.

Cunning-folk, who were both men and women, served both Catholic and Protestant communities in early modern Ireland. Apart from a small number of Catholic priests, they tended to come from the same social order as their clients, the lower orders, and provided three main services: finding lost or stolen goods or treasure; the diagnosis, detection, and curing of witchcraft; and in Gaelic-Irish and Catholic areas, the provision of protection against, and curing of, fairy attack on livestock and humans, including written protective charms. Although a range of magical practices identifiable with cunning-folk were rendered illegal by the 1586 witchcraft Act, no real effort was made by the civil authorities to punish them. The three main religious denominations (and some of the laity), however, regarded cunning-folk as socially and religiously dangerous up until the mid-eighteenth century. In print, opposition to this form of popular magic was articulated in much the same way as counterparts in Britain, while the Presbyterian Church doled out light punishments to individual practitioners in ecclesiastical courts. These concerns of ecclesiastical authorities fed into larger goals of the imposition of their own particular brand of right religion on the laity.

Along with magical healers and fortune-tellers, male and female cunning-folk were a firm part of Irish, rural, popular culture up until at least the early twentieth century. Working a settled client base or 'cold-calling' members of rural poor while wandering the countryside, they were paid in cash or goods for a range of services slightly larger than their early modern counterparts: they healed natural, minor ailments in cattle and humans; found lost or stolen cattle; told fortunes; and diagnosed, protected against, and cured illness in livestock, and occasionally humans, believed to have been caused by the evil-eye, fairies, and witches (often the butter-stealing variety). It was, however, only in Irish Catholic areas that cunning-folk were called upon to resolve cases of suspected changeling abduction. This was a dangerous part of their business that could go dreadfully wrong and terminate in murder charges being brought against them. From the mid-nineteenth century onwards, itinerant wandering cunning-folk were increasingly prosecuted by clients for theft or obtaining money under false pretences, facilitated once more by changes in policing and legal administration. Presbyterian and Catholic clergy, for much the same reasons as their early modern predecessors, warned their flocks against the use of magical practitioners but rarely took disciplinary action.

Notes

Introduction

1. St. John D. Seymour, *Irish Witchcraft and Demonology* (Dublin, 1913, repr., London, 1989). For an earlier, less scholarly, narrative-driven discussion of key Irish witchcraft cases, see: Classon Emmet Porter, *Witches, Warlocks and Ghosts* (Belfast, 1885).
2. *Irish Times*, 3 October 1913; Letter to St. John D. Seymour, c.1913 (NLI, Documents relating to St. John D Seymour, Ms 46, 866); Mrs Astell to St. John D. Seymour, 6 October 1913 (NLI, Ms 46, 866); W. Carrigan to St. John D. Seymour, 8 October 1913 (NLI, Ms 46, 866); D.H. Moutray Read, 'Irish Witchcraft and Demonology', *Folklore*, 27/3 (1916): 322–3.
3. R.W. Dudley Edwards and Mary O'Dowd, *Sources for Modern Irish History, 1534–1641* (Cambridge, 2003): 131–8; Neal Garnham, 'Local Elite Creation in Early Hanoverian Ireland: The Case of the County Grand Juries', *Historical Journal*, 42/3 (1999): 624.
4. Neal Garnham, 'How Violent was Eighteenth-Century Ireland?', *Irish Historical Studies*, 30/119 (1997): 378.
5. The historiography relating to witchcraft in western Europe is vast and its contours and debates have been mapped more incisively and fully elsewhere than could be accomplished here, see: Malcolm Gaskill, *A Very Short Introduction to Witchcraft* (Oxford, 2010); Darren Oldridge (ed.), *The Witchcraft Reader* (Abingdon, 2nd ed., 2008); Richard M. Golden (ed.), *Encyclopaedia of Witchcraft: The Western Tradition* (4 vols, Denver and Oxford, 2007); Brian P. Levack (ed.), *Oxford Handbook of Witchcraft in Early Modern Europe and Colonial America* (Oxford, 2013); idem, *The Witch-hunt in Early Modern Europe* (Edinburgh, 3rd ed., 2006); Wolfgang Behringer, *Witches and Witch-Hunts* (Cambridge, 2004); Robin Briggs, *Witches and Neighbours: The Social and Cultural Context of Witchcraft* (Oxford, 2nd ed., 2002); Bengt Ankerloo and Gustav Henningsen (eds), *Early Modern European Witchcraft: Centres and Peripheries* (Oxford, 1990); Jonathan Barry and Owen Davies (eds), *Witchcraft Historiography* (Basingstoke, 2007). The best study for the intellectual foundations of early modern witchcraft belief remains, Stuart Clark, *Thinking with Demons: The Idea of Witchcraft in Early Modern Europe* (Oxford, 1997). For a short, text-book introduction to English witchcraft, see, James Sharpe, *Witchcraft in Early Modern England* (Edinburgh, 2001). The same author has also produced a highly readable but more detailed and academic study, *Instruments of Darkness: Witchcraft in Early Modern England* (Philadelphia, 1996, repr. 1997). See also, William Monter, 'Re-Contextualizing British Witchcraft', *Journal of Interdisciplinary History*, 35/1 (2004): 105–11.
6. See: Ronald Hutton, 'The Changing Faces of Manx Witchcraft', *Cultural and Social History*, 7/2 (2010): 153–69; James Sharpe, 'Witchcraft in the Early Modern Isle of Man', *Cultural and Social History*, 4/1 (2007): 9–20; Richard

Suggett, 'Witchcraft Dynamics in Early Modern Wales', in Michael Roberts and Simone Clarke (eds), *Women and Gender in Early Modern Wales* (Cardiff, 2000); idem, *A History of Magic and Witchcraft in Wales* (Stroud, 2008), Chapter 3; Sally Parkin, 'Witchcraft, Women's Honour and Customary Law in Early Modern Wales', *Social History*, 31/3 (2006): 295–318; Lizanne Henderson, 'Witch-Hunting and Witch-Belief in the Gàidhealtachd', in Julian Goodare, Lauren Martin, and Joyce Miller (eds), *Witchcraft and Belief in Early Modern Scotland* (Basingstoke, 2008): 97–118.

7. Patrick F. Byrne, *Witchcraft in Ireland* (1969, repr., Dublin, 1973); Bob Curran, *Ireland's Witches: A Bewitched Land* (Dublin, 2005); Edmund Lenihan, *In Search of Biddy Early* (Duboin, 1987); Meda Ryan, *Biddy Early, The Wise Woman of Clare* (Dublin, 1978, repr. 1991); Charles McConnell, *The Witches of Islandmagee* (Carrickfergus, 2000). For more on Biddy Early, see Chapter 7.

8. Andrew Sneddon, 'Witchcraft Belief and Trials in Early Modern Ireland', *Irish Economic and Social History*, 39 (2012): 1–25; Ronald Hutton, 'Witch-Hunting in Celtic Societies', *Past and Present*, 212/1 (2011): 43–71; E.C. Lapoint, 'Irish Immunity to Witch-Hunting, 1534–1711', *Eire-Ireland*, 37 (1992): 76–92; Raymond Gillespie, 'Women and Crime in Seventeenth-Century Ireland', in Margaret MacCurtain and Mary O' Dowd (eds), *Women in Early Modern Ireland* (Edinburgh, 1991): 45–8.

9. Mary McAuliffe, 'Gender, History and Witchcraft in Early Modern Ireland: A Re-Reading of the Florence Newton Trial', in Mary Ann Gialenella Valiulis (ed.), *Gender and Power in Irish History* (Dublin, 2009): 39–58; idem, 'From Alice Kyteler to Florence Newton; Witchcraft in Medieval Ireland', *History Review*, 12 (2001); Andrew Sneddon, *Possessed by the Devil: The Real History of the Islandmagee Witches and Ireland's only Mass Witchcraft Trial* (Dublin, 2013). For more on these trials, see Chapter 5.

10. Raymond Gillespie, 'Imagining Angels in Early Modern Ireland', in Peter Marshall and Alexandra Walsham (eds), *Angels in the Early Modern World* (Cambridge, 2006): 214–32; idem, *Devoted People: Belief and Religion in Early Modern Ireland* (Manchester, 1997); idem, 'Popular and Unpopular Religion: A View from the Early Modern Ireland', in James S. Donnelly and Kerby A. Miller (eds), *Popular Culture in Irleand, 1650–1850* (Dublin, 1998): 30–49.

11. S.J. Connolly, *Priests and People in pre-Famine Ireland, 1780–1845* (1982, repr. Dublin, 2001): 22–9; Timothy Corrigan Correll, 'Believers and Sceptics, and Charlatans: Evidential Rhetoric, the Fairies and Fairy Healers in Irish Oral Narratives and Beliefs', *Folklore*, 116 (2005): 1–18; Richard P. Jenkins, 'Witches and Fairies: Supernatural Aggression and Deviance among the Irish Peasantry', *Ulster Folklife*, 23 (1977): 33–56; Simon Young, 'Some Notes on Irish Fairy Changelings in Nineteenth-Century Irish Newspapers', *Béascna*, 8 (2013): 38–43; Diarmuid Ó Giolláin, 'The Fairy Belief and Official Religion in Ireland', in Peter Narváez (ed.), *The Good People: New Fairylore Essays* (Kentucky, 1991): 199–214; Richard Jenkins, 'The Transformations of Biddy Early: From Local Reports of Magical Healing to Globalised New Age Fantasies', *Folklore*, 118 (2007): 162–82; Angela Bourke, *The Burning of Bridget Cleary: A True Story* (London, 1999). For a rare study of Protestant supernatural belief in the modern period: Andrew R. Holmes, *The Shaping of*

Ulster Presbyterian Belief and Practice, 1770–1840 (Oxford 2006, repr. 2009), Chapter 3.

12. Wanda Wyporska, *Witchcraft in Early Modern Poland, 1500–1800* (Basingstoke, 2013); Jonathan Barry, *Witchcraft and Demonology in South-West England, 1640–1789* (Basingstoke, 2011); idem, *Raising Spirits: How a Conjuror's Tale was Transmitted across the Enlightenment* (Basingstoke, 2013), Chapters 4–7; Owen Davies, *Grimoires: A History of Magic Books* (Oxford, 2009); idem, *Witchcraft, Magic and Culture 1736–1951* (Manchester, 1999); idem, *Popular Magic: Cunning-Folk in English History* (London, 2003, repr. 2007); Behringer, *Witches and Witch-Hunts*; Marian Gibson, *Witchcraft Myths in American Culture* (New York, 2007); Owen Davies and Willem De Blécourt, *Beyond the Witch Trials: Witchcraft and Magic in Enlightenment Europe* (Manchester, 2004); idem, (eds), *Witchcraft Continued: Popular Magic in Modern* Europe (Manchester, 2004); Bob Bushaway, 'Tacit, Unsuspected, but still Implicit Faith: Alternative Belief in Nineteenth-Century Rural England', in Tim Harris (ed.), *Popular Culture in England, 1500–1850* (Basingstoke, 1995): 189–215; Francis Young, *English Catholics and the Supernatural, 1553–1829* (Farnham, 2013); Karl Bell, *The Magical Imagination: Magic and Modernity in Urban England 1780–1914* (Cambridge, 2012).
13. Barry, *Witchcraft and Demonology in South-West England*: 4; Bell, *Magical Imagination*: 19.
14. Jodie Shevlin, 'Catholicism and the Supernatural in Nineteenth-Century Ireland', Ulster University PhD candidate.
15. John Fulton, 'Clerics, Conjurors, and Courtrooms: Witchcraft, Magic and Religion in 18th and 19th century Ireland', Ulster University PhD candidate.
16. Francis Hutchinson, *An Irish–English Almanack for the Year, 1724 ...* (2nd edition, Dublin, 1724): vi.

1 Witchcraft Belief in Early Modern Ireland

1. Briggs, *Witches and Neighbours*: 343.
2. See Peter Elmer, 'Towards a Politics of Witchcraft in Early Modern England', in Stuart Clark (ed), *Languages of Witchcraft: Narrative, Ideology and Meaning in Early Modern Culture* (Hampshire, 2001): 101–18; Andrew Sneddon, *Witchcraft and Whigs: The Life of Bishop Francis Hutchinson* (Manchester, 2008): 99, 125; Behringer, *Witches and Witch-Hunts*: 101–5.
3. See Ian Bostridge, *Witchcraft and its Transformations, c.1650–c.1750* (Oxford, 1997): 36, and Clark, *Thinking with Demons*: vii–viii.
4. Brian P. Levack, *The Witch-hunt in Early Modern Europe* (Harlow, 3rd ed., 2006): 51.
5. Levack, *Witch-hunt in Early Modern Europe*: 51.
6. Clark, *Thinking with Demons*: 527–30, 541; Sharpe, *Witchcraft in Early Modern England*: 18; idem, *Instruments of Darkness*, Chapters 1–3; Norman Cohn, *Europe's Inner Demons: the Demonisation of Christians in Medieval Christendom* (London, 2nd ed., 1993): 144–7; Peter Burke, 'The Comparative Approach to European Witchcraft', in, *Early Modern European Witchcraft: Centres and Peripheries*: 440–1; Christina Larner, *Enemies of God: The Witch-hunt in*

Scotland (London, 1981): 187; Brian Levack, *Witch-hunting in Scotland: Law, Politics, Religion* (Abington, 2008): 7; idem, *Witch-hunt in Early Modern Europe*: 30–1, 37–8; Philip C. Almond, *The Lancashire Witches: A Chronicle of Sorcery and Death on Pendle Hill* (London, 2012): 21–2, 54–5; Edward Bever, 'Popular Witchcraft and Magical Practices', in *Oxford Handbook of Witchcraft*: 50–1.

7. For a discussion of the problems associated with the division of culture into popular and elite traditions: Pieter Spierenburg, *The Broken Spell: A Cultural and Anthropological History of Pre-Industrial Europe* (New Brunswick, 1991): 49–59; and in relation to witchcraft in particular, see Barry Reay, *Popular Culture in England, 1550–1750* (London, 1998): 115–19, and Malcolm Gaskill, *Crime and Mentalities in Early Modern England* (Cambridge, 2000): 18.

8. Barry, *Witchcraft and Demonology in South-West England*: 5.

9. Sharpe, *Instruments of Darkness*: 56–7.

10. E. William Monter, *Witchcraft in France and Switzerland: the Borderlands during the Reformation* (Ithaca and London, 1976), Chapter 6.

11. Bever, 'Popular Witchcraft and Magical Practices': 50–1. For a discussion of how popular witchcraft belief and folklore fused with learned demonology in early modern, Swabian Austria and the Electorate of Trier: Johannes Dillenger, trans. Laura Stokes, *'Evil People': A Comparative Study of Witch Hunts in Swabian Austria and the Electorate of Trier* (1992, repr 2009), Chapter 2.

12. Almond, *Lancashire Witches*: 22–4, 54–5; Sharpe, *Instruments of Darkness*: 70–9; Levack, 'Introduction', in *Oxford Handbook of Witchcraft*: 8; [Thomas Benskin], *A True and Impartial Relation of the Informations against Three Witches, viz. Temperance Lloyd, Mary Trembles, and Susanna Edwards* ... (London, 1682): 11. For a detailed examination of this pamphlet and the religious and political context of the trial it depicts, see Stephen Timmons, 'Witchcraft and Rebellion in Late Seventeenth-century Devon', *Journal of Early Modern History*, 10/4 (2006): 317–22, and Barry, *Witchcraft and Demonology in South-West England*, Chapter 3.

13. James Sharpe, 'Women, Witchcraft and the Legal Process', in Jenny Kermode and Garthine Walker (eds), *Women, Crime and the Courts in Early Modern England* (London, 1994): 108; Orna Alyagon Darr, 'The Devil's Mark: A Socio-Cultural Analysis of Physical Evidence', *Continuity and Change*, 24/2 (2009): 361–87.

14. Larner, *Enemies of God*: 10–11, 138, 200–1.

15. Julian Goodare and Lauren Martin, 'Introduction', in *Witchcraft and Belief in Early Modern Scotland*: 3–9; Stuart Macdonald, 'In Search of the Devil in Fife Witchcraft Cases, 1560–1705', in Julian Goodare (ed.), *The Scottish Witch-hunt in Context* (Manchester, 2002): 51–72; idem, 'Enemies of God Re-visited: Recent Publications on Scottish Witchcraft', *Scottish Economic and Social History*, 23/2 (2003): 71, 73–4.

16. Julian Goodare, 'Witchcraft in Scotland', in *Oxford Handbook of Witchcraft*: 302, 313.

17. Hutton, 'Witch-hunting in Celtic Societies': 43–71; idem, 'The Global Context of the Scottish Witch-hunt', in *Scottish Witch-hunt in Context*: 31–2.

18. Suggett, 'Witchcraft Dynamics in Early Modern Wales': 83–4; idem, *History of Magic and Witchcraft in Wales*: 22–3, 44–5; Sharpe, 'Witchcraft in the Early Modern Isle of Man': 14–16, 19–20.

19. Henderson, 'Witch-hunting and Witch-belief in the Gàidhealtachd': 97–118.

20. Sharpe, 'Witchcraft in the Isle of Man': 14, 16.
21. Suggett, *History of Magic and Witchcraft in Wales*: 84, 45–6, 99–100; idem, 'Witchcraft Dynamics in Early Modern Wales': 84.
22. Bodil Nilden-Wall and Jan Wall, 'The Witch as Hare or the Witch's Hare: Popular Legends and Beliefs in Nordic Tradition', *Folklore*, 104/1–2 (1993): 67–8; Éilís Ní Dhuibhne, '"The Old Woman as Hare": Structure and Meaning in an Irish Legend', *Folklore*, 104/1–2 (1993): 78.
23. For shape-shifting witches see: Briggs, *Witches and Neighbours*: 91; Almond, *Lancashire Witches*: 77–9, 111–13, 119; Monter, *Witchcraft in France and Switzerland*: 144–51; Davies, *Witchcraft, Magic and Culture*: 190, 192.
24. Hutton, 'Witch-hunting in Celtic Societies': 65.
25. Ibid: 69.
26. Hutton, 'Witch-hunting in Celtic Societies': 63.
27. Lapoint, 'Irish Immunity to Witch-hunting': 79, 81–2; Gillespie, 'Women and Crime in Seventeenth-century Ireland': 45–7.
28. Gillian Kenny, *Anglo-Irish and Gaelic Women in Ireland, c. 1170–1540* (Dublin, 2007): 9, 13. I am grateful to Dr Kenny for reading early drafts of this discussion of medieval magic and supplying references.
29. I have argued elsewhere that butter-witches were, in the early modern period at least, a culturally distinct Gaelic-Irish witchcraft belief: Sneddon, 'Witchcraft Belief and Trials in Early Modern Ireland': 10, and idem, *Possessed by the Devil*, Chapter 4. For studies that suggest in the highlands and islands of Scotland witches were less threatening and largely concerned with the disruption of agricultural production rather than with diabolical deeds and endangering human life, and as such culturally distinct from those of low-land Scotland and much of Europe: Francis E. Thomson, *The Supernatural Highlands* (London, 1976): 12, 20–3, and John Gregorson Campbell, *Witchcraft and the Second Sight in the Highlands and Islands of Scotland: Tales and Traditions Collected Entirely from Oral Sources* (Glasgow, 1902), Chapter 1. For a critique of these views, see Henderson, 'Witch-hunting and Witch-belief in the Gàidhealtachd': 100.
30. The first surviving Irish ecclesiastical text is from the fifth century, while the oldest Penitential texts date from the sixth century. Secular law texts, first written in the seventh and eighth centuries, along with examples of early Irish literature, have survived in later medieval and early modern manuscripts. Foreign accounts of early Ireland are nearly non-existent before *Topographia Hibernica, or The History and Topography of Ireland* (1186–7), written by Gerald of Wales (Giraldus Cambrensis). Although the earliest Gaelic-Irish legal tracts date from the medieval period, it is believed that many features of the Gaelic law they describe stretch back centuries to around 1000 b.c., see: 'The Irish Penitentials', ed., Ludwig Bieler, Dublin, 1963: 1–2; Michael Richer, *Medieval Ireland: the Enduring Tradition* (New York, 1988): 75; *The Tain, from, The Táin Bó Cúalnge*, trans, Thomas Kinsella (Dublin, 1969, repr. London, 1970): ix; Fergus Kelly, *A Guide to Early Irish Law* (Dublin, 1988): 1; S.J. Connolly, *The Oxford Companion to Irish History* (Oxford, 2nd ed., 2002): 320.
31. Jacqueline Borsje, *The Celtic Evil Eye and Related Mythological Motifs in Medieval Ireland* (Paris, 2012): 16–17; idem, 'Demonising the Enemy: a Study of Congal Cáech', in Jan Erik Rekdal and Ailbhe Ó Corráin (eds),

Proceedings of the Eighth Symposium of Societas Celtologica Nordica, Studia Celtica Upsaliensia 7, Acta Universitatis Upsaliensis (Uppsala, 2007): 21–38; idem, 'Love Magic in Medieval Irish Penitentials, Law and Literature: A Dynamic Perspective', *Studia Neophilologica* 84, Supplement 1 (2012): 6–23; idem, 'The "Terror of the Night" and the Morrígain: Shifting Faces of the Supernatural', in Mícheál Ó Flaithearta (ed.), *Proceedings of the Seventh Symposium of Societas Celtologica Nordica. Studia Celtica Upsaliensia 6. Acta Universitatis Upsaliensis* (Uppsala 2007): 71–98; idem, 'Druids, Deer and "Words of Power": Coming to Terms with Evil in Medieval Ireland', in Katja Ritari and Alexandra Bergholm (eds), *Approaches to Religion and Mythology in Celtic Studies* (Cambridge, 2008): 122–49; Maeve B. Callan, 'Of Vanishing Fetuses and Maidens-Made Again: Abortion, Restored Virginity, and Similar Scenarios in Medieval Irish Historiography and Penitentials', *Journal of the History of Sexuality*, 21/2 (2012): 289–92; Lisa M. Bitel, *Land of Women: Tales of Sex and Gender from Early Ireland* (Ithaca and London, 1996): 25–7, 216–22.

32. 'The Irish Penitentials': 56–7; Borsje, 'Love Magic in Medieval Irish Penitentials': 6.

33. 'The Irish Penitentials': 79–81. See also, J. Borsje, 'Rules and Regulation on Love Charms in Early Medieval Ireland', *Peritia*, 21 (2010): 173–5.

34. Borsje, 'Rules and Regulation on Love Charms': 175.

35. 'The Irish Penitentials': 101.

36. *Ancient Laws of Ireland* (5 vols, Dublin, 1865–1901): i, 181.

37. Ibid, v, 295, 297.

38. *Ancient Laws of Ireland*: i, 181.

39. Ibid: 203.

40. *Ancient Laws of Ireland*: i, 181.

41. *The Tain*: xii. This text survives in manuscripts produced in the twelve and fourteenth centuries.

42. *The Tain*: 133.

43. 'The Ban-Shenchus [part 1]' ed. Margaret E. Dobbs, *Revue Celtique*, 47 (1930): 333.

44. Gerald of Wales, *Topographia Hibernica, or The History and Topography of Ireland*, trans. John O'Meara, rev. edn (St Ives, 1982): 57–91. See also, John J. O'Meara, 'Giraldus Cambrensis in Topographia Hibernia, "Text of the First Recension"', *Proceedings of the Royal Irish Academy. Section C: Archaeology, Celtic Studies, History, Linguistics, Literature*, 52 (1948–50): 113, and *ODNB*.

45. Borsje, *Celtic Evil Eye*: 48–54, 68–77.

46. 'The historical works of Giraldus Cambrensis, Containing: the Topography of Ireland, and the History of the Conquest of Ireland ... the Itinerary through Wales, and the Description of Wales', ed. Thomas Forester, Richard Colt Hoare, and Thomas Wright (London, 1863): 83; see also, Davies, *Witchcraft, Magic and Culture*: 189–90; Dhuibhne, 'The Old Woman as Hare': 78.

47. *The Register of John Swayne: Archbishop of Armagh and Primate of Ireland, 1418–1439. With Some Entries of Earlier and Later Archbishops*, ed. D.A. Chart (Belfast, 1935): 12; *ODNB*.

48. Clarke Garret, 'Witches and Cunning-folk in the Old Regime', in Jacques Beauroy, Marc Betrand, and Edward T. Gargon (eds), *The Wolf and the Lamb: Popular Culture in France from the Old Regime to the Twentieth Century* (Saratoga, California, 1976): 60; Keith Thomas, *Religion and the Decline of Magic: Studies*

in Popular Beliefs in Sixteenth and Seventeenth Century England (London, 1971, repr. 1997): 186, 436–7, 448; Clive Holmes, 'Women: Witnesses and Witches', *Past and Present*, 140/1 (1991): 49; Timothy R. Tangherlini, '"How do you know she's a Witch?"': Witches, Cunning-folk and Competition in Denmark', *Western Folklore*, 59 (2000): 283.

49. Mary O'Dowd, 'Gaelic Economy and Society', in C. Brady and R. Gillespie (eds), *Natives and Newcomers: the Making of Irish Colonial Society, 1534–1641* (Dublin, 1986): 120–2, 129.

50. William Camden, *Britain, or A Chorographicall Description of the most Flourishing Kingdomes, England, Scotland, and Ireland ... Written first in Latine by William Camden ... Translated Newly into English by Philémon Holland ... Revised, Amended, and Enlarged ...* (London, 1610): 146.

51. Dr Meredith Hanmer, 'Notes on Customs in Ireland', n.d. in R.P. Mahaffy (ed.), *Calendar of State Papers Relating to Ireland, 1601–3* (London, 1912), ii, 687; *ODNB*.

52. Nicholas Canny, *Making Ireland British, 1580–1650* (Oxford, 2001), Chapters 1–3; idem, *From Reformation to Restoration: Ireland, 1536–1660* (Dublin, 1987), Chapter 4; S.J. Connolly, *Contested Island, Ireland 1460–1630* (Oxford, 2009), Chapter 5; Stephen G. Ellis, *Ireland in the Age of the Tudors: English Expansion and the End of Gaelic Rule* (London, 1998), Chapters 11 and 12.

53. Sean Connolly, 'Ag Déanamh Commanding': Elite Responses to Popular Culture, 1650–1850', in J.S. Donnolly and Kerby A. Millar (eds), *Irish Popular Culture, 1650–1850* (Dublin, 1998): 4. See also, Brian MacCuarta, *Catholic Revival in the North of Ireland, 1603–41* (Dublin, 2007); P.J. Corish, *The Catholic Community in the Seventeenth and Eighteenth Centuries* (Dublin, 1985), Chapter 2; and Colm Lennon, 'The Counter-Reformation in Ireland, 1542–1641', *Natives and Newcomers*: 76–78, 87–91.

54. Examination of Anne Dawson, 22 Aug. 1642 (TCD, 1641 depositions, Ms 809, f. 10v.). See also, Chapter 3.

55. Connolly, 'Elite Responses to Popular Culture': 3.

56. Laurence Echard, *An Exact Description of Ireland: Chronologically Surveying all its Provinces and Counties* (London, 1691): 14; *ODNB*.

57. Echard, *An Exact Description of Ireland*: 22. See also, J.F. Fuller, 'An Exact Description of Ireland', *Kerry Archaeological Magazine*, 4/20 (1918): 259.

58. S.J. Connolly, *Religion, Law and Power: the Making of Protestant Ireland, 1660–1760* (Oxford, 1992): 43, 145–7.

59. See Chapter 3.

60. The historiography for Protestant Ascendancy Ireland and the Penal Laws in particular is extremely large and complex, but a good starting place would be a combination of the following: David Hayton, *Ruling Ireland, 1685–1742: Politics, Politicians, and Parties* (Woodbridge, 2004); John Bergin, Eoin Magennis, Lesa Ní Mhunghaile, and Patrick Walsh (eds), *New Perspectives on the Penal Laws: Eighteenth-century Ireland/Iris an dá chultúr, special issue no. 1* (Dublin, 2011); Toby Barnard, *The Kingdom of Ireland, 1641–1760* (Houndsmills, 2004), Chapter 3; David Dickson, *New Foundations: Ireland 1660–1800* (2nd ed., Dublin, 2000), Chapters 1–2; Patrick McNally, *Patriots and Undertakers: Parliamentary Politics in Early Hanoverian Ireland* (Dublin, 1997), Chapters 2–4; Ian McBride, *Eighteenth Century Ireland* (Dublin, 2009),

Chapter 5; D. George Bryce, Robert Eccleshall, and Vincent Geoghegan, 'Preface', in D. George Bryce, Robert Eccleshall, and Vincent Geoghegan (eds), *Political Discourse in Seventeenth- and Eighteenth-century Ireland* (Basingstoke, 2001): viii; Connolly, *Religion, Law and Power*, Chapter 7.

61. Larner, *Enemies of God*: 8.
62. Hutton, 'Witch-hunting in Celtic Societies': 64–5.
63. Borsje, *Celtic Evil-Eye*, Chapters 1 and 2. See also, Alan Dundes (ed.), *The Evil Eye: A Casebook* (London, 1981, repr. 1992): 35, 155. For similar beliefs in Scotland and elsewhere, see idem: 145–6, 39–40, 27, 24.
64. See Chapter 3.
65. Thomas Ady, *A Candle in the Dark or, a Treatise Concerning the Nature of Witches and Witchcraft* ... (London, 1655, repr. 1656): 104; Sharpe, *Instruments of Darkness*: 68; Clark, *Thinking with Demons*: 520, 144–5; Thomas, *Religion and the Decline of Magic*: 537, 570.
66. William Molyneux's Commonplace book, 1683 (TCD, Ms 883/1: 17): 297.
67. Reginald Scot, *The Discoverie of Witchcraft* ... (London, 1584): 64. For Reginald Scot, see: David Wootton, 'Reginald Scot/Abraham Fleming/The Family of Love', in Stuart Clark (ed.), *Languages of Witchcraft: Narrative Ideology and Meaning in Early Modern Culture* (Basingstoke, 2001): 119–38; Sydney Anglo, 'Reginald Scot's Discoverie of Witchcraft: Scepticism and Sadduceeism', in Sidney Anglo (ed.), *The Damned Art: Essays in the Literature of Witchcraft* (London, 1977): 106–39; Phillip C. Almond, *England's First Demonologist: Reginald Scot and 'The Discoverie of Witchcraft'* (London, 2011, repr. 2014).
68. Hutton, 'Witch-hunting in Celtic Societies': 59.
69. Joseph Glanvill, *Saducismus Triumphatus: or, Full and Plain Evidence Concerning Witches and Apparitions* (London, 3rd ed., 1689): 379.
70. Glanvill, *Saducismus Triumphatus*: 386. The third edition of *Saducismus Triumphatus* was compiled anonymously out of the papers and publications of Joseph Glanvill and Henry More and included testimonies and letters sent to the authors: Cameron, *Enchanted Europe*: 276; Peter Elmer, *The Miraculous Conformist: Valentine Greatrakes, the Body Politc, and the Politics of Healing in Restoration Britain* (Oxford, 2013): 114.
71. Jacqueline Borsje, 'Monotheistic to a Certain Extent: The "Good Neighbours" of God in Ireland', in Anne-Marie Korte and Maaike de Haardt (eds), *The Boundaries of Monotheism: Interdisciplinary Explorations into the Foundations of Western Monotheism, Studies in Theology and Religion 13* (Leiden & Boston, 2009): 54–9, 62–3, 74–7.
72. Diarmuid Ó Giolláin, 'Fairy Belief and Official Religion in Ireland', in *The Good People*: 199–200; Hutton, 'Witch-hunting in Celtic Societies': 63–5. For fairy belief in the later period see Chapters 6 and 7.
73. John Cother, *Strange and Wonderful News from the County of Wicklow in Ireland* ... (London, 1678): 1–6.
74. Rev. John Keogh's Account of Co. Roscommon, 1684 (TCD, Transcripts of Dr William Molyneux's Papers, Ms 883/1: 17).
75. Ibid.
76. Hugh Cheape, 'Charms against Witchcraft: Magic and Mischief in Museum Collections', in *Witchcraft and Belief in Early Modern Scotland*: 230–1. See also

Alaric Hall, 'Getting Shot of Elves: Healing, Witchcraft and Fairies in the Scottish Witchcraft Trials', *Folklore*, 116 (2005): 19–36.

77. See Chapter 3.
78. Cohn, *Europe's Inner Demons*: 213–16.
79. For the 'high' magic of the literate and ruling elites, see Chapter 3.
80. Christina Larner, *Witchcraft and Religion: the Politics of Popular Belief* (Oxford, 1984): 40–4; Richard Kieckhefer, *European Witch Trials: their Foundations in Popular and Learned Culture, 1300–1500* (London, 1976): 10–26; Sharpe, *Instruments of Darkness*: 14–17; Levack, *Witch-hunt in Early Modern Europe*: 204–5; Cohn, *Europe's Inner Demons*: 202.
81. Levack, *Witch-hunt in Early Modern Europe*: 204.
82. Hans Peter Brodel, 'Fifteenth-century Witch Beliefs', in *Oxford Handbook of Witchcraft*: 34–5, 48; Larner, *Witchcraft and Religion*: 41; Levack, *Witch-hunt in Early Modern Europe*: 204–5; Cohn, *Europe's Inner Demons*, Chapters 11 and 12.
83. Davies, *Grimoires*: 45.
84. Levack, *Witch-hunt in Early Modern Europe*: 205–9; Larner, *Enemies of God*: 18; Briggs, *Witches and Neighbours*: 169–71, 253.
85. Anne Neary, 'The Origins and Character of the Kilkenny Witchcraft Case of 1324', *Proceedings of the Royal Irish Academy*, 83C (1983): 333–50; *ODNB*; William Renwick Riddell, 'The First Execution for Witchcraft in Ireland', *Journal of Criminal Law and Criminology*, 7/6 (1917): 828–37. For a controversial, radical feminist reading of the Kyteler case, see Anne Llewllyn Barstow, *Witchcraze: A New History of the European Witch Hunts* (New York, 1995), 77: 'Several important European precedents were established by this trial ... women were associated with demonic sex, man-hating and man-harming, and harming of dead infants, and that wives hostile to husbands were witches'.
86. *Statute Rolls of the Parliament of Ireland, Reign of King Henry the Six ...*, ed. Henry F. Berry (Dublin, 4 vols, 1910): ii, 101; Seymour, *Irish Witchcraft and Demonology*: 33–4.
87. The Register of Primate Cromer, 1521–43 (PRONI DIO 4/2/11, f. 103v.); Henry A. Jefferies, 'The Church Courts of Armagh on the Eve of the Reformation', *Seanchas Ardmhacha: Journal of the Armagh Diocesan Historical Society*, 15/2 (1993): 15.
88. 'Red Book of the Privy Council', 1544, in *Historical Manuscripts Commission* [hereafter *HMC*], *15th Report, appendix, part iii, the Manuscripts of Charles Halliday, esq., of Dublin, Acts of the Privy Council in Ireland, 1556–71* (London, 1897): 277; Seymour, *Irish Witchcraft and Demonology*: 59.
89. David Edwards, 'Collaboration without Anglicisation the MacGiollapadraig Lordship and Tudor Reform', in Patrick J. Duffy, David Edwards, and Elizabeth FitzPatrick (eds), *Gaelic Ireland, c.1250–c.1650, Land, Lordship, Settlement* (Dublin, 2001): 77–97.
90. Sir Barnaby Fitzpatrick to [?], 4 May 1571 (Bodleian Library, Oxford, Carte Ms 57: 33v.); *DIB*.
91. Edwards, 'Collaboration without Anglicisation': 92–3; *DIB*.
92. Fitzpatrick to [?], 4 May 1571 (BL, Oxford, Carte Ms 57: 32r.); *DIB*.
93. Fitzpatrick to [?], 4 May 1571 (BL, Oxford, Carte Ms 57: 32v.); Connolly, *Contested Island*: 151–2, 158–9, 161; Ellis, *Ireland in the Age of the Tudors*: 271, 295–7.

94. Christopher Wandesford to [John Bramhall], 4 September 1640 (Huntington Library, San Marino, California, Hastings Collection, Irish papers, HA 15969: 6); Jane H. Olmeyer, *Civil War and Restoration in the Three Stuart Kingdoms: The Career of Randal MacDonnell, Marquis of Antrim, 1609–1683* (Cambridge, 1993): 29–30, 49, 75–6, 195; M. O'Cathain, 'Witchcraft in Ulster 1608–1731', unpublished research paper, University of Ulster, 2006; Raymond Gillespie, *Colonial Ulster: The Settlement of East Ulster, 1600–41* (Cork, 1985): 138; Robert Rock, 'Witchcraft Magic and Politics in Early Modern Ireland, 1563–1699' (MRes thesis, 2012, University of Ulster): 22–4; Breen, *Dunluce Castle*: 164–5.
95. Breen, *Dunluce Castle*: 130–3, 139, 160–3.
96. Wandesford to Bramhall, 4 September 1640 (Huntington Library, HA 15969: 6); John McCafferty, *The Reconstruction of the Church of Ireland: Bishop Bramhall and the Laudian Reforms, 1633–1641* (Cambridge 2007, repr. 2010): 227. For more on Wentworth's religious reforms, see Chapters 2 and 3.
97. For more on Irish JPs, see Chapter 2.
98. Gillespie, *Colonial Ulster*: 102–4. For more on legal structures and criminal prosecution in Ireland, see Chapter 2.
99. S.J. Connolly, *Divided Kingdom: Ireland 1630–1800* (Oxford, 2008): 24–31; McCafferty, *Reconstruction of Ireland*: 193–4, 223.
100. For the 1641 insurrection and its aftermath, see Chapter 4.
101. Breen, *Dunluce Castle*: 164–72.
102. These accusations and prosecutions are dealt with in Chapters 4 and 5.
103. Holmes, 'Women: Witnesses and Witches': 48–50; Laura Gowing, *Common Bodies: Women, Touch and Power in Seventeenth-century England* (New Haven and London, 2003): 74; Alan Macfarlane, *Witchcraft in Tudor and Stuart England: A Regional and Comparative Study* (London, 1970, 2nd ed., 1999): 179–80; Almond, *Demonic Possession*: 14–17; Sharpe, *Instruments of Darkness*: 14, 152–5; Bever, 'Popular Witch Beliefs and Magical Practices': 54–5. For a discussion of demonic possession see Chapter 5.
104. Sneddon, *Possessed by the Devil*: 44–6.
105. Sharpe, *Instruments of Darkness*: 153.
106. Poppets are discussed in, Richard Godbeer, *The Devil's Dominion, Magic and Religion in Early New England* (Cambridge, 1992): 39.
107. Glanvill, *Saducismus Triumphatus*: 373–4, 379, 384, 386.
108. Daniel Higgs, *The Wonderfull and True Relation of the Bewitching a Young Girle in Ireland, What Way she Was Tormented, and a Receipt of the Ointment that she Cured With* (1699): 6. The place of publication is not given in this pamphlet, nor is it listed in the *ESTC*. However, the title page bears the Latin motto of *The Most Ancient and Most Noble Order of the Thistle*, namely, 'Nemo Me Impune Lacessit'. This is an order of knighthood associated with Scotland which was revived in 1687 by James II. The only known copy of this pamphlet is held in University of Glasgow's Special Collections department. It is therefore highly likely that Higgs's pamphlet was printed in Scotland, possibly Glasgow. The *ESTC* states that the copy in Glasgow University is a second edition. The first edition is unfortunately no longer extant. Higgs's pamphlet is summarised in a late eighteenth-century, expanded edition of George Sinclair's *Satan's Invisible*

World Discovered ... (Edinburgh, 1769): 201–3. It is Sinclair's summary that historians have largely based discussions of the Antrim case on, believing Higgs's original pamphlet to be lost: Levack, *Witch-hunting in Scotland:* 127n, and Seymour, *Irish Witchcraft and Demonology*: 197.

109. Higgs, *Wonderful True Relation*: 6. For a discussion of how physicians dealt with witchcraft and demonic possession in the seventeenth century, see Chapter 5.

110. Higgs, *Wonderful True Relation*: 6–8; Sneddon, *Possessed by the Devil*: 51; George Hughes, *Hewn from the Rock, the Story of First Antrim Presbyterian Church* (Antrim, 1996): 32–3.

111. Barnabe Rich, *A New Description of Ireland, wherein is Described the Irish Whereunto they are Inclined* ... (London, 1610): 9; *ODNB*.

112. See Young, *English Catholics and the Supernatural*, Chapters 1 and 4.

113. Euan Cameron, *Enchanted Europe: Superstition, Reason and Religion, 1250–1750* (Oxford, 2010): 237–8.

114. Ezekiel Hopkins, *The Works of the Right Reverend and Learned Ezekiel Hopkins, late lord Bishop of Derry in Ireland, Collected in One Volume* ... (London, 3rd ed., 1710): 105.

115. For Archbishop William King, see Phillip O'Regan, *Archbishop William King of Dublin (1650–1729) and the Constitution in Church and State* (Dublin, 2000), and Christopher J. Fauske (ed.), *Archbishop William King and the Anglican Irish Context* (Dublin, 2004).

116. Cotton Mather was heavily involved in the Salem witch trials in the 1690s, see Cotton Mather, *The Wonders of the Invisible World: Being an Account of the Tryals of Several Witches Lately Executed in New England* ... (London, 1693). The Salem witch-hunt has a large historiography, including John Putnam Demos' seminal treatment, *Entertaining Satan, Witchcraft and the Culture of Early Modern New England* (Oxford, 1982). For an exploration of the social tensions and conflict underpinning the Salem trials, see Paul Boyer and Stephen Nissenbaum, *Salem Possessed: the Social Origins of Witchcraft* (Cambridge, MA, 1974). For the relationship between Salem and political and economic crisis, see Godbeer, *Devil's Dominion*, while gender and witchcraft is examined in Carol F. Karlsen, *The Devil in a Shape of a Woman: Witchcraft in Colonial New England* (New York, 1989).

117. Archbishop William King to Mather [?], 3 October 1693 (TCD, Ms 1995–2008/300); Connolly, *Religion, Law, and Power*: 196.

118. Samuel McSkimmin (ed.), *The Islandmagee Witches: a Narrative of the Suffering of a Young Girl Called Mary Dunbar, Who was Strangely Molested by Spirits and Witches, at Mr James Hattridge's House, Islandmagee, near Carrickfergus, in the County of Antrim and Province of Ulster, and in Some Other Places to which she was Removed during the Time of her Disorder, as also of the Aforesaid Mr. Hattridge's House being Haunted with Spirits in the Latter End of 1710 and the Beginning of 1711* (Belfast, 1822): 17; Sneddon, *Possessed by the Devil*: 92.

119. William Tisdall, 'Account of the Trial of Eight Reputed Witches, 4 April 1711', *Hibernian Magazine* (1775): 50. For Anthony Upton, see F.E. Ball, *The Judges in Ireland, 1221–1921* (2 vols, New York, 1927): ii, 23, 66.

120. Richard Allestree, *The Whole Duty of Man* ... (Dublin, 1714): 69.

121. Stuart Clark, 'Satanic Libraries: Marsh's Witchcraft Books', Muriel McCarthy and Ann Simmons (eds), *The Making of Marsh's Library: Learning, Politics and*

Religion in Ireland, 1650–1750 (Dublin, 2004): 97–116; Thomas Thornton, *A Catalogue of Books, to Be Sold By Auction at Dick's Coffee House ...* (Dublin, 1730): 53, 63. For sceptical witchcraft books in auction catalogues, see Chapter 6.

122. Sneddon, *Possessed by the Devil*: 109. The exception is Higgs, *Wonderful True Relation*. In contrast to England, Scotland also produced few witchcraft pamphlets before the end of the seventeenth century, most of which were devoted to detailing a recent spate of demonic possessions: Goodare, 'Introduction', in *Witch-hunting in Context*: 6.

123. Raymond Gillespie, *Reading Ireland: Print, Reading, and Social Change in Early Modern Ireland* (Manchester, 2005), Chapter 4.

124. Clark, 'Satanic Libraries': 115.

125. Francis Hutchinson, *Historical Essay*, xiii–xiv, 56. See also, Sneddon, *Witchcraft and Whigs*, especially Chapters 5–6.

126. Bishop Francis Hutchinson's Commonplace book, 1731–9 (PRONI, Accessioned 2004: 553–6). See also, *A Catalogue of Books: being in the Library of the Right Rev. Dr Francis Hutchinson, late Bishop of Down and Connor. To be Sold by Auction, by William Ross, at the Coffee House ... the House of Lords, on Monday, the Twenty-Sixth of April 1756 ...* (London, 1756). For a discussion of a portrait painted of Hutchinson in Ireland in the 1720s surrounded by his beloved library, Andrew Sneddon, 'What the Witchcraft Bishop did in Ireland: the Controversial Career of Francis Hutchinson, 1660–1739', *History Ireland*, 18/1 (2010): 22–5. For Hutchinson's estate, see Sneddon, *Witchcraft and Whigs*, Chapter 8.

127. Bishop Hutchinson's Commonplace book, 1731–9 (PRONI, 2004: 553–6).

2 Witchcraft Legislation and Legal Administration in Early Modern Ireland

1. Levack, *Witch-hunt in Early Modern Europe*: 74.

2. Seymour, *Irish Witchcraft and Demonology*: 61–5; Lapoint, 'Irish Immunity to Witch-hunting': 80.

3. Sharpe, *Instruments of Darkness*: 25–31; Julian Goodare, 'The Scottish Witchcraft Act', *Church History*, 74/1 (2005): 50; idem, 'Introduction', *Scottish Witch-Hunt in Context*: 5.

4. Goodare, 'Witchcraft in Scotland', *Oxford Handbook of Witchcraft*: 302.

5. Goodare, 'The Scottish Witchcraft Act': 4–5; idem, 'Introduction': 40–67; Owen Davies, 'A Comparative Perspective on Scottish Cunning-folk and Charmers', *Witchcraft and Belief in Early Modern Scotland*: 193; For a study of events leading up to the passing of the Scottish Witchcraft Act that emphasises an essentially anti-Catholic agenda: P.G. Maxwell-Stuart, *Satan's Conspiracy: Magic and Witchcraft in Sixteenth-century Scotland* (East Linton, 2001): 35–50.

6. 33 Hen. VIII c.8 [Eng.], 'An Act Against Conjurations, Witchcrafts, Sorcery, and Enchantments' (1541/2); Sharpe, *Instruments of Darkness*: 24–30.

7. Marion Gibson (ed.), *Witchcraft and Society in England and America, 1550–1750* (London, 2003): 1–2.

8. 5 Eliz. I, c. 16 [Eng.], 'An Act Against Conjuration, Enchantments and Witchcrafts' (1563).

9. Norman Jones, 'Defining Superstitions: Treasonous Catholics and the Act Against Witchcraft of 1563', Charles Carleton, Robert L. Woods, Mary L. Robertson, and Joseph L. Black (eds), *States, Sovereigns, and Society* (Stroud, 1998): 187–203; James Sharpe, *Witchcraft in Early Modern England* (Harlow, 2001): 16; Gibson, *Witchcraft and Society*: 3. For a study which negates Jones' theory that the 1563 Witchcraft Act was partly a result of fear of Catholic plots: Young, *English Catholics and the Supernatural*: 134–7.
10. Edward Bever, 'Female Aggression, and Power in the Early Modern Community', *Journal of Social History*, 35/4 (2002): 957.
11. Gibson, *Witchcraft and Society*: 3.
12. Davies, *Popular Magic*: 7–8.
13. 5 Eliz.I, c.16 (1563); 28 Eliz. I, c. 2 [Ire.] 'An Act Against Witchcraft and Sorcerie' (1586). The English Act referred to the earlier Henrician statute of 1541–2, but as this had never been passed in Ireland all reference to it was removed from the Irish Act. Some spelling and words were also altered but this did not change the thrust or meaning of the original Act.
14. 28 Eliz.I, c. 2 [Ire.] (1586).
15. Seymour, *Irish Witchcraft and Demonology*: 60–4; *ODNB*.
16. Lord Justice William Drury and Sir Edward Fitton, 4 November 1578 in, J.S. Brewer and William Bullen (eds), *Calendar of the Carew Manuscripts ... 1578–88 ...* (London, 1868): 144; *DIB*.
17. See Chapter 4.
18. See Chapter 3.
19. William Kramer, 'The Effects of Gaelic Culture, Religious Conflict and the Dynamics of Dual Confessionalisation on the Suppression of Witchcraft Accusations and Witch-hunts in Early Modern Ireland, 1533–1670' (California Polytechnic State University, MA Thesis, 2010): 171–3.
20. This point is made by Elwyn Lapoint in passing but not fully developed: Lapoint, 'Irish Immunity to Witch-hunting': 82.
21. Ellis, *Ireland in the Age of the Tudors*: 320–1.
22. Victor Treadwell, 'Sir John Perrot and the Irish Parliament of 1585–6', *Proceedings of the Royal Irish Academy*, Section C, 85 (1985): 299.
23. 'Journal of the Irish House of Lords in Sir John Perrot's Parliament (3 May 1585–13 May 1586)', ed. F.J. Routledge, *English Historical Review*, 29 (1914): 115, 117; Treadwell, 'Sir John Perrot and the Irish Parliament of 1585–6': 299–301.
24. Ellis, *Ireland in the Age of the Tudors*: 321.
25. Jones, 'Defining Superstition': 197–8.
26. I Jas. c.12 [Eng.], 'An Act Against Conjuration, Witchcraft and Dealing with Evil and Wicked Spirits' (1604); Lapoint, 'Irish Immunity to Witch-hunting': 82.
27. Marion Gibson, 'Applying the Act of 1604: Witches in Essex, Northamptonshire and Lancashire before and after 1604', in John Newton and Jo Bath (eds), *Witchcraft and the Act of 1604* (Leiden, 2008): 117–28; Malcolm Gaskill, 'Witchcraft and Imagination in the English Civil War', in idem, 162; Gibson, *Witchcraft and Society*: 5–7.
28. Ireland is not included in a recent book of essays dedicated to the passing and implementation of the 1604 Act: Newton and Bath, *Witchcraft and the Act of 1604*.
29. Connolly, *Contested Island*: 204.

30. See Chapter 4.
31. Hiram Morgan, 'Hugh O'Neil and the Nine Years War in Tudor Ireland', *Historical Journal*, 36/1 (1993): 21–37; idem, *Tyrone's Rebellion: The Outbreak of the Nine Years War in Tudor Ireland* (Woodbridge, 2nd ed., 1999); Raymond Gillespie, *Seventeenth-century Ireland* (Dublin, 2006): 33–44.
32. *JHCI*, i, 16, 51, 55, 63–4.
33. Victor Treadwell, 'The House of Lords in the Irish Parliament of 1613–1615', *English Historical Review*, 70 (1965): 96.
34. Treadwell, 'The House of Lords in 1613–1615': 97.
35. *HCJI*, i, 114–15, 134.
36. 10 Charles I, session 2, c. 19, [Ire.], 'Act for the Triall of Murders and Felonies committed in Severall Counties' (1635). The following discussion is based on an analysis of this act.
37. Similarly, an official publication, printed in Dublin in 1635, when listing those felonies 'excepted out of this pardon' from the King, added 'all offences of Invocations, Conjurations, Witch-Crafts, Sorceries, Inchantments, and charmes' to crimes including rape, murder, robbery, 'buggery', and Burglary: *Act for the Kings Majesties most Gracious, General, and Free Pardon* (Dublin, 1635): 4.
38. Gillespie, *Seventeenth-Century Ireland*, Chapter 5. For more on Wentworth, see Chapter 1, and Chapter 3.
39. W.N. Osborough, 'The Laws and Other Legalities of Ireland, 1689–1850', in Michael Brown and Seán Patrick Donlan (eds), *The Laws and Other Legalities of Ireland, 1689–1850* (Farnham, 2011): 77–96; Margaret MacCurtain, *Tudor and Stuart Ireland* (Dublin, 1972): 70; D.W. Hayton, 'Introduction: the Long Apprenticeship', in David W. Hayton, (ed.), *The Irish Parliament in the Eighteenth Century* (Edinburgh, 2001): 8–12; David Hayton, James Kelly and John Bergin (eds), *The Eighteenth-century Composite State: Representative Institutions in Ireland and Europe, 1690–1800* (Basingstoke, 2010), Chapters 1–5; Neal Garnham, *The Courts, Crime and the Criminal Law in Ireland, 1692–1760* (Dublin, 1996): 10.
40. Neal Garnham, 'The Limits of English Influence on the Irish Criminal Law and the Boundaries of Discretion in the Eighteenth-century Irish Criminal Justice System', in *Laws and Other Legalities of Ireland*: 97; Michael Brown and Sean Patrick Donlan, 'The Laws in Ireland, 1689–1850: A Brief Introduction', in idem: 5.
41. Garnham, 'How Violent was Eighteenth-century Ireland?': 388.
42. Neal Garnham, 'Crime, Policing and the Law, 1600–1900', in Liam Kennedy and Philip Ollerenshaw (eds), *Ulster Since 1600: Politics, Economy and Society* (Oxford, 2013): 90–1. See also, Chapter 4.
43. Garnham, *Courts, Crime and the Criminal Law*: 87–90.
44. Garnham, 'Crime, Policing and the Law, 1600–1900': 91; idem, *Crime, Criminal Law and the Courts*: 32–3, 66, 48. See also, Chapter 1.
45. Garnham, 'Crime, Policing and the Law, 1600–1900': 92.
46. Garnham, *Courts, Crime and the Criminal Law*: 27–32. See also Chapter 3.
47. Garnham, 'Crime, Policing and the Law, 1600–1900': 92–3; idem, *Courts, Crime and the Criminal Law*: 27–9, 31–2.
48. 'Grand Juries ... [are] generally composed of persons of the first rank, and best credit in their country': Richard Ashton, *Charge Given to the Grand Juries*

of the County of the City of Dublin ... Saturday the 3rd Day of December, 1763 (Dublin, 1763), sig. A3; See also, Garnham, *Courts, Crime and Criminal Law*, Chapter 7. See also Chapter 4.

49. Richard Bolton, *A Justice of the Peace for Ireland ...* (Dublin, 2nd ed., 1638): 97; Gillespie, *Women and Crime*: 46; ODNB.

50. Bolton, *Justice of Peace for Ireland*: 97–8. For a detailed examination of the types of evidence used as proof of the crime of witchcraft in early modern England, see: Orna Alyagon Darr, *The Marks of an Absolute Witch: Evidentiary Dilemmas in Early Modern England* (Aldershot, 2013). For the rise of judicial scepticism with regards this evidence, see Chapters 4 and 6.

51. Gaskill, *Crime and Mentalities*: 227.

52. Bolton, *Justice of Peace for Ireland*: 97.

53. Sharpe, *Instruments of Darkness*: 73, 94 n28; Barry, *Witchcraft and Demonology in South-West England*: 47–8.

54. Richard Bolton, *A Justice of Peace for Ireland ...* (Dublin, 1750).

3 Cunning-folk in Early Modern Ireland

1. Davies, 'Scottish Cunning-folk and Charmers': 186–7; idem, *Popular Magic*: 163.

2. Macfarlane, *Witchcraft in Tudor and Stuart England*: 130 n1.

3. Hutton, 'The Global Context of the Scottish Witch-hunt': 19; Briggs, *Witches and Neighbours*: 146.

4. Bever, *Realities of Witchcraft and Popular Magic in Early Modern Europe: Culture, Cognition, and Everyday Life* (Basingstoke, 2008), Chapter 6; Thomas, *Religion and the Decline of Magic*: 177–85, 213–21; Dillenger, 'Evil People': 58–62; Macfarlane, *Witchcraft in Tudor and Stuart England*, Chapter 8; Joyce Millar, 'Devices and Directions: Folk-Healing Aspects of Witchcraft Practice in Seventeenth-century Scotland', in *The Scottish Witch-hunt in Context*: 92–105; Davies, *Popular Magic*, especially Chapters 1, 4–6; idem, 'Scottish Cunning-folk and Charmers': 187–8, 194–8; Robin Briggs, 'Circling the Devil: Witch-doctors and Magical Healers in Early Modern Lorraine', in Stuart Clark (ed.), *Languages of Witchcraft: Ideology and Meaning in Early Modern Culture* (New York, 2001): 162–3; idem, *Witches and Neighbours*: 148–60; Francisco Bethencourt, 'Portugal: a Scrupulous Inquisition', in *Early Modern European Witchcraft*: 410–13; Garret, 'Witches and Cunning-folk in the Old Regime': 53–64; Frederick Valletta, *Witchcraft, Magic and Superstition in England, 1640–70* (Aldershot, 2000), Chapter 5.

5. Godbeer, *Devil's Dominion*: 7, 24, 30–47.

6. Davies, *Popular Magic*: 84–8; Briggs, *Witches and Neighbours*: 146–7.

7. Davies, *Grimoires*, Chapters 1–2; idem, *Popular Magic*, Chapters 5–6; D.P. Walker, *Spiritual and Demonic Magic from Ficino to Campenella* (Pennsylvania, 1958, repr. 2003): ix, 45–60, 75–112; Clark, *Thinking with Demons*, Chapters 14–15; P.G. Maxwell-Stuart, *Witchcraft in Europe and the New World, 1400–1800* (Basingstoke, 2001): 2–3, 5–9; idem, *Astrology from Ancient Babylon to the Present* (Stroud, 2010, repr. 2012), Chapters 10–12; Levack, *Witch-hunt in Early Modern Europe*: 37–9; Bever, *Realities of Witchcraft*: 152–3; Richard Kieckhefer,

'Magic and its Hazards in the Late Medieval West', in *Oxford Handbook of Witchcraft*: 15–19.

8. Davies, *Popular Magic*: 29–34, 163–4; idem, 'Scottish Cunning-folk and Charmers': 188–92; Geoffrey Scarre, *Witchcraft and Magic in 16th and 17th Century Europe* (London, 1987): 31; Briggs, *Witches and Neighbours*: 148.

9. Goodare, 'Introduction': 4–6; Millar, 'Folk-healing': 91, 104; Davies, *Popular Magic*: 9, 14–17, 164–8; idem, 'Scottish Cunning-folk and Charmers': 190–2. For similar clerical opposition to popular magic in seventeenth-century New England, see Godbeer, *Devil's Dominion*: 60–6, 69–74, 83–91.

10. Marko Nenonen, 'Culture Wars: State, Religion and Popular Culture in Europe, 1400–1800', in Jonathan Barry and Owen Davies (eds), *Witchcraft Historiography* (Basingstoke, 2007): 111. Much the same argument is made in relation to seventeenth-century Ireland by Raymond Gillespie: Gillespie, 'Unpopular and Popular Religion': 131–2.

11. Kieckhefer, 'Magic and its Hazards in the late Medieval West': 17.

12. Davies, 'Scottish Cunning-folk and Charmers': 185–205 (quotes at 187, 186). Some historians however conflate the activities of these magical practitioners, see: Millar, 'Devices and Directions': 90–105, and Emma Wilby, *Cunning-folk and Familiar Spirits: Shamanistic Visionary Traditions in Early Modern British Witchcraft and Magic* (Brighton, 2005, repr. 2010): 31–7.

13. Davies, *Witchcraft, Magic and Culture*, Chapter 5; idem, 'Scottish Cunning-folk and Charmers': 187.

14. See Chapter 7.

15. See Chapter 2.

16. See Chapter 1.

17. Thomas Wentworth to John Coke 2 March 1635 (Sheffield City Archives [hereafter SCA], Wentworth Wodehouse Ms, Strafford Letter Books, WWM/Str P/5, f. 190); Gillespie, *Devoted People*: 65.

18. Gillespie, *Seventeenth Century Ireland*: 109–15; J.F. Merritt (ed.), *The Political of Thomas Wentworth, Earl of Strattford, 1621–41* (Cambridge, 1996), Chapters 7–8; John McCafferty, 'The Churches and People of the three Kingdoms, 1603–1641', in Jenny Wormald (ed.), *The Seventeenth Century* (Oxford, 2008, repr. 2013): 67–8, 75–6.

19. George Hill (ed.), *The Montgomery Manuscripts, 1603–1706: Compiled from Family Papers* … (2 vols, Belfast, 1869), i, 205 n38; John M. Dickson, 'The Colville Family in Ulster', *Ulster Journal of Archaeology*, second series 5/3 (1899): 140; Seymour, *Irish Witchcraft and Demonology*: 82–5; Porter, *Witches, Warlocks and Ghosts*: 13–15; J.B Leslie (ed.), *Clergy of Connor: from Patrician Times to the Present day* (Belfast, 1993): 271; Regal Visit of Diocese of Down and Connor, 1634 (PRONI, T/975, 1–3: 9); Harry Jessop St. John Clarke, *Thirty Centuries in South East Antrim: the Parish of Coole or Carnmoney* (Belfast, 1938): 78.

20. Michael Harward, *The Herdsman's Mate; Or a Guide for Herdsman. Teaching How to Cure all Diseases in Bulls, Owen, Cows and Calves* … (Dublin, 1673), sig. A2.

21. Harward, *The Herdsman's Mate*, sig. A2.

22. Harward, *The Herdsman's Mate*, sig. A3. The title of astrologer in Harward's case was self-assigned: Gillespie, *Devoted People*: 131 n23.

23. Hopkins, *Works of the Right Reverend and Learned Ezekiel Hopkins*: 105.

24. Anon, *The Whole Duty of Man, Laid Down in a Plain and Familiar Way for the Use of all, but Especially Meanest Reader* ... (Dublin, 1714): 69–70.
25. See, Gillespie, 'Popular and Unpopular Religion': 33.
26. James Butler, First Duke of Ormond to Henry Bennet, First Earl of Arlington, 26 November 1666, in Robert Pentland Mahaffy (ed.), *Calendar of State Papers Relating to Ireland ... 1666–69* (London, 1908): 247. For Ormond, see Toby Barnard and Jane Fenlon (eds), *The Dukes of Ormond, 1610–1745* (Woodbridge, 2000), Chapters 1, 4, 5, 6, and for his early career see, W.P. Kelly, 'The Early Career of James Butler, Twelfth Earl and First Duke of Ormond (1610–1688), 1610–1643' (PhD diss., University of Cambridge, 1997). For his attitude to witchcraft, see Chapter 4.
27. Gillespie, *Devoted People*: 67–8. See also, Anselm Faulkner, 'Father O'Finaghty's Miracles', *Irish Ecclesiastical Record*, 5th series, 104 (1965): 349–62.
28. Account of Co. Kildare, 1684 [?] (TCD, Ms 883/1: 297).
29. John Dunton, *The Dublin Scuffle* ... (London, 1699): 333; *ODNB*; Samuel Bentley, *Literary Anecdotes of the Eighteenth Century* ... (London, 9 vols, 1812–15), v, 59–76.
30. Stuart Clark, *Thinking with Demons*, Chapter 31; idem, 'Protestant Demonology: Sin, Superstition and Society (c. 1520–1630)', in *Early Modern European Witchcraft: Centres and Peripheries*: 65–9; Davies, *Grimoires*: 45; idem, *Popular Magic*: 29–32.
31. Davies, *Popular Magic*: 35.
32. Ibid: 36.
33. See Davies, *Popular Magic*: 34–5.
34. Keogh's Account of Co. Roscommon, 1684 (TCD, Ms 883/1: 16–17).
35. From the conjuration of spirits for any purpose, to the magical detection of thieves, finding buried treasure lost or stolen goods, and using charms, symbols, incantations, or love magic. See Chapter 1.
36. Cited in, Seymour, *Irish witchcraft*: 77–8. See also, Gillespie, *Devoted People*: 130–1. Seymour states on p. 78 that in the 'Rolls at the Record Office' in Dublin, Aston's trial is said to have occurred in the 'three weeks of Easter in the 6th year of James I'. However on the preceding page, Seymour states that Aston's trial occurred in 1606. I have taken 1609, the date given in the Dublin Rolls, as the correct one, although since the original document is no longer extant, it is impossible to state where this conjecture is correct.
37. Gillespie, *Seventeenth-century Ireland*: 42–4; John McCavitt, *The Flight of the Earls* (Dublin, 2002); idem, 'The Flight of the Earls, 1607', *Irish Historical Studies*, 29/114 (1994): 159–73; Nicholas Canny, 'The Flight of the Earls, 1607', *Irish Historical Studies*, 17/67 (1971): 380–99.
38. Cited in, Seymour, *Irish witchcraft*: 79.
39. See Levack, *Witch-hunting in Scotland*, Chapter 3; Sharpe, *Instruments of Darkness*: 47–50. For James VI's involvement in the two major witch-hunts of the 1590s in Scotland, see: Lawrence Normand and Gareth Roberts, *Witchcraft in Early Modern Scotland: James VI's Demonology and the North Berwick Witches* (Exeter, 2000), and Julian Goodare, 'The Scottish Witchcraft Panic of 1597', in *Scottish Witch-hunt in Context*, Chapter 4; idem, 'The Framework for Scottish Witch-hunting in the 1590s', *The Scottish Historical Review*, 81/212 (2002): 247–50; idem, 'The Aberdeenshire Witchcraft Panic of 1597', *Northern Scotland*, 21 (2001): 17–38.

40. Sharpe, *Instruments of Darkness*: 160–1, 271; Davies, *Popular Magic*: 103–9; Gaskill, *Witchfinders*: 105; Macfarlane, *Witchcraft in Tudor and Stuart England*: 122–3; Peter Elmer, 'Medicine, Witchcraft and the Politics of Healing in Late Seventeenth-century England', in Ole Peter Grell and Andrew Cunnigham (eds), *Medicine and Religion in Enlightenment Europe* (Aldershot, 2007): 237–40.
41. http://ingeniousireland.ie/2012/11/dublins-weird-witch-bottle/ [last accessed 3 September 2014].
42. Glanville, *Saducismus Triumphatus*: 380. For use of similar counter-magic in early eighteenth-century England, see: Francis Bragge, *Witchcraft Further Display'd ...* (London, 1712): 23–4.
43. Glanville, *Saducismus Triumphatus*: 381; Elmer, *Miraculous Conformist*: 131.
44. Higgs, *Wonderful True Relation*: 13.
45. Ibid: 14.
46. Higgs, *Wonderful True Relation*: 15; Johannes Janssen, *History of the German People at the Close of the Middle Ages* (17 vols, London, 1896–1910), xii, 290; Davies, *Grimoires*: 48–9; Walker, *Spiritual and Demonic Magic*: 96–106.
47. Higgs, *Wonderful True Relation*: 15.
48. Ibid: 16.
49. A detailed search of indexes, records, and registers held at the Royal College of Physicians of Ireland, Dublin has yielded no trace of Higgs. Likewise, I have not been able to find his name in matriculation records of contemporary universities in Britain and Ireland, nor in surviving genealogical sources such as parish registers.
50. Higgs, *Wonderful True Relation*: 3–16.
51. Ibid: 12, 16.
52. Higgs, *Wonderful True Relation*: 3–6, 16; Cameron, *Enchanted Europe*, Chapters 16–17; Levack, *Witch-hunting in Scotland*: 125–8. Saducee was a pejorative term, used particularly in the seventeenth century, that referred to those sceptical of the existence of spiritual essences as traditionally conceived. The term was derived from an ancient Jewish sect active in biblical times. See Levack, *Witch-hunting in Scotland*: 125.
53. Sneddon, *Possessed by the Devil*, Chapter 8. See also Chapter 5 for a detailed account of the case.
54. Anon, 'The Islandmagee Witches': 25.
55. Tisdall, 'Account of the Trial': 48.
56. Anon, 'The Islandmagee Witches': 25.
57. Tisdall, 'Account of the Trial': 49.
58. Anon, 'The Islandmagee Witches': 25.
59. Porter, *Congregational Memoir of Larne*: 45; Fred Rankin (ed.), *Clergy of Down and Dromore* (Belfast, 1996), part II, 95,195.
60. Anon, 'The Islandmagee Witches': 25.
61. Tisdall, 'Account of the Trial': 49.
62. J. O'Laverty, *An Historical Account of Diocese of Down and Connor, Ancient and Modern* (5 vols, Dublin, 1878–95), iii, 109–10.
63. See pp 48–9.
64. See p. 47.
65. Anon, 'The Islandmagee Witches': 26.
66. For the only example of a referral of cunning-folk to ecclesiastical courts see below.

67. Davies, 'Scottish Cunning-folk and Charmers': 192; Davies and de Blécourt, *Beyond the Witch Trials*, Chapters 4, 5, 8.
68. Gillespie, 'Popular and Unpopular Religion': 31.
69. Connolly, *Religion, Law and Power*: 161, 167; J.C. Beckett, *Protestant Dissent in Ireland, 1687–1780* (1948, repr. 2008): 24; Toby Barnard, 'Enforcing the Reformation in Ireland, 1660–1704', in Elizabethanne Boran and Crawford Gribben (eds), *Enforcing Reformation in Ireland and Scotland, 1550–1700* (Manchester, 2006): 202–3, 219, 224; Ian McBride, *Eighteenth Century Ireland* (Dublin, 2009): 169, 286, 290–1; idem, 'Ulster Presbyterianism and the Confessional State, 1688–1733', in D. George Boyce, Robert Eccleshall, Vincent Geoghegan (eds), *Political Discourse in Seventeenth and Eighteenth Century Ireland* (Basingstoke, 2001): 170, 176; Robert Whan, 'Presbyterianism in Ulster, c1680–1730: a Social and Political Study' (Queen's University, Belfast, PhD thesis, 2009): 10, 90–1, 133; Robert Armstrong, 'The Irish Alternative: Scottish and English Presbyterianism in Ireland', in Robert Armstrong and Tadhg Ó hAnnracháin (eds), *Insular Christianity: Alternative Models of the Church in Britain and Ireland, c.1570–c.1700* (Manchester, 2013): 208–14.
70. Connolly, *Religion, Law and Power*: 167.
71. McBride, *Eighteenth-century Ireland*: 294.
72. See David Hayton, 'The Development and Limitations of Protestant Ascendancy: the Church of Ireland Laity in Public Life, 1660–1740', in Raymond Gillespie and W.G. Nealy (eds), *The Laity and the Church of Ireland, 1000–2000: all Sorts and Conditions* (Dublin, 2002): 118–21; idem, 'Presbyterians and the Confessional State: the Sacramental Test as an Issue in Irish Politics, 1704–80', *Bulletin of the Presbyterian Historical Society of Ireland*, 26 (1997): 11–31; idem, *Ruling Ireland*, 196–203; Whan, *Presbyterians in Ulster*: 134, 216–19, 223–5; Barnard, 'Enforcing the Reformation in Ireland, 1660–1704': 206, 217–18; McBride, *Eighteenth-Century Ireland*: 287–8, 293; idem, 'Presbyterians in the Penal Era', *Bulletin of the Presbyterian Historical Society of Ireland*, 27 (1998–2000): 14–28, 15–16; idem, 'Ulster Presbyterians and the Confessional State': 177–8; Connolly, *Religion, Law and Power*: 162; Beckett, *Protestant Dissent*: 27–9, 40–1, 53, 141; Holmes, *The Shaping of Ulster Presbyterian Belief and Practice*: 213.
73. Hayton, *Ruling Ireland*: 203–5; Whan, 'Presbyterians in Ulster': 133; McBride, 'Presbyterians in the Penal Era': 18, 21, 25; Robert Armstrong, 'Of Stories and Sermons: Nationality and Spirituality in the later Seventeenth-Century', in Tadhg Ó hAnnracháin, Robert Armstrong (eds), *Community in Early Modern Ireland* (Dublin, 2006): 230–1; Barnard, 'Enforcing the Reformation in Ireland, 1660–1704': 208.
74. Davies, 'Scottish Cunning-folk and Charmers': 186; idem, 'Charmers and Charming in England and Wales from the 18th to 20th Centuries', *Folklore*, 109 (1998): 41–53.
75. Antrim Presbytery minutes, 3 September 1672 (PRONI, D1759/1/A/2: 54).
76. Patrick Adair, *A True Narrative of the Rise and Progress of the Presbyterian Church in Ireland … 1623–70*, ed.W.D. Killen (Belfast, 1866): 299–300.
77. Antrim Presbytery minutes, 5 February 1673 (PRONI, D1759/1/A/2: 72).
78. Minutes of the Laggan Presbytery, 4 November 1699 (PRONI, D/1759/1/E/2: 505).
79. Aghadowey Session minutes, 25 April 1703 (PHS, Aghadowey Session minutes, 1701–1765: 8).

80. Aghadowey Session minutes, 9 May 1703 (PHS, Aghadowey Session minutes: 8).
81. Ibid: 9.
82. Thomas, *Religion and the Decline of Magic*: 213–21; Godbeer, *Devil's Dominion*: 37, 41; Sharpe, 'Witchcraft in the early Modern Isle of Man': 17; Jo Bath, 'The Treatment of Potential Witches in North-east England, c.1649–1680', in *Witchcraft and the Act of 1604*: 129–30.
83. Davies, *Popular Magic*: 100.
84. Aghadowey Session minutes, 11 May 1703 (PHS, Aghadowey Session minutes: 9).
85. Carnmoney Session minutes, 1 August 1703 (PRONI, Presbyterian Church Records, Minutes of the Presbyterian Church of Carnmoney, 1686–1748, MIC 1P/37/4: 34). This session book is not in chronological order and contains both paginated and un-paginated sections.
86. Carnmoney Session minutes, 1 August 1703 (PRONI, MIC 1P/37/4: 34).
87. Carnmoney Session minutes, 13 April 1709 (PRONI, MIC 1P/37/4, un-paginated section).
88. Carnmoney Session minutes, 15 June, 18 August, 11 September 1709 (PRONI, MIC 1P/37/4, un-paginated section).
89. Carnmoney Session minutes, 24 October 1731 (PRONI, MIC 1P/37/4, un-paginated section).
90. Bishop Hutchinson's Commonplace book, 1721–30 (PRONI, Down Diocesan Papers, MS DIO/1/22/1, un-paginated section, page entitled 'witchcraft').
91. See Sneddon, *Witchcraft and Whigs*, Chapters 2, 3, 6, 7, and Bostridge, *Witchcraft and its Transformations*, Chapter 6.
92. See Chapter 1.
93. Bishop Hutchinson's Commonplace book, 1731–9 (PRONI, 2004: 131).
94. Hutchinson was aware that popular magic was illegal under the 1563 English witchcraft statute, see Hutchinson, *Historical Essay*: 111.
95. Legal Notebook of Sir Richard Cox, Hillary term 1711, Easter term 1712 (NLI, Ms 4245). For Cox see, Garnham, *Courts, Crime and the Criminal Law*: 15, 78–9, 90, 94, 99.
96. Camden, *Britain*, 1610: 146.
97. Ibid.
98. Camden, *Britain*, 1610: 146; Gillespie, *Devoted People*: 65.
99. Camden, *Britain*, 1610: 147; Gillespie, *Devoted People*: 65.
100. Camden, *Britain*, 1610: 146.
101. See, Davies, *Popular Magic*, Chapter 6.
102. Nicholas Bernard, *The Whole Proceedings of the Siege of Drogheda* ... (London, 1642): 84. For Bernard in Ireland, see Peter Marshall, *Mother Leakey and the Bishop: A Ghost Story* (Oxford, 2007, repr. 2008), Chapter 5.
103. Bernard, *Whole Proceedings of the Siege of Drogheda*: 85–8.
104. Bernard, *Whole Proceedings of the Siege of Drogheda*: 84. See also, idem, 86 for another example of this type of written charm.
105. Bernard, *Whole Proceedings of the Siege of Drogheda*: 85–8.
106. Cited in, Gillespie, *Devoted People*: 120.
107. Charles Lamotte, *An Essay upon Poetry and Painting, with Relation to the Sacred and Profane History with and Appendix Concerning Obscenity in Writing and Painting* (London, 1730, repr. Dublin, 1742): 76–77. See also, Walter D. Sweeting, *Northamptonshire: Notes and Queries* ... (1896): 78.

108. Jeanne Foster Cooper, *Ulster Folklore* (Belfast, 1951): 59; *Irish Independent*, 19 September 1925.
109. Gillespie, 'Popular and Unpopular Religion': 35, 45.
110. 'Brussels Ms 3947: Donatus Moneyus De Provinicia Hiberniae S. Francisci', ed. Brendan Jennings in, *Analecta Hibernica*, 6 (1934): 43–4; Gillespie, 'Popular and Unpopular Religion': 31.
111. Malachy Hartry, *Triumphalia Chronologica Monstarii Sanctae Crucis in Hibernia ...*, ed. Denis Murphy (Dublin, 1891): 127–9.
112. Bernard, *Whole Proceedings of the Siege of Drogheda ...* (London, 1642): 53.
113. Gillespie, *Devoted People*: 115.
114. *The Annals of Clonmacnoise*, ed. Denis Murphy (Dublin, 1896): 96; Gillespie, *Devoted People*: 115.
115. Davies, *Grimoires*: 62.
116. Antoin Gearnon, *Parrthas An Anma*, ed. Anselm Ó Fachtna (Dublin, 1953): 70.
117. Gillespie, 'Popular and Unpopular Religion': 31.
118. 'Synod of Drogheda, Statutes of Armagh: Summary of the Provincial Consultation, 19 Feb. 1614' ed. Daniel McCarthy in, *Collections on Irish Church History from the Mss of the later v. Rev. Laurence F. Renehan ...* (2 vols, Dublin, 1861), i, 433.
119. Alison Forrestal, *Catholic Synods in Ireland, 1600–1690* (Dublin, 1998): 69.
120. Cited in, Forrestal, *Catholic Synods in Ireland*: 71.
121. Corish, *Catholic Community*: 50–1.
122. Cited in, Forrestal, *Catholic Synods in Ireland*: 85.
123. Forrestal, *Catholic Synods in Ireland*: 126.
124. Ibid.

4   Witchcraft Accusations in Early Modern Ireland

1. The last person, Alice Molland, to be executed in England was in 1685 in Exeter, while the last conviction, of Jane Wenham, occurred in Hertfordshire in 1712.
2. Monter, 'Re-contextualizing British Witchcraft': 106; Gaskill, *Crime and Mentalities:* 79n.
3. *The Survey of Scottish witchcraft*, http://www.shc.ed.ac.uk/Research/witches/; Levack, *Witch-hunting in Scotland*: 1–2.
4. Goodare, 'Witchcraft in Scotland': 302.
5. See Chapter 5.
6. Lapoint, 'Irish Immunity to Witch-hunting': 79, 81–2; Gillespie, 'Women and Crime in Seventeenth-century Ireland': 45–7.
7. Lapoint, 'Irish Immunity to Witch-hunting': 83.
8. Ibid: 76–82.
9. Raymond Gillespie, 'Ireland', *Encyclopaedia of Witchcraft*: ii, 568.
10. Gillespie, 'Women and Crime': 43–7; idem, 'Ireland': 568.
11. Jonathan Barry, 'Introduction: Keith Thomas and the Problems of Witchcraft', in J. Barry, M. Hester, and G. Roberts (eds), *Witchcraft in Early Modern Europe: Studies in Culture and Belief* (Cambridge, 1996): 8–9. For the 'charity-refused' model, see Thomas, *Religion and the Decline of Magic*, Chapter 17, and Macfarlane, *Witchcraft in Tudor and Stuart England*.
12. See Chapter 1.

13. See Chapter 2.
14. Gaskill, *Crime and Mentalities*: 34–6, 37–8, 46–9, 55–64; idem, 'Witchcraft in Early Modern Kent: Stereotypes and the Background to Accusations', in *Witchcraft in Early Modern Europe*: 263–5, 271–6; Sharpe, *Instruments of Darkness*: 169.
15. Sally Parkin, 'Witchcraft, Women's Honour and Customary Law in Early Modern Wales', *Social History*, 31/3 (2006): 298–9.
16. See p. 63.
17. For witchcraft and old age, see p. 60. For witchcraft accusations in children and adolescents, see James Sharpe, 'Disruption in the Well-Ordered Household: Age, Authority and Possessed Young People', in Paul Griffiths, Adam Fox, and Steve Hindle (eds), *The Experience of Authority in Early Modern England* (London, 1996): 187–216. Furthermore, Lyndal Roper argues that by the end of the witch-hunts in Europe, when old women were no longer deemed credible witches, attention shifted fleetingly towards self-confessed child and adolescent witches: Lyndal Roper, 'Evil Imaginings and Fantasies: Child Witches and the end of the Witch-craze', *Past and Present*, 167/1 (2000): 107–39.
18. See pp 58, 60, 90–91.
19. See pp 61–2.
20. See Larner, *Enemies of God*.
21. Stuart MacDonald, 'Enemies of God Re-visited: Recent Publications on Scottish Witchcraft', *Scottish Economic and Social History*, 23/2 (2003): 76–7; Levack, *Witch-hunting in Scotland*, Chapter 6.
22. Levack, *Witch-hunting in Scotland*: 1, 8; Lauren Martin, 'The Devil and the Domestic: Witchcraft, Quarrels and Women's Work in Scotland', in *Scottish Witch-hunt in Context*: 74–77, 84–9; James Sharpe, 'Witch-hunting and Witch Historiography: Some Anglo-Scottish Comparisons', in ibid: 185–6; Lauren Martin, 'Some Findings from the Survey of Scottish Witchcraft', in *Witchcraft and Belief in Early Modern Scotland*: 59–61.
23. See Behringer, *Witches and Witch-Hunts*, Chapter 4; Briggs, *Witches and Neighbour*, Chapters 4–6, 8; Levack, *Witch-hunt in Early Modern Europe*, Chapters 5–6.
24. See Chapter 1 and, Sneddon, 'Witchcraft Belief and Trials in Early Modern Ireland': 10.
25. Larner, *Witchcraft and Religion*: 4; Suggett, 'Witchcraft Dynamics in Early Modern Wales': 75; Levack, *Witch-hunting in Early Modern Scotland*: 127–8. Lapoint however argues that witchcraft accusation came early to Ireland, in the fourteenth century, but this is because she regards the Kyteler case as a witchcraft trial rather than a sorcery-cum-treason plot: Lapoint, 'Irish Immunity to Witch-hunting': 77–8. For a study of the Kyteler case which argues that it represents the 'dawn of the devil-worshipping witch', see, Maeve Callan, *The Templars, the Witch, and the Wild Irish: Vengeance and Heresy in Medieval Ireland* (New York, 2015), Chapters 2–3.
26. Bath, 'Treatment of Potential Witches in North-East England': 137–9; James Sharpe, 'Witchcraft in Seventeenth-century Yorkshire: Accusations and Countermeasures', in *Borthwick Papers* (1992): 11–17; idem, *Witchcraft in Early Modern England*: 37, 52–7.

27. Copy of Ms containing collections of Sir James Ware, 4 October 1630 (Dublin City Archives [hereafter DCA], Gilbert Ms 169, ii, f. 204).
28. Thomas Jervis to Humphrey Owen, Dublin, 21 March 1668 in W.J. Smith (ed.), *Herbert Correspondence: the Sixteenth and Seventeenth-Century Letters of the Herberts of Chirbury* (Dublin, 1963).
29. See Chapter 3.
30. Sneddon, *Possessed by the Devil*: 35, 144–5.
31. Crawford Gribben, *God's Irishmen: Theological Debates in Cromwellian Ireland* (Oxford, 2007): 140.
32. Bath, 'Treatment of Suspected Witches in North-East England': 137.
33. Diocese of Killaloe Court Book, 10 August 1704 (BL, Add. Ms 31881, f. 150r.).
34. Yvonne Petry, '"Many Things Surpass our Knowledge": An Early Modern Surgeon on Magic, Witchcraft and Demonic Possession', *Social History of Medicine*, 25/1 (2011): 55.
35. Archbishop of Dublin, Michael Boyle to James Butler, duke of Ormond, 17 November 1668 (Bodleian Library, Oxford, Carte MS 36, f. 568). I thank Dr Peter Elmer for providing this source.
36. T.C. Barnard, *Cromwellian Ireland: English Government and Reform in Ireland, 1649–1660* (Oxford, 1975, repr. 2000): 66n; Aidan Clarke, *Prelude to Restoration in Ireland: the End of the Commonwealth, 1659–1660* (Cambridge, 1999): 208, 231n, 232n.
37. James Butler, duke of Ormond, to Archbishop of Dublin, Michael Boyle, 8 May 1669 (Bodleian Library, Oxford, Carte MS 50, f. 28r.).
38. R. Bolton, 'Griffith Williams, bishop of Ossory, 1641–72', *Journal of Butler Society*, 2/3 (1984): 333–4; *ODNB*.
39. Raymond Gillespie, 'The Religion of the First Duke of Ormond', in *The Dukes of Ormond*: 101–13.
40. Duke of Ormond to Captain George Matthews, 25 May 1669 (Bodleian Library, Oxford, Carte MS 50, f. 34). Thanks to Peter Elmer for providing a transcript of this letter.
41. Ohlmeyer, *Civil War and Restoration in the Three Stuart Kingdoms*: 101.
42. Suggett, *Magic and Witchcraft in Wales*: 91; Levack, *Witch-hunting in Scotland*, Chapter 4; Malcolm Gaskill, *Witchfinders: a Seventeenth-Century English Tragedy* (London, 2006).
43. For the 1641 rebellion, see: Brian Mac Cuarta, *Ulster 1641: Aspects of the Rising* (Belfast, 1993, rev. ed. 1997); Eamon Darcy, *The Irish Rebellion of 1641 and the Wars of the Three Kingdoms* (London, 2013); Joseph Cope, *England and the 1641 Irish Rebellion* (Woodbridge, 2009); John Gibney, 'Protestant Interests? The 1641 Rebellion and State Formation in Early Modern Ireland', *Historical Research*, 84/223 (2011): 67–8; Micheál Ó Siochrú, 'Civil Autonomy and Military Power in Early Modern Ireland', *Journal of Early Modern History*, 15 (2011): 37; Robert Armstrong, *Protestant War: the 'British' of Ireland and the Wars of the Three Kingdoms* (Manchester, 2006), Chapters 1 and 2; M. Perceval-Maxwell, *The Outbreak of the Irish Rebellion of 1641* (Dublin, 1994).
44. Mary O'Dowd, *A History of Women in Ireland, 1500–1800* (Harlow, 2005): 174.
45. Examination of Anne Dawson, 26 April 1653 (TCD, 1641 depositions, Ms 836, f. 228r.). For the 1641 depositions and their strengths and weakness

as a historical source, see: Eamon Darcy, Annaleigh Margey, and Elaine Murphy, *The 1641 Depositions and the Irish Rebellion* (London, 2012); Marie-Louise Coolahan, '"And this Deponent Further Sayeth": Orality, Print and the 1641 Depositions', in Marc Caball and Andrew Carpenter (eds), *Oral and Print Cultures in Ireland 1600–1900* (Dublin, 2009): 69–84; Nicholas Canny, 'What Really Happened in 1641?', in Jane H. Ohlmeyer (ed.), *Ireland from Independence to Occupation, 1641–1660* (Cambridge, 1995): 26–42.

46. McAuliffe, 'Gender, History and Witchcraft': 47–55.
47. O'Dowd, *A History of Women in Ireland*: 243, 246–7, 252.
48. For studies which proceed from the sex-specific view of witchcraft prosecution, Marianne Hester, *Lewd Women and Wicked Witches: A Study in the Dynamics of Male Domination* (London, 1992), Chapters 6–8, and Barstow, *Witchcraze: a New History of the European Witch-hunt*. Marianne Hester argues that 'using a revolutionary feminist approach it may be shown that the witch-hunts provided one means of controlling women socially within a male supremacist society, using violence or the threat of violence, and relying on a particular construct of female sexuality' (Hester, *Wicked Witches and Lewd Women*: 108). For an overview of the complex historical debates concerning gender and witchcraft, especially for those coming to it for the first time: Darren Oldridge, *The Witchcraft Reader* (London, 1st ed., 2002), Chapters 20–3; idem, *The Witchcraft Reader* (London, 2nd ed., 2008), Chapters 25–9; and Garthine Walker, 'Witchcraft and History', *Women's History Review*, 7/3 (1998): 425–32.
49. See Malcolm Gaskill, 'The Devil in the Shape of a Man: Witchcraft, Conflict and Belief in Jacobean England', *Historical Research*, 71 (1998): 144–5; idem, 'Masculinity and Witchcraft in Seventeenth-century England', in Alison Rowlands (ed.), *Witchcraft and Masculinities in Early Modern Europe* (Basingstoke, 2009): 171–2; Alison Rowlands, 'Witchcraft and Old Women in Early Modern Germany', *Past and Present*, 173 (2001): 50–8; Peter Maxwell-Stuart, 'Witchcraft and Magic in Eighteenth Century Scotland', *Beyond the Witch-Trials*: 83.
50. Karen Jones and Michael Zell, '"The Divels Speciall Instruments": Women and Witchcraft before the "Great Witch-Hunt"', *Social History*, 30/1 (2005): 45–63; Frances Timbers, 'Witches' Sect or Prayer meeting? Matthew Hopkins Revisited', *Women's History Review*, 17/1 (2008): 21–37.
51. Examination of Elleanor Stringer, 8 August 1653 (TCD, 1641 depositions, Ms 826, ff. 243r.–243v.).
52. Examination of Elleanor Stringer, 8 August 1653 (TCD Ms 826, f. 244r.).
53. Ibid.
54. Maxwell, *Outbreak of the Irish Rebellion*: 232. See also, Mary O'Dowd, 'Women and War in Ireland in the 1640s', in *Women in Early Modern Ireland*: 92, 94–6.
55. Ohlmeyer, *Civil War and Restoration in the Three Stuart Kingdoms*: 107–8; Colin Breen, *Dunluce Castle: History and Archaeology* (Dublin, 2012): 164, 167–9; Armstrong, *Protestant War*: 33.
56. Examination of Allen McRee, 9 March 1653 (TCD, 1641 depositions, Ms 838, ff 73r–73v). See also, Raymond Gillespie, *Colonial Ulster: the Settlement of East Ulster 1600–1641* (Cork, 1985): 161. For Archibald Stewart, see: Ohlmeyer, *Civil War and Restoration in the Three Stuart Kingdoms*: 23, 41, 49n, 57, 65n, 75n, 106–7.

57. Examination of John McCart, 15 March 1653 (TCD, 1641 depositions, Ms 838, f. 79r.).
58. Raymond Gillespie, 'Destabilising Ulster, 1641–2', in *Ulster 1641*:116–18.
59. For a discussion of this case: Dianne Purkiss, 'Desire and its Deformities: Fantasies of Witchcraft in the English Civil War', *The Journal of Medieval and Early Modern Studies*, 27/1(1997): 103–5; Gaskill, *Crime and Mentalities*: 47; idem, *Witchfinders*: 147–8.
60. Anon, *A Most Certain, Strange, and True Discovery of a Witch. Being Taken by some of the Parliament Forces, as she was standing on a Small Planck Board and Sayling on it on the River of Newbury ...* (1643): 3–7; Purkiss, 'Desire and Its Deformities': 103–4.
61. Hugh Trevor-Roper, *The European Witch-Craze of the Sixteenth and Seventeenth Centuries* (London, 1969): 177.
62. Trevor-Roper, *Witch-Craze*: 160; Sharpe, *Instruments of Darkness*: 176; Gaskill, *Crime and Mentalities*: 48.
63. Jonathan B. Durrant, *Witchcraft, Gender and Society in Early Modern Germany* (Boston, 2007), xiii–xiv; Rowlands, 'Witchcraft and Old Women': 50–1; Edward Bever, 'Old Age and Witchcraft in Early Modern Europe', in Peter N. Stearns (ed.), *Old Age in Pre-Industrial Europe* (New York, 1982): 157, 178, 181.
64. Rowlands, 'Witchcraft and Old Women': 88.
65. Bever, 'Old Age and Witchcraft in Early Modern Europe': 154–90.
66. Lyndal Roper, *Witch-Craze: Terror and Fantasy in Baroque Germany* (New Haven, 2004): 177.
67. James Turner, 'Memoirs of his Own Life and Times, 1632–70', ed. T. Thomson (Edinburgh, 1829): 22; *ODNB*. See also, Thomas Fitzpatrick, *The Bloody Bridge, and Other Papers Relating to the Insurrection of 1641 ...* (Dublin, 1903): 127, and 'Proceedings of the Scottish and English Forces in the North of Ireland, A.D. 1642', *Ulster Journal of Archaeology*, first series, 8 (1860): 85.
68. See Chapter 1, and Chapter 5.
69. O'Dowd, *A History of Women in Ireland*: 251. See also, Andrea Knox, '"Barbarous and Pestiferous Women": Female Criminality, Violence and Aggression in Sixteenth- and Seventeenth-century Scotland and Ireland', Yvonne Galloway Brown and Rona Ferguson, *Twisted Sisters: Women, Crime and Deviance in Scotland since 1400* (Phantassie, East Lothian, 2002): 21–5.
70. See Peter Elmer, 'Towards a Politics of Witchcraft in Early Modern England', in *Languages of Witchcraft*: 103–10.
71. See Micheál Ó Siochrú, *Confederate Ireland 1641–1649: A Constitutional and Political Analysis* (Dublin, 1999, repr. 2008), and Pádraig Lenihan, *Confederate Catholics at War, 1641–9* (Cork, 2001).
72. See Chapter 2.
73. Arthur Annesley and William Beale, to the committee of both houses, Belfast, 12 January 1646, in Charles McNeil (ed.), *The Tanner Letters: Original Documents and Notices of Irish Affairs in the Sixteenth and Seventeenth-Centuries* (Dublin, 1943): 206.
74. Sharpe, *Witchcraft in Early Modern England*: 24–5, 27–31; idem, *Instruments of Darkness*: 233; idem, *The Betwitching of Anne Gunter* (London, 2001): 71; Levack, *Witch-hunting in Scotland*: 27; Malcolm Gaskill, 'Witchcraft and Evidence in Early Modern England', *Past and Present*, 198 (2008): 39–45.

75. For the witch-hunting activities of Matthew Hopkins in East Anglia in the 1640s, see Gaskill, *Witchfinders*, and James Sharpe, 'The Devil in East Anglia: the Matthew Hopkins Trials Reconsidered', in *Witchcraft in Early Modern Europe*: 237–54. For a study which places gender conflict at the centre of the first set of accusations handled by Hopkins, see Timbers, 'Witches' Sect or Prayer Meeting?': 21–37.

76. Sharpe, *Instruments of Darkness*: 128–46, 215–16, 227–34; Davies, *Witchcraft, Magic and Culture*: 79–84.

77. See Chapter 6.

78. Levack, *Witch-hunting in Scotland*: 4, 17–30, 135–9.

79. Garnham, 'Crime, Policing and the Law': 91.

80. See Chapter 5.

81. Davies, *Witchcraft, Magic and Culture*: 82.

82. Christopher Crofts to Sir John Perceval, 15 March 1686 in *HMC, Egmont Manuscripts* (2 vols, Dublin, 1909), ii, 181).

83. Crofts to Perceval, 15 March 1686 in *HMC*: 182.

84. See Chapter 5.

85. Sharpe, *Witchcraft in Early Modern England*: 45; Gaskill, *Crime and Mentalities*: 57–8; Rowlands, 'Witchcraft and Old Women': 79–85; Bath, 'Potential Witches in North-East': 135–6.

86. Sharpe, *Instruments of Darkness*, Chapter 7.

87. Holmes, 'Women: Witnesses and Witches': 45–8.

88. Crofts to Perceval, 15 March 1686: 182.

89. Garnham, *Courts, Crime and the Criminal Law*: 104.

90. Elmer, *Miraculous Conformist*: 132–3. See also Chapter 5.

91. Memoirs of Roger Boyle, first earl of Orrery, c.1558/9 (BL, Sloane Ms 4227, f. 81r.). Thanks to Dr Peter Elmer for providing this reference.

92. Davies, *Popular Magic*: 106, 108; Almond, *Demonic Possession*: 16.

93. For more on this, especially in relation to the Islandmagee witch case of 1711, see Chapter 5.

94. See Chapter 5.

95. Transcript of Commonwealth papers, 9 February, 15 November 1656 (Allen Library, Dublin, Jennings Ms J2/Box 263, item 14); St. John D. Seymour, *The Puritans in Ireland, 1647–61* (Oxford, 1912, repr. Oxford, 1969): 140–1.

96. Owen Davies, 'Decriminalising the Witch: The Origin and Response to the 1736 Witchcraft Act', in *Witchcraft and the Act of 1604*: 209.

97. See, Bishop Hutchinson's Commonplace book, 1721–30 (PRONI, MS DIO/1/22/1, 'witchcraft' page); Killaloe Court Book, 10 August 1704 (BL, Add. Ms 31881, f. 150r.).

98. Archbishop William King to Cotton Mather [?], 3 Oct. 1693 (TCD, Archbishop King papers Ms 1995-2008/300).

99. Julian Goodare, 'Witch-hunting and the Scottish State', in *Scottish Witch-hunt in Context*: 139; Davies, 'Decriminalising the Witch': 209–10; Maxwell-Stuart, 'Witchcraft and Magic in Scotland': 85.

100. For how slander cases in relation to witchcraft and popular magic were handled in Church of England church courts, see: Peter Rushton, 'Women, Witchcraft and Slander in Early Modern England: Cases from the Church Courts at Durham, 1560–1675', *Northern History* 18 (1982): 116–32.

101. See p. 54.

102. Higgs, *Wonderfull and True Relation*: 7.
103. Templepatrick minutes, 27 July 1647 (PRONI, Templepatrick Non-Subscribing Presbyterian Church Records, CR4/12/B/1: 23); Armstrong, 'The Irish Alternative': 210.
104. Antrim Presbytery minutes, 14 February 1656 (PRONI, MS D/1759/1/A/1: 93–4).
105. Mark S. Sweetnam (ed.), *The Minutes of the Ministers' Meeting 1654–8* (Dublin, 2012): 14.
106. This reading of the Kennedy/Etkin case contrasts with that of Mark Sweetnam who argues that the case is indicative of the Antrim Meetings' reluctance to deal with witchcraft because it was a 'capital crime' and did not 'fall within' its 'ambit', as well as being indicative of 'the general lack of hysteria about witchcraft in Ireland': Sweetnam, *Minutes of the Ministers' Meeting*: 17.
107. See Chapter 3.
108. Strabane Presbytery minutes, 2 July, 13 August 1718, 4 March 1719 (UTC, minutes of Strabane Presbytery, 1717–40, CR 3/26/2/1: 35, 36, 42, 88.
109. See Chapter 3.
110. Minutes of Connor Session, 5 May 1701 (PHS, Minutes of the Connor Session, 1693–1713: 11).
111. Minutes of Connor Session, 8 May 1701 (PHS, Minutes of the Connor Session, 1693–1713: 11).
112. See Chapter 5.
113. Carnmoney Session minutes, 5 April 1721 (PRONI, MIC 1P/37/4).
114. Aghadowey Session minutes, 26 November 1724 (PHS., Aghadowey Session minutes: 132).
115. Aghadowey Session minutes, 1 April 1724 (PHS., Aghadowey Session minutes: 133).
116. Strabane Presbytery minutes, 12 October 1731 (UTC, CR 3/26/2/1: 284).
117. For an articulation of this argument, see Gaskill, *Crime and Mentalities*: 50–4.
118. Alison Rowlands, 'Not "the Usual Suspects"? Male Witches, Witchcraft, and Masculinities in Early Modern Europe', in *Witchcraft and Masculinities in Early Modern Europe*: 13.
119. Davies, 'Decriminalising the Witch': 209–13; Gaskill, *Crime and Mentalities*: 118.
120. Levack, *Witch-hunt in Early Modern Europe*: 74, 289–90.
121. Higgs, *Wonderfull and True Relation*: 6–7.
122. Ibid: 8.
123. Higgs, *Wonderfull and True Relation*: 9–11.
124. See Chapters 1 and 3.
125. Adair, *A True Narrative of the Rise and Progress of the Presbyterian Church in Ireland*: 299–300; George Hughes, *Hewn from the Rock, The story of first Antrim Presbyterian Church* (Antrim, 1996): 32–3; W.S. Smith, *Historical Gleanings in Antrim and Neighbourhood* (Belfast, 1888): 32–3.
126. See Seymour, *Irish Witchcraft and Demonology*: 196; Levack, *Witch-hunting in Scotland*: 127–8.
127. Porter, *Witches, Warlocks and Ghosts*: 18–19.
128. Higgs, *Wonderfull and True Relation*: 6–8.
129. Higgs, *Wonderfull and True Relation*: 8–14. See also Chapters 1 and 3.

130. Marion Gibson, *Reading Witchcraft: Stories of Early English Witches* (London and New York, 1999): 113–17.
131. Higgs, *Wonderfull and True Relation*: 8–16.
132. Higgs, *Wonderfull and True Relation*: 3–16. See Chapter 2 for the legal steps involved in bringing a suspected witch to court.
133. Higgs, *Wonderfull and True Relation*: 7.
134. Robert Dunlop (ed.), 'Ireland Under the Commonwealth ... 1651 to 1659' (2 vols, Manchester, 1913), i, 252; Raymond Gillespie, 'The Burning of Ellen NíGilwey, 1647: a Sidelight on Popular Belief in Meath', *Journal of the County Meath Historical Society*, 10 (1999): 74.

5 Witchcraft Trials and Demonic Possession in Early Modern Ireland

1. Lapoint, 'Irish Immunity to Witch-Hunting': 77n.
2. Seymour, *Irish Witchcraft and Demonology*: 25–52, 59–61, 77–4, 105–13, 194–220.
3. See Chapters 2 and 3.
4. This figure is a corrective of a previous calculation by the author of four trials and three executions, arrived at by the inclusion of the Kilkenny witches of 1578: Sneddon, 'Witchcraft Belief and Trials in Early Modern Ireland': 17.
5. Holmes, 'Women: Witnesses and Witches': 59–65; Kathleen R. Sands, *Demon Possession in Elizabethan England* (London, 2004): 1–5; Phillip C. Almond, *Witches of Warboys: an Extraordinary Story of Sorcery, Sadism and Satanic Possession* (London, 2008): 25–7; idem, *Demonic Possession*: 1–2, 26–37; Ivan Bunn and Gilbert Geis, *A Trial of Witches: a Seventeenth-century Witchcraft Prosecution* (London, 1997): 65–6; Sharpe, *Anne Gunter*: 7–9, 139–42; idem, *Instruments of Darkness*: 195; Brian P. Levack, *The Devil Within: Possession and Exorcism in the Christian West* (Yale, 2013), Chapters 1–2; A. Cambers, 'Demonic Possession, Literacy and Superstition in Early Modern England', *Past and Present*, 202/1 (2009): 13–14. For a discussion of how early modern witchcraft writers dealt with possession see, Clark, *Thinking With Demons*, Chapters 26–8, and Clive Holmes, 'Witchcraft and Possession at the Accession of James I: the Publication of Samuel Harsnett's A Declaration of Egregious Popish Impostures', in *Witchcraft and the Act of 1604*: 69–90.
6. Almond, *Demonic Possession*: 14–17, 24; idem, *Witches of Warboys*: 44; Holmes, 'Women: Witnesses and Witches': 62; Sharpe, *Anne Gunter*: 145.
7. Levack, *Demon Within*: 3.
8. Almond, *Demonic Possession*: 1, 22–3. For more on demonic possession and gender, see Sarah Ferber, 'Possession and the Sexes', in *Witchcraft and Masculinities in Early Modern Europe*: 214–38.
9. See Anon, *The Most Strange and Admirable Discoverie of the Witches of Warboys* ... (London, 1593); Almond, *Witches of Warboys*; idem, *Demonic Possession*, Chapter 3.
10. Thomas, *Religion and the Decline of Magic*: 479; Sharpe, *Anne Gunter*: 141–2.
11. Thomas, *Religion and the Decline of Magic*: 478. See also, Michelle Marshman, 'Exorcism as Empowerment: a New Idiom', *The Journal of Religious History*, 23/3 (1999): 269–71.

12. Thomas, *Religion and the Decline of Magic*: 478–9; Sharpe, *Anne Gunter*: 142–3, 146–7, 152; idem, *Instruments of Darkness*: 194. For the use in early modern Europe of demonic possession and exorcism in anti-Protestant Propaganda and as a way to target moderate Catholics, see: Jonathan L. Pearl, *The Crime of Crimes: Demonology and Politics in France 1560–1620* (Ontario, 1999): 42–51.

13. Sands, *Demon Possession*, Chapter 13; Marion Gibson, *Possession, Puritanism and Print* (London, 2006): 1–5; Thomas, *Religion and the Decline of Magic*: 485–7; Sharpe, *Anne Gunter*: 147–53; idem, *Instruments of Darkness*: 194–5. De-possession was used in a number of seventeenth-century possessions, including those of Richard Rothwell and John Fox (1612), the children of George Muschamp (1650), and Richard Dugdale (1690). For Dugdale, see Hutchinson, *An Historical Essay Concerning Witchcraft*: 124–8, while for the Muschamp children, see Almond, *Demonic Possession*, Chapter 3.

14. Anon, *Sadducismus Debellatus, or a True Narrative of the Sorceries and Witchcrafts Exercis'd by the Devil and his Instruments Upon Mrs Christian Shaw …* (London, 1698): 1–38; Levack, *Witch-hunting in Scotland*, Chapter 7. Levack's research into the Shaw case builds on issues first raised in an article by Hugh McLachlan and Kim Swales, 'The Bewitchment of Christian Shaw: A Reassessment of the Famous Paisley Witchcraft Case of 1697', in *Twisted Sisters*: 54–83. For a discussion of late seventeenth-century anti-Sadduceeism demonology, see Chapter 3.

15. Exceptions are Gillespie, *Devoted People*: 7, 67–8, 76, 120, 161, and Sneddon, *Possessed by the Devil*.

16. Gillespie, *Devoted People*: 7.

17. Ibid.

18. Dunton, *The Dublin Scuffle*: 333–5; Gillespie, *Devoted People*: 7.

19. Dunton, *The Dublin Scuffle*: 333.

20. Robert Blair, 'The Life of Mr Robert Blair, minister of St Andrews, Containing his Autobiography, from 1593 to 1636 …', ed. Thomas McCrie (Edinburgh, 1848): 89; Thomas Witherow, *Historical and Literary Memorials of Presbyterianism in Ireland* (London and Belfast, 1879): 7–10.

21. Copy of Ms containing collections of Sir James Ware, 25 March 1630 (DCA Gilbert Ms 169, ii, f. 200).

22. 'The "Brevis Relatio" of the Irish Discalced Carmelites, 1625–70', ed. Paul Browne, Marcellus Glynn, F.X. Martin, *Archivium Hibernicum*, 25 (1962): 137.

23. Sir James Ware collections, 30 August 1630 (DCA Gilbert Ms 169, ii, f. 202); 'The "Brevis Relatio"': 138.

24. Mark Empey, '"We are not yet Safe, for they Threaten us with More Violence": a Study of the Cook Street Riot, 1629', in William Sheehan and Maura Cronin (eds), *Riotous Assemblies: Rebels, Riots and Revolts in Ireland* (Dublin, 2011): 64–76. For Andrea Knox however there is nothing overtly political, harsh or unorthodox about Browne's treatment at the hands of Protestant authorities. She argues instead that the case demonstrates 'the apparent liberality of imported judges and courts' who were unable to decide who was worthy of more censure, the girl who had faked her possession or a Catholic priest: Andrea Knox, 'Female Criminality and Subversion in Early Modern Ireland', in Louis A. Knafla (ed.), *Crime, Gender and Sexuality in Criminal Prosecutions* (London, 2002): 230. This reading however does not take into account the dictates of the 1586 Witchcraft Act, the political

context surrounding the trial, and the legal limitations of the court in which the case was heard. Furthermore, there is no documentary evidence support- ing Knox's claim that the girl was imprisoned along with Browne.

25. Sir James Ware collections, March 1631 (DCA Gilbert Ms 169, ii, f. 205).
26. 'The "Brevis Relatio"': 138, 150–2.
27. Allan Makcouldy, *A True Perpetuall Prognostication for the Yeare 1632, being Leape Yeare, and for all Years to Come* ... (Dublin, 1632): 4. For almanacs, astrology and fortune-telling in Ireland, see Chapters 6 and 7.
28. Empey, 'A Study of the Cook Street Riot': 77.
29. 'The "Brevis Relatio"': 138. For Bolton and witchcraft, see Chapter 2.
30. Sir James Ware collections, 11 February 1635 (DCA Gilbert Ms 169, ii, f. 214).
31. Garnham, *Courts, Crime, and the Criminal Law*: 71. For the star chamber in England, see J.A. Sharpe, *Crime in Early Modern England, 1550–1750* (Edinburgh, 1999): 31.
32. Wentworth to Coke, 2 March 1635 (SCA, Strafford Letter Books, WWM/Str P/5, f. 190).
33. Wentworth to Coke, 2 March 1635 (SCA, WWM/Str P/5, f.190); Garnham, *Courts, Crime and the Criminal Law*: 72–3.
34. Jeremy Taylor, *A Dissuasive from Popery to the People of Ireland* ... (Dublin, 2nd ed., 1664): 135.
35. Taylor, *A Dissuasive from Popery to the People of Ireland*: 141.
36. Sir James Ware collections, 11 February 1635 (DCA Gilbert Ms 169, ii, f. 214); 'The "Brevis Relatio"': 138.
37. Wentworth to Coke, 2 March 1635 (SCA, WWM/Str P/5, f.190).
38. King Charles I to Thomas Wentworth, 7 August 1636 in *Calendar of State Paper Relating to Ireland of the Reign of Charles I, 1633–47* (London, 1901): 139; 'The "Brevis Relatio"': 138.
39. William Laud to John Bramhall, 1637/8 (PRONI, Transcripts, T/415/12).
40. See Chapter 4.
41. Glanvill, *Saducismus Triumphatus*: 423–7; Elmer, *Miraculous Conformist*: 128–9.
42. P.G. Maxwell Stuart, *Witch-hunters* (Stroud, 2006): 103–4; Barbara Rosen, *Witchcraft in England, 1558–1618* (Massachusetts, 1969, repr. 1991): 227.
43. Richard Baxter, *The Certainty of the World of Spirits. And Consequently, of the Immortality of Souls* ... (London, 1691): 218–20.
44. Gillespie, *Devoted People*: 118.
45. Elmer, *Miraculous Conformist*: 42, 64n39.
46. William Petty, *Reflections Upon Some Persons and Things in Ireland, by Letters to and from Dr Petty: With Sir Hierome Sankey's Speech in Parliament* (London, 1660): 101. See also, Raymond Gillespie, '"Into Another Intensity", Prayer in Irish Non-conformity, 1650–1700', in Kevin Herlihy (ed.), *The Religion of Irish Dissent, 1600–1800* (Dublin, 1996): 44.
47. Petty, *Reflections Upon Some Persons and Things*: 102.
48. For demonic possession and blood-letting, see: Sands, *Demon Possession*: 11–12.
49. See Chapter 4.
50. Seymour, *Irish Witchcraft and Demonology*: 107, 127; Lapoint, 'Irish Immunity to Witch-hunting': 75.
51. Seymour, *Irish Witchcraft and Demonology*, Chapter 5; Bob Curran, *Ireland's Witches: a Bewitched Land* (Dublin, 2005): 39–59.

52. McAuliffe, 'Gender, History and Witchcraft': 39–58. See also p. 58, and p. 82.
53. Elmer, *Miraculous Conformist*: 114, 127–32.
54. Corporation records for Youghal and Cork, which may have thrown more light on the local political elites involved in the trial, are missing for the years of 1660–1, see: 'The Council Book of the Corporation of Youghal, from 1610 to 1659, from 1666 and 1687, and from 1690 to 1800', ed. Richard Caulfield, Guildford, 1878, and 'The Council Book of the Corporation of the City of Cork, from 1609 to 1643, and from 1690 to 1800', ed. Richard Caulfield, Guildford, 1876.
55. Bragge, *Witchcraft Further Display'd*. For the trial of Jane Wenham see: P. J Guskin, 'The Context of Witchcraft: the Case of Jane Wenham (1712)', *Eighteenth-Century Studies*, 15/1 (1981): 48–71; Mark Knights, *The Devil in Disguise: Deception, Delusion and Fanaticism in Early Enlightenment Period* (Oxford, 2011), Chapter 6; and Bostridge, *Witchcraft and Transformations*: 132–8, 143–4.
56. This trial transcript has some small additional sections and is structured slightly differently to Glanvill's published account of the Youghal trial (Elmer, *Miraculous Conformist*: 127n).
57. Glanvill, *Saducismus Triumphatus*: 373–8, 384–6.
58. Ibid: 373.
59. Ibid. For early modern, popular attitudes to the Devil, in particular examples of his earthly manifestations in the form of a man: Darren Oldridge, *The Devil in Early Modern England* (2000), Chapter 4; Joyce Miller, *Magic and Witchcraft in Scotland* (Musselburgh, 2004): 86–9; P.G. Maxwell-Stuart, *Satan: A Biography* (Stroud, 2008, repr. 2011): 116–26; Philip C. Almond, *The Devil: a New Biography* (New York, 2014), Chapters 6–7.
60. Almond, *Demonic Possession*: 17–18.
61. Glanvill, *Saducismus Triumphatus*: 373–6, 378.
62. Glanvill, *Saducismus Triumphatus*: 374. See also Bragge, *Witchcraft Farther Display'd*: 16.
63. Richard Chamberlain, *Lithobolia, or, the Stone-throwing Devil. Being an Exact and True Account (by the Way of Journal) of the Actions of Infernal Spirits, or (Devils Incarnate) Witches or Both* … (London, 1698): 3–16; George Lincoln Burr (ed.), *Narratives of the New England Witchcraft Cases, 1648–1706* (New York, 1914): 53–77; Owen Davies, *The Haunted: A Social History of Ghosts* (Basingstoke, 2007): 31–2; P.G. Maxwell-Stuart, *Poltergeists: A History of Violent Ghostly Phenomena* (Stroud, 2011): 78, 110, 126–7.
64. Glanvill, *Saducismus Triumphatus*: 375, 378–9.
65. Elmer, *Miraculous Conformist*: 128.
66. Glanvill, *Saducismus Triumphatus*: 375.
67. Almond, *Demonic Possession*: 1–8; Davies, *Popular Magic*: 105–7; Sharpe, *Anne Gunter*: 141; Clark, *Thinking with Demons*: 390–1; Judith Bonzol, 'The Medical Diagnosis of Demonic Possession in an Early Modern Community', *Parergon*, 26/1 (2009): 117–20.
68. See Chapter 4.
69. Anon, *Strange and Terrible News from Ireland* … (London, 1673): 3; A second, enhanced edition appeared later, replete with further warnings against the use of profane language, and with 'severall historical instances in the like kind': Anon, *A Full Account from Ireland of the Maid at Dublin* … (London, 1700). See also, Gillespie, *Devoted People*: 108.

70. Anon, *Strange and Terrible News from Ireland*: 4; K. Theodore Hoppen, *The Common Scientist in the Seventeenth Century: a Study of the Dublin Philosophical Society, 1683–1704* (London, 1970, repr. 2013): 18–20.
71. Anon, *Strange and Terrible News from Ireland*: 4.
72. Anon, *Vertue Rewarded; Or the Irish Princess, a New Novel* (London, 1692, repr. 1992): 21. Raymond Gillespie, however, argues that this novel indicates a more general decline in belief in the devil in educated Protestant culture in the late seventeenth century (Gillespie, *Devoted People*: 41).
73. Historians of medicine and witchcraft are often wary of retrospective diagnosis because doing so involves the imposition of diagnostic labels taken from modern medicine, which can gloss over the fact that such diagnoses are often at best educated guesses based on their own, time-bound views of disease: not only does the way in which diseases are described and defined change over time, symptoms are not often described accurately or in great detail in surviving sources. Furthermore, diseases themselves may even change over time, so that symptoms from one era may not map directly onto their modern counterparts. See, John Thielmann, 'Disease or Disability? The Conceptual Relationship in Medieval and Early Modern England', in Wendy J. Turner and Tory Vandeventer Pearman (eds), *The Treatment of Disabled Persons in Medieval Europe* ... (Lewiston, New York, 2010): 200–1, and Jon Arrizabalaga, 'Problematizing Retrospective Diagnosis in the History of Disease', *Ascelpio*, 54 (2002): 55–67.
74. Almond, *Demonic Possession*, Chapter 2; Sands, *Demon Possession*, Chapter 6.
75. See Sharpe, *Anne Gunter*, and Bonzol, 'Medical Diagnosis of Demonic Possession': 115–18, 132–8.
76. [Richard Baddeley], *The Boy of Bilson* ... (London, 1622): 45–75; Hutchinson, *Historical Essay*: 217–24; Almond, *Demonic Possession*, Chapter 3.
77. Hutchinson, *Historical Essay*: 46. There is no mention of this case in *The Proceedings of the Old Bailey, 1674–1913*, http://www.oldbaileyonline.org/ [last accessed June 2014].
78. Anon, *The Tryal of Richard Hathaway Upon an Information for Being a Cheat and Imposter* ... (London, 1702): 1–30; C. L'Estrange Ewen, *Witch-hunting and Witch Trials: The Indictments for Witchcraft from the Records of 1313 Assizes Held for the Home Circuit, 1559–1736* (New York, 1929): 264–5; *ODNB*; Knights, *Devil in Disguise*: 217–19.
79. Sharpe, 'Disruption and Possessed Young People': 198–205; idem, *Anne Gunter*: 156–7. For research which explores social, cultural, and political restrictions, both in society at large and within the family itself, placed on women of all religious and ethnic backgrounds, including young Protestants servants such as Mary Longdon, in hierarchical, male-dominated, early modern Irish society, see: MacCurtain and O'Dowd, *Women in Early Modern Ireland*, Chapters 1–3, 10, 14, 18; and O'Dowd, *A History of Women in Ireland, 1500–1800*, Chapters 1, 3–4, 7.
80. Thomas, *Religion and the Decline of Magic*: 480.
81. Almond, *Demonic Possession*: 14–15, 22–6; Sharpe, 'Disruption and Possessed Young People': 118–19; Levack, *Witch-hunt in Early Modern Europe*: 139–40.
82. Gibson, *Possession, Puritanism, and Print*: 105.
83. Valletta, *Witchcraft, Magic and Superstition in England*: 45.
84. Elmer, 'Politics of Witchcraft': 104.

85. Elmer, *Miraculous Conformist*: 128–32.
86. Ibid: 128–31.
87. See Chapter 4.
88. McAuliffe, 'Gender, History and Witchcraft': 40, 48–54.
89. Glanvill, *Saducismus Triumphatus*: 383.
90. Elmer, *Miraculous Conformist*: 130.
91. Higgs, *Wonderful True Relation*: 7.
92. A term used by James Sharpe to describe the swimming test: Sharpe, *Instruments of Darkness*: 218.
93. Glanvill, *Saducismus Triumphatus*: 383.
94. Davies, *Magic, Witchcraft and Culture*: 86–91; Sharpe, *Instruments of Darkness*: 218–19; Knights, *Devil in Disguise*: 224.
95. The full narrative of the Islandmagee witchcraft trial can be found elsewhere: Porter, *Witches, Warlocks and Ghosts*: 1–12; Seymour, *Irish Witchcraft and Demonology*, 200–21; Curran, *Ireland's Witches: a Bewitched Land*: 60–79. A treatment of the trial has also been published which fictionalises substantial portions of dialogue and events, as well as names, ages and professions of people involved: McConnell, *The Witches of Islandmagee*: 2, 4–6, 10–14, 16, 17, 28, 29, 31, 34, 35, 43, 46, 47, 51, 54, 63–65, 67.
96. Anon, *The Islandmagee Witches*: 2–7; Sneddon, *Possessed by the Devil*, Chapter 1; Dixon Donaldson, *Historical, Traditional and Descriptive Account of Islandmagee* (1927, repr. Newtonabbey, 2002): 42.
97. Anon, *The Islandmagee Witches*: 8–31; Deposition of Mary Dunbar, 12 March 1711 (TCD, Transcripts of the Papers of William Molyneux, 1662–1745, Ms 883/2: 274–6); Sneddon, *Possessed by the Devil*, Chapters 2, 3, 5–7.
98. *The Fly-Post, or the Post Master*, 14 April 1711; Porter, *Witches, Warlocks and Ghosts*: 11; Sneddon, *Possessed by the Devil*, Chapter 9.
99. Sir Thomas Browne, 'Religio Medici', 1642, ed. Robin Robbins (Oxford, 1972): 32–3; Bonzol, 'Medical Diagnosis of Demonic Possession'; Almond, *Demonic Possession and Exorcism*: 2–7; Ronald C. Sawyer, '"Strangely Handled in All Her Lyms": Witchcraft and Healing in Jacobean England', *Social History*, 22/3 (1989): 461–85; Garfield Tourney, 'The Physician and Witchcraft in Restoration England', *Medical History*, 16/2 (1972): 143–55; Peter Elmer, 'Medicine, Witchcraft and the Politics of Healing in Late-seventeenth-century England', in Ole Peter Grell and Andrew Cunnigham (eds), *Medicine and Religion in Enlightenment Europe* (Aldershot, 2007): 237–40; Sharpe, *Instruments of Darkness*: 10–11, 271.
100. For an overview of the medical profession and practice in seventeenth and eighteenth-century Ireland, see Fiona Clark and James Kelly (eds), *Ireland and Medicine in the Seventeenth and Eighteenth Centuries* (Farnham, 2010), Chapters 1, 4, 5, 6, 8. See also James Kelly, 'The Emergence of Scientific and Institutional Medical Practice in Ireland, 1650–1800', in Greta Jones, Elizabeth Malcolm (eds), *Medicine, Disease and the State in Ireland* (Cork, 1999): 21–39, idem, '"Bleeding, Vomiting and Purging": the Medical Response to Ill-Health in Eighteenth-Century Ireland', in Catherine Cox and Maria Luddy (eds), *Cultures of Care in Irish Medical history, 1750–1970* (Basingstoke, 2010): 13–36, and T.C. Barnard, *A New Anatomy of Ireland: the Irish Protestants, 1649–1770* (New Haven and London): 129–42. For an overview of Presbyterian medical profession in Ulster see, Robert Whan,

The *Presbyterians in Ulster, 1680–1730* (Woodbridge, 2013), Chapter 5, while Roman Catholic physicians in Dublin are detailed in Patrick Fagan, *Catholics in a Protestant Country: the Papist Constituency in Eighteenth-century Dublin* (Dublin, 1998): 77–100. The best overview of the first charitable hospitals in Ireland can be found in Laurence M. Geary, *Medicine and Charity in Ireland, 1718–1851* (Dublin, 2004), Chapter 1.

101. OSMI, *vol. 10, Islandmagee*: 43; Anon, *The Islandmagee Witches*: 6–7; Sneddon, *Possessed by the Devil*: 34–5, 65–6.
102. Sharpe, *Instruments of Darkness*: 199, 222–6; Sneddon, *Possessed by the Devil*, Chapter 2; Knights, *Devil in Disguise*: 224.
103. Anon, *The Islandmagee Witches*: 10.
104. Deposition of Dunbar, 12 March 1711 (TCD Ms 883/2: 275).
105. Sneddon, *Possessed by the Devil*: 52–61.
106. Anon, *The Islandmagee Witches*: 12–28; Examinations and Depositions, March 1711 (TCD, Ms 883/2: 273–85); Sneddon, *Possessed by the Devil*, Chapters 2, 3, 5, 7. For Bolton's book, see Chapter 2.
107. Sneddon, *Possessed by the Devil*, Chapter 6.
108. Levack, *Scottish Witch-hunting*: 115–128, 145–58; Maxwell-Stuart, 'Witchcraft and Magic in Scotland': 84–5; idem, *Witch-hunters: Professional Prickers, Unbewitchers and Witch Finders of the Renaissance* (Stroud, 2003, repr., 2006), Chapter 4; Sharpe, *Anne Gunter*: 7–8, 62–3; Demos, *Entertaining Satan*; Karlsen, *Devil in the Shape of a Woman*; Sands, *Demon Possession*, Chapter 11; Almond, *Demonic Possession*: 38–9, 240–3; Raymond Gillespie, 'The World of Andrew Rowan: Economy and Society in Restoration Antrim', in Brenda Collins, Philip Ollerenshaw and Trevor Parkhill (eds), *Industry, Trade and People in Ireland, 1690–1750: Essays in Honour of W.H. Crawford* (Belfast, 2005): 18.
109. Examinations and Depositions, March 1711 (TCD, Ms 883/2: 273–85).
110. Anon, *The Islandmagee Witches*: 11.
111. Samuel Molyneux to Thomas Molyneux, 14 May 1711 (TCD, Ms 889, f.31v).
112. Tisdall, 'Account of the Trial': 48.
113. Anon, *The Islandmagee Witches*: 13, 16, 22–3, 11. See also, Sneddon, *Possessed by the Devil*: 14–16.
114. Samuel McSkimmin, *The History and Antiquities of the County of the Town of Carrickfergus* (Belfast, 2nd ed., 1823): 75–7; Hayton, *Ruling Ireland*: 202; Sneddon, *Possessed by the Devil*, Chapter 9.
115. Tisdall, 'Account of the Trial': 50; Hayton, *Ruling Ireland*: 202; Sneddon, *Possessed by the Devil*: 153–5.
116. Tisdall, 'Account of the Trial': 50.
117. Sharpe, *Instruments of Darkness*: 191, 226. For a detailed account of this trial see Geis and Bunn, *A Trial of Witches*.
118. Ball, *Judges in Ireland, 1221–1921*, ii, 17, 23, 51–2, 66–7.
119. Anon, *The Islandmagee Witches*: 32–3; Tisdall, 'Account of the Trial': 47, 49.
120. Anon, *The Islandmagee Witches*: 33.
121. See, Rowlands, *Witchcraft and Masculinities in Early Modern Europe*, Chapters 1, 3, 6, 7; idem, *Witchcraft Narratives in Germany: Rothenburg, 1561–1652* (Manchester, 2003): 160–1; Rolf Schulte, *Man as Witch: Male Witches in Central Europe* (Basingstoke, 2009): 246–50; Karlsen, *Devil in the*

Shape of a Woman: 40; Lara Apps and Andrew Gow, *Male Witches in Early Modern Europe* (Manchester, 2003), Chapters 1, 2, 5.

122. Robert Walinski-Kiehl, 'Males, "Masculine Honour", and Witch Hunting in Seventeenth-century Germany', *Men and Masculinities*, 6/3 (2004): 265.
123. Gaskill, 'Masculinity and Witchcraft in Seventeenth-century England': 182.
124. Anon, *The Islandmagee Witches*: 33.
125. Almond, *Demonic Possession*: 42.
126. Anon, *The Islandmagee Witches*: 33.
127. Normand and Roberts, *Witchcraft in Early Modern Scotland*: 135–6, 138–9; *Survey of Scottish Witchcraft Database*; P.G. Maxwell-Stuart, *Satan's Conspiracy: Magic and Witchcraft in Sixteenth-Century Scotland* (East Linton, 2001): 142–6.
128. For Sir Patrick Dun, see: J.D.H. Widdess, *A History of the Royal College of Physicians of Ireland, 1654–1963* (Dublin, 1963), and T.P.C. Kilpatrick, *Sir Patrick Dun* (Dublin, 1945).
129. Goodare, 'The Scottish Witchcraft Panic of 1597': 51–72; idem, 'The Framework for Scottish Witch-hunting in the 1590s', *The Scottish Historical Review*, 81/212 (2002): 247–50; idem, 'The Aberdeenshire Witchcraft Panic of 1597', *Northern Scotland*, 21 (2001): 17–38; *Survey of Scottish Witchcraft Database*; *The Miscellany of The Spalding Club* (5 vols, Aberdeen, 1841–52), i, 164–7, 169–70; idem, v, 66; *Memoir of Sir Patrick Dun ... ed. T.W. Belcher (Dublin, 2nd ed., 1866): 15–18; William Temple, *The Thanage of Fermartyn ...* (Aberdeen, 1894): 538–40; Lauren Martin, 'Scottish Witchcraft Panics Re-examined', in *Witchcraft and Belief in Early Modern Scotland*: 119; Levack, *Witch-hunting in Scotland*: 41–2.
130. Seymour, *Irish Witchcraft and Demonology*: 147–8; Gillespie, 'Women and Crime in Seventeenth-century Ireland': 45; John Millar, A *History of the Witches of Renfrewshire. Who were burned on the Gallow Green of Paisley* (Paisley, 1809): 41–7; *Survey of Scottish Witchcraft Database*.
131. Cotton Mather, *Memorable Providences Relating to Witchcrafts and Possessions ...* (Boston, 1689): 1–44; Seymour, *Irish Witchcraft and Demonology*, Chapter 7; David Harley, 'Explaining Salem: Calvinist Psychology and the Diagnosis of Possession', *The American Historical Review*, 101/2 (1996): 307–30; David D. Hall (ed.), *Witch-hunting in Seventeenth Century New England: A Documentary History, 1638–1693* (Durham, NC, 2005): 266; Karlsen, *Devil in the Shape of a Woman*: 33–5, 51, 232–33, 244, 260; Demos, *Entertaining Satan*: 7–9, 71, 75, 280.

6 Witchcraft in Modern Ireland: After the Trials

1. Davies, '*Decriminalising the Witch*': 207–9; Levack, '*Witch-hunting in Scotland*', Chapter 8; idem, '*Witch-hunt in Early Modern Europe*', Chapter 8; Sharpe, *Instruments of Darkness*, Chapter 9; idem, *Witchcraft in Early Modern England*, Chapter 5; Behringer, *Witches and Witch-hunts*: 186–9; Cameron, *Enchanted Europe*, Chapter 17; Brian P. Levack, 'The Decline and End of Witchcraft Prosecutions', in Marijke Gijswijt-Hofstra and Roy Porter (eds), *The Athlone History of Witchcraft and Magic in Europe: Volume 5, the Eighteenth*

and Nineteenth Centuries (London, 1999): 3–33; Edward Bever, 'Witchcraft Prosecutions and the Decline of Magic', *Journal of Interdisciplinary History*, 40/2 (2009): 264–72, 291–2. Bever also suggests that the decline in witchcraft trials occurred as a result of a questioning in European culture of the level of threat witchcraft was believed to pose. This was in its turn engendered by a general crisis of authority in the seventeenth century, increased secularisation in legal and political administrations, and ongoing social, economic, and technological change and improvement: idem, 292.

2. See, Trevor-Roper, *Witch-Craze*: 97–112; Thomas, *Religion and the Decline of Magic*, Chapters 18, 22; Barbara Shapiro, *Probability and Certainty in Seventeenth-Century England* (Princeton, 1983), Chapter 6; Joseph Klaits, *Servants of Satan: The Age of the Witch-hunts* (Bloomington, 1985): 173–5; and Brian Easlea, *Witch-hunting, Magic, and the New Philosophy: An Introduction to Debates of the Scientific Revolution, 1450–1750* (Suffolk, 1980): 197.

3. Bostridge, *Witchcraft and its Transformations*: 4; Bever, 'Witchcraft Prosecutions and the Decline of Magic': 264; Levack, 'Witch-hunt in Early Modern Europe': 266; Barry, *Witchcraft and Demonology in South-west England*: 4; Michael Hunter, 'The Royal Society and the Decline of Magic', *Notes and Records of The Royal Society*, 65 (2011): 1–12; Peter Elmer, 'Science and Witchcraft', in *Oxford Handbook of Witchcraft*: 555–8; Clark, *Thinking with Demons*, Chapters 10, 19; Roy Porter, 'Witchcraft and Magic in Enlightenment, Romantic and Liberal Thought', in *Athlone History of Witchcraft and Magic in Europe*: 197–9.

4. Michael Wasser, 'The Mechanical World-view and the Decline of Witch-beliefs in Scotland', in *Witchcraft and Belief in Early Modern Scotland*: 206–26. For a critique of Wasser based on a misinterpretation of 'scientific' change in early modern Scotland, see Elmer, 'Science and Witchcraft': 558n.

5. Levack, *Witchcraft in Early Modern Europe*: 268. See also idem, 'The Decline and End of Witchcraft Prosecutions': 36–40.

6. Sharpe, *Witchcraft in Early Modern England*: 79.

7. Levack, *Witch-hunt in Early Modern Europe*: 270–1.

8. Sharpe, *Instruments of Darkness*, Chapter 10; idem, *Witchcraft in Early Modern England*: 82–5; Porter, *Enlightenment*: 99–105, 219–23; idem, 'Witchcraft and Magic in Enlightenment, Romantic and Liberal Thought': 199–204, 240–2; Phillip C. Almond, *Heaven and Hell in Enlightenment England* (Cambridge, 1994); Paul C. Davies, 'The Debate on Eternal Punishment in late Seventeenth and Eighteenth-century English Literature', *Eighteenth-century Studies*, 4/3 (1971): 257–76; D.P. Walker, *The Decline of Hell: Seventeenth-century Discussions of Eternal Torment* (London, 1964).

9. Maxwell-Stuart, 'Witchcraft and Magic in Scotland': 81–95.

10. Knights, *Devil in Disguise*: 240.

11. Bostridge, *Witchcraft and its Transformations*: 107–63. See also, Sneddon, *Witchcraft and Whigs*, Chapter 5. Peter Elmer anticipated Bostridge's thesis by suggesting that witchcraft discourse was marginalised in educated culture after the Restoration due to its politicisation during the previous decade, which rendered it incapable of use as a tool to forge unity or consensus in the body politic: Peter Elmer, '"Saints or Sorcerers": Quakerism, Demonology and the Decline of Witchcraft in Seventeenth-century England', in *Witchcraft in Early Modern Europe*: 145–82.

12. Ian Bostridge 'Witchcraft Repealed', in *Witchcraft in Early Modern Europe*: 316. See also, idem, *Witchcraft and Whigs*, Chapter 7.
13. Michael Hunter, 'The Decline of Magic: Challenge and Response in Early Enlightenment England', *Historical Journal*, 55/2 (2012): 399–425. See also, idem, 'Witchcraft and the Decline of Belief', *Eighteenth Century Life*, 22 (1998): 144–6.
14. Davies, 'Decriminalising the Witch': 214.
15. Davies, *Witchcraft, Magic and Culture*: 8.
16. Ibid: 7.
17. Owen Davies, 'Methodism, the Clergy, and the Popular Belief in Witchcraft and Magic', *History*, 82/266 (1997): 255, 257–8, 260, 263–4, 266; idem, *Witchcraft, Magic and Culture*: 12–17, 76.
18. Young, *English Catholics and the Supernatural*, Chapter 5.
19. Gaskill, *Crime and Mentalities*: 107.
20. Gaskill, *Crime and Mentalities*: 118. For a 'breakdown' of the 'stereotyped polarities between "believers" (the great majority) and "sceptics" (a beleaguered minority)' and one that emphasises 'the partial hold of witchcraft beliefs even in the most intense periods of witch-hunting' see, Barry, *Witchcraft and Demonology in South-west England*: 4.
21. Davies, *Witchcraft, Magic and Culture*, chapters 2–4; See also, Behringer, *Witches and Witch-hunts*: 186–8, 194; Marijke Gijswijt-Hofstra, 'Witchcraft after the Witch Trials': 97, 105–18, 146–54, 157–62, 170–4; Bushaway, 'Tacit, Unsuspected, but Still Implicit Faith: Alternative Belief in Nineteenth-century Rural England': 201–5.
22. Owen Davies, *America Bewitched: The Story Witchcraft after Salem* (Oxford, 2013), Chapter 1.
23. Suggett, *Magic and Witchcraft in Wales*: 84, 107–12, 116, 136.
24. Davies, 'Decriminalising the Witch': 213, 232; Sharpe, *Witchcraft in Early Modern England*: 83.
25. Davies, *Witchcraft, Magic and Culture*: 93–116, 193.
26. For a summary of this historiography see, Porter, 'Witchcraft and Magic in Enlightenment, Romantic and Liberal Thought': 207, 211.
27. Davies, 'Decriminalising the Witch': 218–28; Bostridge 'Witchcraft Repealed': 317–34. See also, idem, *Witchcraft and its Transformations*, Chapter 8.
28. Connolly, *Priests and People*: 16–17, 111; Correll, 'Believers, Sceptics and Charlatans': 1–2.
29. Maureen Wall, 'The Penal Laws 1691–1760', in Gerald O'Brien and Tom Dunne (eds), *Catholic Ireland in the Eighteenth Century: Collected Essays of Maureen Wall* (Dublin, 1989): 17–30; McNally, *Parties, Patriots and Undertakers*: 26. For more on the Penal Laws see Chapter 1.
30. Thomas Bartlett, *The Fall and Rise of the Irish Nation: The Catholic Question 1690–1830* (Dublin, 1992): 24–9; Connolly, *Religion, Law, and Power*: 287–90; Patrick J. Corish, *The Irish Catholic Experience: A Historical Survey* (Dublin, 1985): 123–6; Patrick Fagan, *Divided Loyalties: the Question of the Oath for Irish Catholics in the Eighteenth Century* (Dublin, 1997): 72, 74; Michael A. Mullet, *Catholics in Britain and Ireland, 1558–1829* (London, 1998): 135–7; McBride, *Eighteenth Century Ireland*, Chapter 6.
31. Connolly, *Religion, Law, Power*: 154–5; Michael P. Carroll, *Irish Pilgrimage: Holy Wells and Popular Catholic Devotion* (Baltimore and London, 1999): 23–4,

30, 44–6; Ronan Foley, *Healing Waters: Therapeutic Landscapes in Historic and Contemporary Ireland* (2010): 20–23, 29–34. Foley argues that belief in the curative power of wells continued into the twenty-first century: idem, Chapter 2.

32. David Miller, 'Irish Catholicism and the Great Famine', *Journal of Social History*, 9 (1975): 81–98; Kevin Whelan, 'The Regional Impact of Irish Catholicism, 1700–1850', in W.J. Smyth and Kevin Whelan (eds), *Common Ground: Essays in the Historical Geography of Ireland presented to T. Jones Hughes* (Cork, 1998): 253–77; James O'Shea, *Priest, Politics, and Society in Post Famine Ireland: A Study of Co. Tipperary, 1850–1891* (New Jersey, 1983), Chapter 1; Corish, *Irish Catholic Experience*: 151–91; Emmet Larkin, 'The Devotional Revolution in Ireland, 1850–75', *American Historical Review*, 77/3 (1972): 625–52; Ambrose McCauley, *William Crolly: Archbishop of Armagh, 1835–49* (Dublin, 1994): 111–12; Sean Connolly, *Religion and Society in Nineteenth-Century Ireland* (Dundalk, 1985, repr. 1994), idem, *Priests and People*: 112–27; Timothy G. McMahon, 'Religion and Popular Culture in Nineteenth-century Ireland', *History Compass*, 5/3 (2007): 845–64; John Newsinger, 'The Catholic Church in Nineteenth Century Ireland', *European History Quarterly*, 25 (1995): 247–67.

33. Connolly, *Priests and People*: 17.

34. Gijswijt-Hofstra, 'Witchcraft after the Witch Trials': 141–4; Catherine Cox, 'The Medical Marketplace and Medical Tradition in Nineteenth Century Ireland', in Ronnie Moore and Stuart McClean (eds), *Folk Healing and Health Care Practices in Britain and Ireland: Stethoscopes, Wands and Crystals* (Oxford and New York, 2010): 56; Simon Young, 'Some Notes on Irish Fairy Changelings in Nineteenth-Century Newspapers', *Béascna* 8 (2013): 34–47; Correll, 'Believers and Sceptics, and Charlatans': 1–3; Bourke, *Burning of Bridget Cleary*, Chapter 2; Seymour, *Irish Witchcraft and Demonology*, Chapter 9; J.T. Westropp, 'A Study of the Folklore on the Coast of Connacht, Ireland (Continued)', *Folklore*, 33/4 (1922): 389; Francis McPolin, 'Fairy Lore in the Hilltown District Co. Down', *Ulster Folklife*, 9 (1963): 80–8; Jenkins, 'Witches and Fairies': 33–56; idem, 'Transformations of Biddy Early': 165; Connolly, *Priests and People*: 16–17, 72–4, 114–15. Diarmuid Ó Gioilláin has argued that in Irish-Catholic popular culture belief in fairies and witches, along with other aspects of the non-christian supernatural, declined dramatically after the Great Famine of the 1840s, first among the rising Catholic middle class and then among the Catholic rural poor. This decline has been attributed to changes in the Irish economy, agriculture, the nature of popular religion, and educational provision (Ó Gioilláin, 'Fairy Belief and Official Religion': 205–8). For a discussion of continuing belief in popular magic in Ireland in the eighteenth and nineteenth centuries, see Chapter 7.

35. Edward MacLysaght, *Irish Life in the Seventeenth-Century* (Cork, 2nd ed., 1950): 177; Ignatius Murphy, *The Diocese of Killaloe in the Eighteenth Century* (Dublin, 1991): 201; idem, *Diocese of Killaloe, 1850–1904* (Dublin, 1995): 279; Connolly, *Priests and People*: 113–14; Jenkins, 'Witches and Fairies': 42.

36. Elaine Farrell, *'A Most Diabolical Deed': Infanticide and Irish Society, 1850–1900* (Manchester, 2013): 30.

37. See, Bourke, *Burning of Bridget Cleary*.

38. Young, 'Some Notes on Irish Fairy Changelings': 34–47; Connolly, *Priests and People*: 114.
39. Andrew Sneddon and John Privilege (eds), 'The Supernatural in Ulster Scots Folklore and Literature Reader': 41–50, http://www.arts.ulster.ac.uk/ulster-scots/works/supernatural/ [last accessed May 2014].
40. Jenkins, 'Witches and Fairies': 37–40. See also: G.W. Saunderson, 'Butterwitches and Cow Doctors', *Ulster Folklife*, 7 (1961): 72–3; J.T. Westropp, 'A Folklore Survey of County Clare (Continued)', *Folklore*, 22/4 (1911): 449; Kevin Danhaher, *In Ireland Long Ago* (Cork, 1962): 103; and, idem, *The Year in Ireland: Irish Calendar Customs* (Cork, 1972): 100–19.
41. See also Chapter 7.
42. For the link between the evil-eye and butter-stealing witches, see pp 102, 104 and Chapter 1.
43. Cited in Mary Jane Cryan Pancani, 'Ireland in 1787: an Italian View', *Books Ireland*, 3 (1987): 52.
44. Thomas Crofton Croker, *Researches in the South of Ireland ...* (1824, repr. Dublin, 1969): 92; *DIB*. For a critical discussion of Croker's work, see: Bo Almqvist, 'Irish Migratory Legends on the Supernatural: Sources Studies and Problems', *Béaloideas*, 59 (1991): 5, 8–9.
45. Croker, *Researches in the South of Ireland*: 93.
46. Ibid: 94.
47. Croker, *Researches in the South of Ireland*: 94.
48. Anon, 'Crofton Croker's Fairy Legends', *The Dublin Penny Journal*, 3/125 (1834): 163.
49. The OSMI are parish accounts collated in the 1830s to accompany the new 6-inch ordnance Survey Maps. The project was abandoned before completion and consequently the OSMI only covers parishes in the North of Ireland.
50. OSMI, J. Stokes, 1835, *Parishes of Londonderry XIII, vol. 3, Parish of Clandermot*: 32.
51. OSMI, C.W. Ligar, July 1836, *Parishes of Londonderry I, vol. 6, Parish of Termoneeny*: 126.
52. For more examples, see Chapter 7.
53. *Cork Examiner*, 5 July 1844.
54. W.R. Wilde, *Irish Popular Superstitions* (Dublin, 1852): 50–1, 54–9. For similar descriptions of the methods employed by witches to steal butter in the north of Ireland in the nineteenth century, see: OSMI, J. Butler Williams, J. Bleakly, C.W. Ligar, May 1835, *Parishes of County Londonderry II, vol. 9, Parish of Drumachose*: 126; Hugh Dorian, *The Outer Edge of Ulster: A Memoir of Social Life in Nineteenth-century Donegal*, eds. Breandán Mac Suibhne and David Dickson (Dublin, 2000): 259.
55. *Nenagh Guardian*, 26 October 1864.
56. William Smith O'Brien, Ms Paper on the Traditions of the Irish Peasantry [n.d., c.1858?] (NLI, Ms G 1,252 (1)). For William Smith O'Brien, see: Robert Sloan, *William Smith O'Brien and the Young Ireland Rebellion of 1848* (Dublin, 2000); Richard P. Davies, *Revolutionary Imperialist: William Smith O'Brien, 1803–64* (Dublin, 1998); and Carmel Heaney, *William Smith O'Brien, 1803–64* (Dublin, 2004).
57. *Irish Times*, 7 July 1894.

58. Leland L. Duncan, 'Notes from Co. Leitrim', *Folklore*, 5/3 (1894): 184–6; Barney Whelan, Anne Whelan, and Edward McVitie, 'Fairy belief and Other Folklore Notes from Co. Leitrim', *Folklore*, 7/2 (1896): 177–8.
59. *Anglo-Celt*, 11 July 1908.
60. James McCaffrey [complainant], Mary McCaffrey [defendant], Belturbet Petty Sessions, Co. Cavan, 4 July 1908 (NAI, Court Order Books: Co. Cavan Petty Session Books, CS/PS 1/2574).
61. Thomas Johnson Westropp, 'A Folklore Survey of County Clare (Continued)', *Folklore*, 22/3 (1911): 339.
62. Diarmaid Ó Muirithe and Deirdre Nutall (eds), *Folklore of County Wexford* (Dublin, 1999); 75, 77–8, 97. See also, Gearóid Ó Crualaoich, 'Reading the Bean Feasa', *Folklore*, 116/1 (2005): 42–3, 46.
63. See Introduction. The best overview of this subject can at present be found in Connolly, *Priests and People*: 122–8.
64. 'Dr Nicholas Madgett's "Constitutio Ecclesiastica"' ed. Michael Manning, *Journal of the Kerry Archaeological and Historical Society*, 9 (1976): 75; *Finn's Leinster Journal*, 31 August 1774; Murphy, *Diocese of Killaloe in the Eighteenth Century*: 88–90. See also Chapter 7.
65. Manning, 'Dr Nicholas Madgett's "Constitutio Ecclesiastica"': 77.
66. Ibid: 78.
67. *Belfast Newsletter*, 15 December 1829.
68. Andrew Holmes provides a brief, tantalising glimpse into Presbyterian, popular belief in fairies, witches, and the evil-eye, tracing their demise to shortly before the Famine for a number of reasons: increased access to education nurturing a widespread naturalisation of outlook; economic hardship in the 1830s sparking a gradual decline in customary activity; and increased sectarian tensions persuading Presbyterians to back-away from traditional beliefs and practices deemed 'superstitious' and Catholic (Holmes, *The Shaping of Ulster Presbyterian Belief and Practice*: 101–3).
69. For more on print culture, reading, and the print trade in eighteenth-century Ireland: Raymond Gillespie and Andrew Hadfield (eds), *The Oxford History of the Irish Book: Volume III, the Irish Book in English 1550–1800* (Oxford, 2006), especially Chapters 3, 5, 9, 12; Niall Ó Ciosáin, *Print and Popular Culture in Ireland 1750–1850* (Basingstoke, 1997, repr. Dublin, 2010); Mary Pollard, *Dublin's Trade in Books, 1550–1800* (Oxford, 1989); Robert Munter, *The History of the Irish Newspaper, 1685–1760* (Cambridge, 1967).
70. Jonathan Barry, 'Public Infidelity and Private Belief?: The Discourse of Spirits in Enlightenment Bristol', in *Beyond the Witch Trials*: 120; James W. Phillips, *Printing and Bookselling in Dublin, 1670–1800* (Dublin, 1998); Richard Cargill Cole, *Irish Booksellers and English Writers, 1740–1800* (London, 1986).
71. See Chapters 4 and 5, and Sneddon, *Possessed by the Devil*, Chapter 9.
72. Gillespie, *Devoted People*: 10–11. See also, idem, 'De-stabilising Ulster, 1641–2', in *Ulster 1641*: 116; idem, 'Imagining Angels in Early Modern Ireland': 214.
73. Cited in *The Irish Quarterly Review* (Dublin, 1853): 267.
74. *JHLI*, iii, 366, 401, 414; David Ryan, *Blasphemers and Blackguards: the Irish Hellfire Clubs* (Dublin, 2012): 2–3, 15–17, 30–6, 40–8, 52–3. For a recent study of English Hell-Fire clubs, see: Evelyn Lord, *The Hell-Fire Clubs: Sex, Satanism and Secret Societies* (London, 2008).

75. Gillespie, *Devoted People*, 133; Bridgit A. Fitzpatrick, 'The Development of the Irish Almanac, 1612–1724' (Master's Thesis, TCD, 1990); Sneddon, *Witchcraft and Whigs*: 72; Patrick Curry, *Prophecy and Power, Astrology in Early Modern England* (Cambridge, 1989): 7, 11–12, 19–57, 105–12, 155–7; J.R.R. Adams, *The Printed Word and the Common Man, 1700–1900* (Belfast, 1987): 84.
76. Gillespie, *Devoted People*: 114–21.
77. Thomas Riggs, *The Tryal and Conviction of Thomas Riggs and John Woods Pretended Prophets, who were Try'd at Drogheda, April 13, 1712. With the Recorder's Speech to the Jury, and Several Speeches Made by the Judge* (Dublin, 1712); 'Council Book of the Corporation of Drogheda, volume 1, 1649–1734' ed. T. Gogarty (Drogheda, 1915): 307, 312–13; Hillel Schwartz, *The French Prophets: the History of a Millenarian Group in Eighteenth-Century England* (California, 1980): 136, 154–5. For overviews of the French Prophets, see: Clarke Garrett, *Spirit Possession and Popular Religion: from the Camisards to the Shakers* (Baltimore, 1997), and Hillel Schwartz, *Knaves, Fools, Madmen and that Subtile Effluvium: a Study of the Opposition to the French Prophets in England, 1706–1710* (Gainesville, 1978).
78. *DIB*.
79. See Sneddon, *Witchcraft and Whigs*, Chapters 7–8.
80. Francis Hutchinson, *A Letter to a Member of Parliament, Concerning the Imploying and Providing for the Poor* (Dublin, 1723): 16.
81. Bishop Hutchinson's *Commonplace book*, 1721–30 (PRONI, MS DIO/1/22/1, 'witchcraft' page).
82. Bishop Hutchinson's *Commonplace book*, October 1726 (PRONI MS DIO/1/22/1, un-paginated section); Francis Hutchinson to Arthur Chartlett, 17 July 1718 (Bodleian Library, Oxford, Ballard Ms 38: f. 27).
83. The second edition of Bishop Hutchinson's *Historical Essay* was published in 1720.
84. *Flin's Sale Catalogue of Books for the Year 1767 ... Part 1 ...* (Dublin, 1767): 22, 25, 53; *Flin's Sale Catalogue of Books for the Year 1766 ... Part 1 ...* (Dublin, 1765): 16; *A Catalogue of the Libraries of John Fergus, MD, and Son, both deceased ...* (Dublin, 1766): 38; *A Catalogue of Books. Being the Entire Library of the Right Reverend Father in God, Robert Downes, Lord Bishop of Raphoe, Deceas'd ...* (Dublin, 1764): 14; *A Catalogue of the Libraries of Richard Terry, Francis Bindon, Esqrs. And part of the library of a late Right Revd. And Learned Prelate ...* (Dublin, 1768): 20, 27; *Catalogue of Books, Prints and Books of Print Being the Libraries of the Late Reverend Doctor Osher ... Mr Clarendon and Another Gentlemen ...* (Dublin, 1796), item 1009; *Freeman's Journal*, 9, 14 August 1813; *Freeman's Journal*, 28 June 1815.
85. Lesa Ní Mhunghaile, 'An Eighteenth-Century Gaelic Scribe's Private Library: Muiris ÓGormáin's Books', *Proceedings of the Royal Irish Academy. Section C: Archaeology, Celtic Studies, History, Linguistics, Literature*, 110c (2010): 239–40, 242, 249n30, 250, 265–6, 274.
86. Bishop Hutchinson's *Commonplace book*, 1731–9 (PRONI, accessioned, 2004: 536); see also, idem: 534.
87. *Dublin Weekly Journal*, 30 October 1725. I thank Dr Richard Holmes for providing me with an initial copy of this essay (a digitised version is now available on Google Books), and for suggesting that it may have been written by Bishop Hutchinson.

88. David Berman, 'Enlightenment and Counter Enlightenment in Philosophy', *Archiv fur Geschichte der Philosophie*, 54 (1982): 150; idem, 'The Culmination and Causation of Irish philosophy', idem: 257–61, 278–9; Michael Brown, *Francis Hutcheson in Dublin, 1719–30* (Dublin, 2002): 50, 99; idem, 'Francis Hutchinson and the Molesworth Connection', *Eighteenth-century Ireland*, 14 (1999): 63, 65–6; idem, 'The Biter Bitten: Ireland and the Rude Enlightenment', *Eighteenth-Century Studies*, 45/3 (2012): 395–8; Richard Holmes, 'James Arbuckle: A Whig Critic of the Penal Laws', in *New Perspectives on the Penal Laws*: 93–5, 97, 110–12; John F. Woznak, 'James Arbuckle and the Dublin Weekly Journal', *Journal of Irish Literature*, 22 (1993): 46–52; M.A. Stewart, 'John Smith and the Molesworth Circle', *Eighteenth-Century Ireland*, 2 (1987): 89–90, 92–3; McBride, *Eighteenth Century Ireland*: 54; DIB.
89. Francis Hutcheson to his father, 4 August 1726, in *Christian Moderator*, 2 (1827–1828): 353; Brown, *Francis Hutcheson in Dublin*: 99, 106.
90. Sneddon, *Witchcraft and Whigs*, Chapters 4–5; Hunter, 'Decline of Magic': 419–22. David Whooton has argued that Francis Hutchinson was 'the first of the skeptics to deploy probability theory ... to measure the reliability of historical testimony': David Whooton, 'Hutchinson, Francis (1660–1739)', *Encyclopaedia of Witchcraft*, ii, 531.
91. *Dublin Weekly Journal*, 30 October 1725. Compare with: 'the credulous multitude will ever be ready to try their tricks, and swim the old women, and wonder at and magnify every unaccountable symptom and odd accident' (Hutchinson, *Historical Essay*: viii). See also, Francis Hutchinson to Sir Hans Sloane, 3 April 1712 (BL Sloane Ms 4043: f. 38): 'Two or three dayes ago I met with the tryal of the suppos'd witch at Hartford. I know not what judgement the town made of it but to me it appears, that as there are many of those circumstances which some or other have never been wanting to swear at all past tryals of witches, so there is a very great deal of the same folly and imprudence in the manage[ment] which, when suffer'd, have never fail'd to bring great trouble and disturbance, not only to the poor old creatures, but to all timerous persons, and the whole neighbourhoods where they are'.
92. Hutchinson, *Historical Essay*, vii: 'For if any wicked person affirms, or any crack'd brain girl imagines, or any lying spirit makes her believe, that she sees any old woman, or other person pursuing her in her visions, the defenders of the vulgar witchcraft tack an imaginary, unprov'd compact to the deposition, and hang the accus'd parties for things that were doing, when they were perhaps, asleep upon their beds, or saying their prayers; or, perhaps, in the accusers own possession, with double irons upon them'.
93. *Dublin Weekly Journal*, 30 October 1725.
94. Francis Hutchinson to William Wake, 14 April 1720 (Christ Church Library, Oxford [hereafter CC], Oxford, Wake Letters, vol. 21, no. 215). See also, Sneddon, *Witchcraft and Whigs*: 133.
95. Timothy Godwin to William Wake, 28 December 1720 (CC, Wake Letters, vol. 13, no. 216).
96. Anon, *An Excellent New Ballad* (Dublin, 1726). This ballad, of which portions stray from the realm of satire into that of outright libel, was published by Thomas Harbin. Harbin left Ireland shortly after the ballad's publication to escape controversy created by a seditious pamphlet he had recently printed: M. Pollard, *A Dictionary of Members of the Dublin Book Trade, 1550–1800* (London, 2000): 274.

97. See Chapters 3 and 4. Clerical elites in early eighteenth-century Isle of Man also took the activities of cunning-folk more seriously than witchcraft: Hutton, 'The Changing Faces of Manx Witchcraft': 115.

98. Anon, *The Irish Spelling Book; Or, Instruction for the Reading of English, Fitted for the Youth of Ireland* ... (Dublin, 1740): 111; George Fox, Ellis Hookes, and Andrew Sowle, *Instructions for Right Spelling, and Plain Directions for Reading and True English* ... (Dublin, 3rd ed., 1726): 23, 102; Thomas Dyche, William Pardon, *A New General English Dictionary; Peculiarly Calculated for the Use and Improvement of such as are Unacquainted with the Learned Languages* ... *Originally Begun by the late Reverend Mr. Thomas Dyche,* ... *and now Finish'd by William Pardon, Gent* (Dublin, 4th ed., 1744); Thomas Wilson, *The Knowledge and Practice of Christianity Made Essay to the Meanest Capacity* ... (Dublin, 1760): 54.

99. See p. 33.

100. *JHCI*, iv, part 1, 1731–48; *JHLI*, iii, 1727–52; *Irish Legislation Database* (http://www.qub.ac.uk/ild/); Robert Burns, *Irish Parliamentary Politics in the Eighteenth Century* (2 vols, Washington, 1989–90), ii, 29–34. For the Irish parliament and improvement in the mid-eighteenth century: Gordon Rees, 'Pamphlets, Legislators and the Irish Economy, 1727–49: a Reconsideration', *Irish Economic and Social History*, 41 (2014): 20–35; Andrew, Sneddon, 'Legislating for Economic Development: Irish Fisheries as a Case Study in the Limitations of "Improvement"', in David Hayton, James Kelly, and John Bergin (eds), *The Eighteenth-century Composite State: Representative Institutions in Ireland and Europe, 1689–1800* (Basingstoke, 2010): 136–59.

101. T.C. Barnard, 'The Language of Politeness and Sociability in Eighteenth century Ireland', in David George Boyle, Robert Eccleshall, and Vincent Geoghegan (eds), *Political Discourse in Seventeenth and Eighteenth-century Ireland* (Palgrave, 2001): 193–221; T.C. Barnard, 'Reforming Irish Manners: the Religious Societies in Dublin During the 1690s', *Historical Journal*, 35/4 (1992): 805–38; idem, *Improving Ireland? Projectors, Prophets and Profiteers 1641–1786* (Dublin, 2008); David A. Fleming, 'Diversions of the People: Sociability among the Orders of Early Eighteenth-century Ireland', *Eighteenth-Century Ireland*, 17 (2002): 99–111; Ian McBride, 'The Edge of Enlightenment: Ireland and Scotland in the Eighteenth Century', *Modern Intellectual History*, 10/1 (2013): 135–51; idem, *Eighteenth Century Ireland*, Chapter 2; Michael Brown, 'Configuring the Irish Enlightenment: Reading the Transactions of the Royal Irish Academy', in James Kelly and Martyn J. Powell (eds), *Clubs and Societies in Eighteenth-century Ireland* (Dublin, 2010): 163–78.

102. See Michael Brown, 'Was There an Irish Enlightenment? The Case of the Anglicans', in R. Butterwick, S. Davies, and G. Espinosa Sanchez (eds), *Peripheries of the Enlightenment* (Oxford, 2008): 49–63; Sean D. Moore, 'Introduction: Ireland and Enlightenment', *Eighteenth-century Studies*, 45/3 (2012): 345–8.

103. Connolly, *Religion and Society in Nineteenth-century Ireland*, Chapter 3; Nigel Yates, *The Religious Condition of Ireland, 1770–1850* (Oxford, 2006), Introduction and Chapters 1–2.

104. See: Davies, *America Bewitched*, Chapter 1; idem, *Witchcraft, Magic and Culture*, chapter 1; De Blécourt, 'Continuation of Witchcraft': 344–5; and

Hutton, 'Changing Faces of Manx Witchcraft': 156–8. For studies which concentrate on the characterisation and responses to early modern witchcraft trials in English and American culture from the eighteenth century onwards: Diane Purkiss, *The Witch in History* (London, 1996); Gibson, *Witchcraft Myths in American Culture*, Chapters 1–3; idem, 'Retelling Salem Stories: Gender Politics and Witches in American Culture', *European Journal of American Culture*, 25/2 (2006): 85–107; and Bernard Rosenthal, *Salem Story: Reading the Witch-Trials of 1692* (Cambridge, 1995). For a dissection of the how the late seventeenth-century story of Thomas Perks' conjuration spirits was re-cast by various authors in Enlightenment England see, Barry, *Raising Spirits*, Chapters 4–7.

105. *Munster Journal*, 14 June 1750; Richard Robert Madden, *The History of Irish Periodical Literature* ... (2 vols, Newby, 1867), ii, 205; Benjamin Bankhurst, *Ulster Presbyterians and the Ulster Scots Diaspora, 1750–64* (Basingstoke, 2013): 154; D.A. Fleming, *Politics and Provincial People: Sligo and Limerick, 1691–1761* (Manchester, 2010): 129, 208. I thank Professor James Kelly for sending me a copy of the *Munster Journal* article.

106. 'One sort of such as are said to bee witches, are bleare-eied, pale, fowle, and full of wrinkles; poor, sullen, superstitious ... these go from house to house, and from doore to doore for a pot of milke, yest, drinke, pottage' (Scot, *The Discoverie of Witchcraft*: 7).

107. *Munster Journal*, 14 June 1750.

108. George Stayley, *The Life and Opinions of an Actor* ... (2 vols, Dublin, 1762), i, 147; *ODNB*.

109. Anon, *A Colloquial Essay on the Liberal Education, and Other Interesting Subjects* ... (2 vols, Dublin, 1764), ii, 82.

110. *Belfast Newsletter*, 13 November 1767.

111. Richard Mead, *The Medical Works of Richard Mead* ... (London, 1762, Dublin, 1767): 444–5, 470–7; David Gentilcore, *Healers and Healing in Early Modern Italy* (Manchester, 1998): 160–1.

112. *Freeman's Journal*, 13 November 1787. For Robert Marchbank, see: Rowena Dudley, *The Irish Lottery, 1780–1801* (Dublin, 20050: 33 n80, 62 n65; and, Phillips, *Printing and Bookselling in Dublin*: 36.

113. *Freeman's Journal*, 16 August 1788.

114. Bernard C. Faust, *Catechism of Health: for the Use of Schools and for Domestic Instruction* ... (Dublin, 1794): 71; Ian Green, '"The Necessary Knowledge of the Principles of Religion": Catechisms and Catechising in Ireland, c. 1560–1800', in A. Ford, J. McGuire, and K. Milne (eds), *As By Law Established: The Church of Ireland Since the Reformation* (Cambridge, 1995): 88.

115. *Belfast Newsletter*, 17 January 1764; idem, 3 April 1764.

116. *Belfast Newsletter*, 3 April 1764. This case was reported in the same newspaper almost a century later but by this time the children's possession was attributed to natural causes: 'Many cases of this description have, from time to time, been recorded, which were at one time attributed to witchcraft, but have been since discovered to result from the imprudent use of damaged or imperfectly ripened grain' (*Belfast Newsletter*, 16 November 1849).

117. OSMI, Lieutenant G.H. Mallock, April 1832, *Parishes of County Antrim XIV, vol. 37, Parish of Carrickfergus*: 77. See also, OSMI, James Boyle and T.C. Hannyngton, 4 February 1837, *Parishes of County Antrim I, vol. 2, Parish*

of Ballymartin: 11. For nineteenth-century literary and popular portrayals of the devil: *Belfast Newsletter*, 28 December 1830; idem, 20 June 1845; and Cecil Frances Alexander, *The Legend of Stumpie's Brae*, in 'Ulster-Scots Folklore and Literature Reader': 75–9.

118. Connolly, *Priests and People*: 127.
119. Owen Davies, *Witchcraft, Magic and Culture*: 18–28; Young, *English Catholics and the Supernatural*, Chapter 6. For a case study of late eighteenth-century Bristol demoniac, George Lutkins, which throws light on the different positions contemporaries took in relation to possession: Barry, *Witchcraft and Demonology in South-west England*, Chapter 7.
120. Maria Tausiet, 'From Illusion to Disenchantment: Feijoo versus the "Falsely" Possessed in Eighteenth-century Spain', in *Beyond the Witch Trials*: 44–60.
121. See, H.C. Erik Midlefort, *Exorcism and Enlightenment: Johann Joseph Gassner and the Demons of Eighteenth-century Germany* (New Haven and London, 2005).
122. *Hibernian Magazine*, November 1781: 564.
123. *Belfast Monthly Magazine*, August 1809: 105. The Islandmagee trial was mentioned in the press on only one occasion before McSkimmin's article appeared, when Rev. William Tisdall's letter was published in January 1775: Tisdall, 'Account of the Trial': 47–51. This article was advertised in the *Belfast Newsletter* a month later, adding that Tisdall was 'grandfather to the present Attorney General': *Belfast Newsletter*, 7–10 February 1775.
124. Samuel McSkimmin, *The History and Antiquities of the County of the Town of Carrickfergus, Co. Antrim* ... (Belfast, 1811): 21–2.
125. OSMI, James Boyle, April 1840, *Parishes of County Antrim III, vol. 10, Parish of Islandmagee*: 40–1. For Presbyterian belief in fairies, see: Holmes, *The Shaping of Ulster Presbyterian Belief and Practice*: 95–7.
126. *Belfast Newsletter*, 12 February 1762.
127. *Walker's Hibernian Magazine*, May 1799: 326. Much the same argument had been used a few years earlier: 'The Witch of Endor is introduced as an old woman [in the Bible], and in every subsequent period, historians, painters, and poets, have all exhibited their witches as old women' (*Walker's Hibernian Magazine*, July 1791: 57). The argument that the Scriptures had been mistranslated and misinterpreted by witch-hunters was a typical sceptical argument: Sneddon, *Witchcraft and Whigs*: 101–2.
128. *Walker's Hibernian Magazine*, August 1791: 144.
129. *Belfast Monthly Magazine*, 13 December 1791.
130. 'Detached Anecdotes and Observations', *Belfast Monthly Magazine*, 11/60 (1831): 56. For a later, more overtly politicised version of the notion of Irish immunity to witchcraft: Peter Finlay, 'Witchcraft', *Irish Monthly*, 2 (1874): 525. The *Irish Monthly* was founded in 1873 by Jesuit Mathew Russell and dedicated to issues affecting 'Catholic Ireland': Andrew McCarthy, 'Publishing for Catholic Ireland', in *The Oxford History of the Irish Book, Volume V: The Irish Book in English, 1891–2000* (Oxford, 2011): 253. For more mid-nineteenth-century, Protestant condemnations of early modern, English witchcraft trials see: *Nenagh Guardian*, 6, 9 November 1844, and *Tuam Herald*, 31 October 1846.
131. *Freeman's Journal*, 17 June 1814.
132. *Southern Reporter and Cork Courier*, 23 October 1827.

133. *Belfast Newsletter*, 13 December 1754.
134. *Belfast Newsletter*, 9 March 1759. For the Hannokes case, see Robert Dodsley, *The Annual Register, or a View of the History, Politicks and Literature of the Year* (London, 1760): 73. For the Osborne case, see Davies, *Witchcraft, Magic and Culture*: 95–6, 111, and W.B. Carnochan, 'Witch-hunting and Belief in 1751: The Case of Thomas Colley and Ruth Osborne', *Social History*, 4/4 (1971): 389–404. A similar 'instance of folly' was published in the *Belfast Newsletter* in 1792 concerning an elderly, poverty-stricken woman from the parish of Stanningfield, Suffolk, who was swum as a witch after neighbours were unable to convince local clergyman to weigh her against the Church Bible (*Belfast Newsletter*, 13–17 July 1792).
135. *Belfast Newsletter*, 12 December 1769.
136. *Freeman's Journal*, 17 November 1808. For a detailed discussion of this case: Stephen A. Mitchell, 'A Case of Witchcraft Assault in Early Nineteenth-century England as Ostensive Action', in *Witchcraft Continued*: 14–28; idem, 'Witchcraft Persecutions in the Post-Craze Era: The Case of Ann Izzard of Great Paxton, 1808', *Western Folklore*, 59/3–4 (2000): 304–28, and Davies, *Witchcraft, Magic and Culture*: 39–50, 111–12, 195, 197–8.
137. *Belfast Newsletter*, 1 December 1809. See also, *Belfast Monthly Magazine*, November 1809: 400, and Davies, *Witchcraft, Magic and Culture*: 112.
138. *Belfast Newsletter*, 4 April 1809.
139. 'The Annals of Yorkshire: From the Earliest Period to the Present Time', ed. John Mayhall (Leeds, 1861): 218–20.
140. *Belfast Monthly Magazine*, November 1810.
141. *Belfast Newsletter*, 12–15 December 1775.
142. Ibid, 6–9 February 1787.
143. *Freeman's Journal*, 9 April 1789.
144. *Belfast Newsletter*, 9 October 1789.
145. Ibid, 15 August 1815.
146. Davies, *America Bewitched*: 3–4, 7–10.
147. *Belfast Newsletter*, 1 November 1806.
148. Ibid, 9 December 1818.
149. Journal of Sir William Power, 29 December 1840 (PRONI, Arnnaghmakerrig Papers, Ms D3585/B/10).
150. David Hayton, 'Introduction: The long Apprenticeship', in David Hayton (ed.), *The Irish Parliament in the Eighteenth Century: The Long Apprenticeship* (Edinburgh, 2001): 10–11; James Kelly, 'Monitoring the Constitution: the Operation of Poynings' Law in the 1760s' in idem: 87–106; idem, *Poynings' Law and the Making of Law in Ireland, 1660–1800* (Dublin, 2007): 156–7, 210–11, 217, 240, 309, 343–4, 357, 361.
151. For the Union: Dáire Keogh and Kevin Whelan (eds), *Acts of Union: The Causes, Contexts and Consequences of the Act of Union* (Dublin and Portland, 2001), and Michael Brown, Patrick Geoghegan, and James Kelly (eds), *The Irish Act of Union, 1800: Bicentennial Essays* (Dublin, 2003).
152. Bostridge, *Witchcraft and its Transformations*: 197.
153. House of Commons Sitting, 7 March 1821, Hansard, Second series, vol. 2, George IV, year 2, columns 1129–1161. See also, *The Times*, 8 March 1821, *Freeman's Journal*, 12 March 1821, and Bostridge, *Witchcraft and its Transformations*: 196.

154. *Finn's Leinster Journal*, 17 March 1821.
155. *Journal of the House of Commons*, vol. 76, 7 March 1821: 147; *Belfast Newsletter*, 16 March 1821; *ODNB*.
156. *Journal of the House of Commons*, vol. 76, 9 March 1821: 154.
157. 2 Geo. IV, 1821 (204) [Ire.], '*A Bill to Repeal an Act, made in the Parliament of Ireland, in the 28th year of the Reign of Queen Elizabeth, Against Witchcraft and Sorcery*'.
158. *Journal of the House of Commons*, vol. 76, 21 March 1821: 190. See also, *The Times*, 24 March 1821.
159. *Finn's Leinster Journal*, 31 March 1821; *Freeman's Journal*, 28 March 1821.
160. *Journal of the House of Commons*, vol. 76, 27 March 1821: 205.
161. *Finn's Leinster Journal*, 4 April 1821. For Castlereagh see, John Bew, *Castlereagh: Enlightenment, War and Tyranny* (London, 2011).
162. *Journal of the House of Commons*, vol. 76, 3 April 1821: 230; *Journal of the House of Lords*, vol. 54, 28, 30 March, 2, 3 April 1821: 144, 151, 156, 158; *The Times*, 29 March, 3 April 1821; *Freeman's Journal*, 3 April 1821.
163. *Journal of the House of Commons*, vol. 76, 6 April 1821: 237; *The Times*, 7 April 1821; *Freeman's Journal*, 6 April 1821; *The Statutes of the United Kingdom of Great Britain and Ireland, 1 & 2, George IV, 1821* (London, 1821); Bostridge, *Witchcraft and its Transformations*: 196.
164. Anon, *Antipas; a Solemn Appeal to the Right Reverend the Archbishops and Bishops of the United Churches of England and Ireland: With Reference to Several Bills Passed, Or Passing Through the Imperial Parliament; Especially that Concerning Witchcraft and Sorcery* (London, 1st ed., 1821): 41, 43; *Morning Chronicle*, 5 April 1821; Bostridge, *Witchcraft and its Transformations*: 196–7.
165. Anon, *Antipas; A Solemn Appeal*: 17.
166. Anon, *Antipas; A Solemn Appeal*: 34; Bostridge, *Witchcraft and its Transformations*: 197.
167. Anon, *Antipas; A Solemn Appeal*: 39.
168. Davies, 'Decriminalising the Witch': 227–8; Bostridge, *Witchcraft and its Transformations*: 197–201; idem, 'Witchcraft Repealed': 320.
169. Davies, *Witchcraft, Magic and Culture*: 46–50.
170. Anon, *Antipas; A Solemn Appeal*: 17. See also, idem: 26.
171. Anon, *Antipas; A Solemn Appeal*: 18. See also, idem: 19–26.
172. Anon, *Antipas; A Solemn Appeal*: 18, 21–2.
173. Anon, *Antipas; A Solemn Appeal*: 31. See also, idem: 34.
174. Anon, *Antipas; A Solemn Appeal*: 34–6.
175. Ibid: 35.
176. Anon, *Antipas; A Solemn Appeal*: 36.
177. *Freeman's Journal*, 21 April 1821; *ODNB*.
178. Garnham, 'Crime, Policing and the Law, 1600–1900': 95.
179. A selection of these cases are discussed below and were identified using browsing facilities and keyword searches (of the words 'witch' and 'witchcraft') in the three main online newspaper databases, the NCN, BNA, and INA. This was complemented by browsing hard copies of post-1750 issues of the *Belfast Newsletter* and the *Freeman's Journal*. Identified cases were then followed up in surviving court records. More cases would no doubt come to light through detailed study of un-digitised Irish provincial newspapers. For an exploration of the explosion of reported witchcraft cases

in nineteenth-century English newspapers, see: Davies, 'Newspapers and Popular Belief': 142–5.

180. Ó Ciosáin, *Print and Popular Culture in Ireland*: 35–6, 64–5; Desmond McCabe, 'Open Court: Law and the Expansion of Magisterial Jurisdiction at Petty Sessions in Nineteenth-century Ireland', in N.M. Dawson (ed.), *Reflections on Law and History: Irish Legal History Society Discourses and Other Papers, 2000–2005* (Dublin, 2006): 126, 130, 138–40, 150; idem, 'Magistrates, Peasants and the Petty Session Courts, Mayo, 1823–50', *Cathair na Mart*, 5 (1985): 45–53; Griffin, *The Bulkies*: 5; Catherine Cox, *Negotiating Insanity in the Southeast of Ireland, 1820–1900* (Manchester, 2012): 98–9.
181. *Irish Times*, 6 October 1894.
182. See Chapter 7.
183. *Freeman's Journal*, 4 September 1812.
184. *Freeman's Journal*, 24 August 1815. For an obituary of Stamer, see *Gentleman's Magazine*, April 1838: 428.
185. Griffin, *The Bulkies*: 1–2; B. Henry, *Dublin Hanged: Crime, Law Enforcement and Punishment in Late Eighteenth Century Dublin* (Dublin, 1994), chapter 7.
186. *Freeman's Journal*, 9 September 1830; *North Wales Chronicle*, 30 September 1830; *The Morning Post*, 15 September 1830; idem, 16 September 1830.
187. *The Morning Post*, 16 September 1830; Anon, *The Assembled Commons; or, Parliamentary Biographer, with an Abstract of the Law of Election, by a Member of the Middle Temple* (London, 1838): 229–30.
188. Owen Davies and Willem de Blécourt, 'Introduction: Beyond the Witch Trials', in *Beyond the Witch Trials*: 6–7; Owen Davies, 'Newspapers and the Popular Belief': 139–46.
189. *Belfast Newletter*, 31 March 1837. For a sceptical report of alleged witchcraft in Marylebone, London, printed in an Irish newspaper in the same year: *Tuam Herald*, 12 August 1832.
190. *Nenagh Guardian*, 9 October 1895; Thomas Meehan [complainant], William Burke [defendant], 19 September 1895 (NAI, Court Order Books: Cahir Petty Sessions, Co. Tipperary, CS/PS 1/2789).
191. Thomas Meehan [complainant], William Burke [defendant], 3 October 1895 (NAI, CS/PS 1/2789).
192. *Belfast Newsletter*, 9 June 1870.
193. Thomas Johnson Westropp, 'Witchcraft in County Limerick', *The Journal of the Royal Society of Antiquaries*, 5th series, 2/3 (1892): 291.
194. Davies, 'Newspapers and Popular Belief': 145.

7 Cunning-folk in Modern Ireland

1. These types of sources have been used by historians to provide insight into witchcraft and magical beliefs in eighteenth- and nineteenth-century England and Europe: Davies, 'Newspapers and Popular Belief': 139–65; De Blécourt, 'On the Continuation of Witchcraft': 343–5; idem, 'The Witch, her Victim, the Unwitcher and the Researcher: The Continued Existence of Traditional Witch', in Bengt Akarloo and Stuart Clark (eds), *Witchcraft and Magic in Europe: The Twentieth Century* (Philadelphia): 158–62.

2. Magical healers should not be confused with faith or miraculous healers who transmitted God's power in order to heal and cure sickness, often by means of laying on of hands, see: Anthony D. Buckley, 'Unofficial Healing in Ulster', *Ulster Folklife*, 26 (1980): 26–9, and Laurence M. Geary, 'Prince Hohenlohe, Signor Pastorini and Miraculous Healing in Early Nineteenth-century Ireland', in *Medicine, Disease and the State in Ireland*: 40–58. For the activities of famed faith-healer, Valentine Greatrakes in the mid-1660s, see Gillespie, *Devoted People*: 121, and Elmer, *Miraculous Conformist*.
3. Ronnie Moore, 'A General Practice, A Country Practice: The Cure, the Charm and Informal Healing in Northern Ireland', in *Folk Healing And Health Care Practices in Britain and Ireland*: 104–29; Erin Kraus, *Wise-Woman of Kildare: Moll Anthony and Popular Tradition in the East of Ireland*: 25. For folklore studies that also describe charms, magical healing and healers: Buckley, 'Unofficial Healing in Ulster': 15–26; Patrick Logan, 'Folk Medicine in Cavan-Leitrim Area, II', *Ulster Folklife*, 11 (1965): 52–3; Foster, *Ulster Folklife*: 56–60; Linda-May Ballard, 'An Approach to Traditional Cures in Ulster', *Ulster Medical Journal*, 78/1 (2009): 26–33; Simon Woods-Panzaru et al., 'An Examination of Antibacterial and Antifungal Properties of Constituents Described in Traditional Ulster Cures and Remedies', in idem: 13–15; Doherty, 'Folklore of Cattle Diseases': 52–4. For a discussion of magical healers in modern Spain: Enrique Perdiguero, 'Magical Healing in Spain (1875–1936): Medical Pluralism and the Search for Hegemony', *Witchcraft Continued*: 136.
4. For example, see: Owen Davies, 'Cunning-folk in the Medical Market-place during the Nineteenth-century', *Medical History Journal*, 43/1 (1999): 55–73, and Cox, 'Medical Marketplace and Medical Tradition': 56–73.
5. Magical healers were identified in nineteenth- and twentieth-century newspapers through 'browse' searches conducted in the BNA, INA, and NCN databases.
6. *Belfast Newsletter*, 16 August 1856.
7. Inquest, death of James Stewart, 12 January 1897 (PRONI, Belfast City Coroner's Record of Inquests, BELF/6/1/2/4); *Belfast Newsletter*, 13 January 1897; *North Eastern Daily Gazette*, 9 January 1897.
8. *Belfast Newsletter*, 13 January 1897.
9. *Irish Times*, 28 October 1905.
10. *Belfast Newsletter*, 30 September 1853. For cholera in nineteenth-century Belfast, see Nigel Sean Farrell, 'Asiatic Cholera and the Development of Public Health in Belfast 1832–78' (University of Ulster PhD thesis, 2014).
11. Joseph Meehan, 'The Cure of Elf-Shooting in the North-West of Ireland', *Folklore*, 17/2 (1906): 201.
12. Thomas J. Westropp, 'A Folklore of County Clare', *Folklore*, 23/2 (1912): 213. For other early twentieth-century magical healers see, Seymour, *Irish Witchcraft and Demonology*: 243–5.
13. Cited in Ó Muirithe and Nutall, *Folklore of County Wexford*: 101. For a tale of a travelling beggar woman who possessed a written charm for toothache, which her clients later believed was derived from the Devil, see idem, 74–5.
14. Holmes, *The Shaping of Ulster Presbyterian Belief and Practice*: 95.
15. See Sneddon, Privilege, 'Ulster-Scots Folklore and Literature Reader': 55.
16. *Hibernian Journal*, 24 May 1773; idem, 7 February 1776.
17. Connolly, *Priests and People*: 122.

18. OSMI, James Boyle, April 1840, *Parishes of County Antrim III, vol. 10, Parish of Islandmagee*: 41.
19. *Belfast Newsletter*, 21 September 1876. For the use of fortune-tellers by nineteenth-century English domestic servants, to 'see if the promises being made by predatory male house hold staff were true or whether, consenting to sex, their future prospects working in the industry would be undone', see: Bell, *Magical Imagination*: 177–8, quote at p. 177.
20. In March 1787, the *Freeman's Journal* reported that Abigail McGuire was transported for 'telling of fortunes, imposing on and giving evil example to others, and for being a vagabond and person of bad fame' (*Freeman's Journal*, 27 March 1787).
21. The fortune-tellers discussed in this chapter were identified in nineteenth- and twentieth-century newspapers through 'keyword' searches of the word 'fortune-teller' conducted in the BNA, INA, and NCN databases. Surveys of hard copies of the *Belfast Newsletter* and the *Freeman's Journal* were also conducted. Once more, cases have been followed up in surviving court records, particularly petty session records.
22. *Vindicator*, 7 September 1844.
23. *Cork Examiner*, 9 July 1849.
24. *Belfast Newsletter*, 2 June 1860.
25. *Belfast Newsletter*, 3 April 1863. See also, *Armagh Guardian*, 3 April 1863.
26. *Cork Examiner*, 5 March 1867.
27. *Belfast Newsletter*, 28 July 1869. See also, *Nenagh Guardian*, 28 July 1869.
28. *Cork Examiner*, 20 January 1854; Mary Bresnihan [complainant], Ellen Leahy [defendant], 19 November 1853 (NAI, Court Order Books: Kanturk Petty Sessions, Co. Cork, CS/PS 1/4959).
29. *Belfast Newsletter*, 3 November 1854.
30. Ibid, 23 June 1856.
31. *Freeman's Journal*, 13 October 1857.
32. *Northern Whig*, 18 May 1860.
33. Davies, *Witchcraft, Magic and Culture*: 246–65. For a case study of fortune-teller, Joseph Powell, who was sentenced to six months imprisonment with hard labour for vagrancy in early nineteenth-century London on charges brought by the Society of the Suppression of Vice, see: Maureen Perkins, 'The Trial of Joseph Powell, Fortune-teller: Public and Private in Early Nineteenth-century Magic', *Journal of Victorian Culture*, 6/1 (2001): 27–45.
34. Gillespie, *Devoted People*: 132.
35. Saunderson, 'Butter-witches and Cow Doctors': 72–3; Ó Giolláin, 'Fairy Belief and Official Religion in Ireland': 203; Meehan, 'The Cure of Elf-Shooting in the North-West of Ireland': 200, 202–5; Young, 'Some Notes on Irish Fairy Changelings': 38–43; Correll, 'Believers and Sceptics, and Charlatans': 2, 11–12; Jenkins, 'Witches and Fairies': 33–56; idem, 'Transformations of Biddy Early': 165–70; Connolly, *Priests and People*: 115–17; Byrne, *Witchcraft in Ireland*: 69–70; Cox, 'Medical Marketplace and Medical Tradition': 55–6, 73; Bourke, *Burning of Bridget Cleary*, Chapter 2; Seymour, *Irish Witchcraft and Demonology*: 236–7, 239–42; Michael L. Doherty, 'The Folklore of Diseases: a Veterinary Perspective', *Bealoideas*, 69 (2001): 53, 55; Schmitz, 'An Irish Wise Woman – Fact and Legend', *Journal of the Folklore Institute*, 14/3 (1977): 169–79; Kraus, *Wise-Woman of Kildare*: 26–9; Byrne, *Witchcraft*

in Ireland: 69; See also Ó Crualaoich, 'Reading the Bean Feasa': 37–50. See also Chapter 6.

36. Jenkins, 'Transformations of Biddy Early': 165.
37. Ibid: 166.
38. Ó Crualaoich, 'Reading the Bean Feasa': 37. Using the Irish Folklore Commission archive collections from the 1920s and 1930s, Ó Crualaoich has argued elsewhere that the Irish bean feasa were not 'flesh and blood' women but mythical, legendary figures: Gearóid Ó Crualaoich, *The Book of Cailleach: Stories of the Wise-Woman Healer* (Cork, 2003, repr. 2007): 93–4.
39. Richard Jenkins is an exception, as he regards the magical practitioners who served rural Ireland up until the twentieth century in a broader European context, although he does not go as far as to the use the term 'cunning-folk': Jenkins, 'Transformations of Biddy Early': 165.
40. Davies, *Witchcraft, Magic, and Culture*: 214.
41. Davies, *Witchcraft, Magic, and Culture*: 214–29. See also, idem, *Popular Magic*: 187–8, and Chapter 3.
42. Davies, *Popular Magic*: 21–4.
43. Holmes, *The Shaping of Ulster Presbyterian Belief and Practice*: 93.
44. Ibid: 95–7.
45. Owen Davies and Willem De Blécourt, 'Introduction: beyond the Witch Trials', *Beyond the Witch Trials*: 5.
46. Andrew Holmes has identified only four instances of this occurring between 1770 and 1840: Holmes, *The Shaping of Ulster Presbyterian Belief and Practice*: 94.
47. *Records of the General Synod of Ulster, 1691–1820* (3 vols, Belfast, 1890–98); *Minutes of the General Synod of Ulster* (Belfast, 1821–40).
48. Holmes, *The Shaping of Ulster Presbyterian Belief and Practice*: 98.
49. 'Archbishop Butler's Visitation Book, Volume I' ed. Christopher O'Dwyer, *Archivium Hibernicum*, 33 (1973): 27.
50. 'Archbishop Butler's Visitation Book, volume II' ed. Christopher O'Dwyer, *Archivium Hibernicum*, 34 (1973): 27.
51. James Coombes, *A Bishop of Penal Times: The Life and Times of John O'Brien, Bishop of Cloyne and Ross, 1701–1769* (Cork, 1981): 50. O'Brien's manual of pastoral practice written in 1755 and preached before his clergy the following year, *Monita Pastoralia et Statuta Ecclesiastica Pro Unitis Dioecesbus Cloynensi et Rossensi*, contained a whole section on the problem of popular superstition: idem, 45, 50, 117.
52. Manning, 'Dr Nicholas Madgett's "Constitutio Ecclesiastica"': 72.
53. Ibid: 76.
54. Manning, 'Dr Nicholas Madgett's "Constitutio Ecclesiastica"': 75.
55. Ibid: 76.
56. Manning, 'Dr Nicholas Madgett's "Constitutio Ecclesiastica"': 77.
57. Ibid: 78.
58. Manning, 'Dr Nicholas Madgett's "Constitutio Ecclesiastica"': 78.
59. 'The Diocesan Manuscripts of Ferns during the Rule of Bishop Sweetman (1745–1786)' ed. W.H. Grattan Flood, *Archivium Hibernicum*, 3 (1914): 117.
60. Thomas Vincent, *A Daily Exercise of the Devout Christian, Containing Several Moving Practices of Piety in Order to Live Holily and Die Happily* (Dublin, 15th ed., 1793): 162.

61. Cited in Connolly, *Priests and People*: 122.
62. S.J. Connolly, 'The "Blessed Turf": Cholera and Popular Panic in Ireland, June 1832', *Irish Historical Studies*, 23/91 (1983): 214–31; Timothy P. O'Neill, Fever and Public Health in pre-Famine Ireland', *Journal of the Royal Society of Antiquaries of Ireland*, 103, part 1 (1973): 1–34; Farrell, 'Asiatic Cholera in Belfast', Chapters 1–2.
63. *Clare Journal*, 1 October 1832.
64. *Freeman's Journal*, 4 June 1900; *Irish Times*, 10 October 1903; M.J. Malone, 'Recollections of a County Dispensary', *The Irish Monthly*, 6 (1878): 76–9; Curran, *A Bewitched Land*: 118–19; Murphy, *Diocese of Killaloe*: 281–2; Schmitz, 'An Irish Wise Woman': 169–75; Jenkins, 'Transformations of Biddy Early': 167–9; John Rainsford, 'Feakle's Biddy Early: a Victim of Moral Panic', *History Ireland*, 20/1 (2012): 28–31; Ryan, *Biddy Early – Wise Woman of Clare*: 7, 13, 23, 24, 30, 43–4, 52–60, 75–8, 81–2; Edmund Lenihan, *In Search of Biddy Early* (Cork and Dublin, 1987), Chapters 2, 4–6; Murphy, *Diocese of Killaloe*: 281–2.
65. *Freeman's Journal*, 27 October 1840; Patrick Kennedy, *Legendry Fictions of the Irish Celts* (London, 1866): 181; Kraus, *Wise-Woman of Kildare*: 11–12, 20–35; Jenkins, 'Transformations of Biddy Early': 116. In contrast to Ireland, in England after 1650 magical healers and cunning-folk very rarely claimed that their powers were derived from fairies: Owen Davies, 'Angels in Elite and Popular Magic, 1659–1790' in, *Angels in the Early Modern World*: 302.
66. OSMI, James Boyle, 28 April 1839, *Parishes of County Antrim I, 1838–9, Parish of Carnmoney*: 42, 44–5, 52, 54, 56; Seymour, *Irish Witchcraft and Demonology*: 225.
67. Jenkins, 'Witches and Fairies': 34–6; OSMI, James Boyle, 28 April 1839, Parish of Carnmoney: 58.
68. Jenkins, 'Witches and Fairies': 35.
69. *Belfast Newsletter*, 21 August 1807.
70. *Belfast Newsletter*, 21 August 1807. Unlike the newspaper report, W.O. McGaw, who wrote his short memoir of the 'Carnmoney Witch' in the mid-nineteenth century, places this event after Butters arrival: W.O. McGaw, 'Tragic Occurrence which took place in the Parish of Carnmoney and County of Antrim in the Year 1807 Through Belief in Witchcraft', *Ulster Journal of Archaeology*, third series, 19 (1955): 113.
71. McGaw, 'Tragic Occurrence': 113. Witch-stones were amulets used against the evil-eye and butter-stealing witches. They usually came in the form of a holed pebble made of flint and hung in loops of string in byres or about the necks of cattle. See, J.G. Dent, 'The Witchstone in Ulster and England', *Ulster Folklife*, 10 (1964), 46–8, and Roisin O'Reilly, 'The Material Evidence of Irish Fairy Folk Beliefs: Regarding Superstition and Witchcraft (Final year thesis, QUB, 2010)': 54–65. In the parish of Ballymoney, Co. Antrim, in the 1830s, rowan branches were tied to the tails of cows as 'a charm against witchcraft and fairyism': OSMI, Lieutenant J. Greatorex, James Boyle, 1832, *Parishes of County Antrim V, vol. 16, Parish of Ballymoney*: 19.
72. *Belfast Newsletter*, 21 August 1807.
73. For a description of these, see: Henry Mackle, 'Fairies and Leprechauns', *Ulster Folklife*, 10 (1964): 51–4; MacLysaght, *Irish Life*: 177–8; Gillespie,

Devoted People: 50–1, 65, 109, 112; Leland L. Duncan, 'Folklore Gleanings from County Leitrim', *Folklore* 4/2 (1893): 180; idem, 'Notes from County Leitrim', *Folklore* 5/3 (1894): 193; Dundes, 'Evil-eye': 31; Jenkins, 'Witches and Fairies': 44–5; Caoimhín Ó Danchair, 'The Luck of the House', *Studies in Folklife Presented to Emyr Estyn Evans* (Belfast, 1970): 20–4; Eammon P. Kelly, 'Trapping Witches in Wicklow', *Archaeology Ireland*, 26/3 (2012): 17–18; Wilde, *Irish Popular Superstitions*: 50–1, 54–9.

74. OSMI, J. Stokes, 1835, *Parishes of Londonderry xiii, vol. 34, Parish of Clandermot*: 32.

75. *Belfast Newsletter*, 21 August 1807.

76. *Caledonian Mercury*, 24 August 1807.

77. *Belfast Newsletter*, 21 August 1807. For a full transcription of a contemporary song about the Mary Butters case, see: John S. Crone (ed.), 'Witchcraft in Antrim', *Ulster Journal of Archaeology, Second Series*, 14/1 (1908): 35–7.

78. Fair Sheets by Thomas Fagan, Ordnance Survey Memoirs, February–April 1839 (PRONI, MIC 6C/REEL 2/Box 6, Antrim VI (Carnmoney)): 35.

79. McGaw, 'Tragic Occurrence': 113.

80. *Belfast Newsletter*, 21 August 1807.

81. McGaw calls him Kernohan: McGaw, 'Tragic Occurrence': 114.

82. *Belfast Newsletter*, 21 August 1807.

83. Seymour, *Witchcraft and Demonology*: 226; *Belfast Newsletter*, 21 August 1807; McGaw 'Tragic Occurrence': 113–14.

84. *Belfast Newsletter*, 21 August 1807; McGaw, 'Tragic Occurrence': 114.

85. Seymour, *Witchcraft and Demonology*: 227.

86. McGaw, 'Tragic Occurrence': 115.

87. *Belfast Newsletter*, 21 August 1807.

88. Jenkins, 'Witches and Fairies': 320; Cooper, *Ulster Folklore*: 90. See also: *Liverpool Mercury*, 6 January 1871; *Belfast Newsletter*, 10 December 1833. For a full transcription of the *Belfast Newsletter* article, see Sneddon and Privilege, 'Ulster-Scots Folklore and Literature Reader': 62–4.

89. *Belfast Newsletter*, 21 August 1807. These men are listed as: Robert Hutcheson, William Fee, Hugh Giffin, James Hill, Mathew Biggar, Andrew Douglas, James Little, James Biggar, [Thomas Clifton?], John Smith, Samuel Waters, and John McHollam.

90. *Belfast Newletter*, 21 August 1807.

91. McGaw, 'Tragic Occurrence': 115.

92. Ibid.

93. *Belfast Newsletter*, 15 April 1808. See also, *Belfast Telegraph*, 18 August 1958.

94. S[amuel] M[cSkimmin], 'An Essay on Witchcraft', *The Belfast Monthly Magazine*, 3/17 (1809): 416.

95. McSkimmin, 'An Essay on Witchcraft': 415.

96. OSMI, Lt. G.H. Mallock, April 1832, *Parishes of County Antrim XIV, vol. 37, Parish of Carrickfergus*: 77.

97. OSMI, Thomas Fagan, 28 July 1836, *Parishes of County Londonderry V, vol. 18, Parish of Tamlaght O'Crilly*: 48.

98. OSMI, James Boyle, June 1838, *Parishes of County Antrim VI, vol. 19, Parish of Drummond*: 60.

99. Account of Unsuccessful Attempt at Witchcraft, Carnmoney, August 1807 (PRONI, Ms D3113/7/237).

100. Seymour, *Irish Witchcraft and Demonology*: 226; *Belfast Newsletter*, 21 August 1807; McGaw, 'Tragic Occurrence': 113–16. Mary Butters was still alive in 1839 when OSMI collector Thomas Fagan visited Carnmoney: Fair Sheets by Fagan, OSMI, February–April 1839 (PRONI, MIC 6C/REEL 2/Box 6, Antrim VI (Carnmoney)): 37–8.

101. J.L.L., 'The Fairy Woman of Balrath: A Tale founded on Fact', *The Dublin Penny Journal*, 2/63 (1833): 82.

102. *Belfast Newsletter*, 10 December 1833.

103. T.J. Westropp, 'A Study of the Folklore on the Coast of Connacht, Ireland (Continued)', *Folklore*, 33/4 (1922): 395. See also, Anon, 'Orhohoo – The Fairy Man a Reminiscence of Connaght', *Irish Penny Journal*, 1/11 (1840): 85–7.

104. *Northern Whig*, 9 September 1843.

105. J.B. Doyle, *Tours in Ulster: A Handbook to the Antiquities and Scenery of the North of Ireland* (Dublin 1854): 278–9.

106. G.H. Kinahan, 'Notes on Irish Folklore', *The Folk-lore Record*, 4 (1881): 102.

107. Duncan, 'Folklore Gleanings from County Leitrim': 181.

108. Nathaniel Colgan, 'Witchcraft in the Aran Islands', *Journal of the Royal Society of Antiquaries of Ireland*, 25 (1895): 84.

109. This assertion is founded upon an examination of a selection of cases found in the BNA, INA and NCN databases, as well as a search of post 1,750 hard copies of the *Belfast Newsletter* and the *Freeman's Journal*. The databases were searched using keywords including, 'fairy doctor', 'fairy man/woman', 'bean feasa', 'cunning-folk', and 'wise woman/man'.

110. *Belfast Morning News*, 11 August 1862.

111. *Freeman's Journal*, 9 September 1864; *Jackson's Oxford Journal*, 17 September 1864; *Daily Southern Cross*, 14 December 1864; *Glasgow Herald*, 17 September 1864; *Liverpool Mercury*, 19 September 1864; *Belfast Newsletter*, 25 October 1864; *The Caledonian Mercury*, 27 October 1864; Clonmel Gaol Register, 6 May 1872 (NAI, Prison Records, Clonmel Gaol Registers, 1870–8, Book Number 1/7/10, item 1, microfilm, MFGS 51/007).

112. *Belfast Newsletter*, 25 July 1870.

113. *Irish Times*, 21 August 1886.

114. *Belfast Newsletter*, 11 April 1834; *ODNB*.

115. *Belfast Newsletter*, 2 June 1860. Constable Hamilton must have been particularly eager to root out magical practitioners at this time because he brought action against a fortune-teller in the same session, see p. 127.

116. *Belfast Newsletter*, 28 February 1861; List of Assize Papers Received in Crown Office, Enniskillen, 6 February 1861 (PRONI, Co. Fermanagh Crown and Peace Records, FER/1/2/D/1).

117. *Belfast Newsletter*, 14 August 1871.

118. *Belfast Newsletter*, 14 August 1871. This story was first reported in the *Newtownards Independent*.

119. For other changeling murder cases not involving cunning-folk, see, Young, 'Some Notes on Irish Fairy Changelings', and Sneddon and Privilege, 'Ulster-Scots Folklore and Literature Reader': 41–9.

120. *The Watchman and Wesleyan Advertiser*, 18 September 1850; Patrick Logan, *Irish Country Cures* (Belfast, 1981): 7.

121. *Belfast Newsletter*, 28 March 1851.
122. *Belfast Newsletter*, 15 April 1856. This case was first reported in the *Kilkenny Moderator*. For Thomas Izod, see: *The Presentments of the Grand Jury ... County of Kilkenny, Discharged Queries, at Lent Assizes, 1837 ...* (Kilkenny, 1838): 62.
123. Bourke, *Bridget Cleary*: 22–3, 75–7, 89, 115–17, 119; Cox, 'Medical Marketplace': 55.
124. This also occurred in nineteenth-century England, where cunning-folk sought legal redress when assaulted by disgruntled clients or to sue for damages or settle unpaid debts: Davies, *Popular Magic*: 25–6.
125. *Liverpool Mercury*, 6 January 1871.

Select Bibliography

Almond, Philip C., *Demonic Possession and Exorcism in Early Modern England: Contemporary Texts and their Cultural Contexts* (Cambridge, 2007).

———, *Witches of Warboys: An Extraordinary Story of Sorcery, Sadism and Satanic Possession* (London, 2008).

———, *England's First Demonologist: Reginald Scot and 'The Discoverie of Witchcraft'* (London, 2011, repr. 2014).

———, *The Lancashire Witches: A Chronicle of Sorcery and Death on Pendle Hill* (London, 2012).

———, *The Devil: A New Biography* (New York, 2014).

Ankerloo, Bengt, and Gustav Henningsen (eds), *Early Modern European Witchcraft: Centres and Peripheries* (Oxford, 1990).

Barnard, Toby, *The Kingdom of Ireland, 1641–1760* (Houndsmills, 2004).

Barry, Jonathan, *Witchcraft and Demonology in South-West England, 1640–1789* (Basingstoke, 2012).

———, *Raising Spirits: How a Conjuror's Tale was Transmitted across the Enlightenment* (Basingstoke, 2013).

——— with, Hester, M. and Roberts, G. (eds), *Witchcraft in Early Modern Europe: Studies in Culture and Belief* (Cambridge, 1996).

——— with, Davies, Owen (eds), *Witchcraft Historiography* (Basingstoke, 2007).

Bath, Jo, and John Newton (eds), *Witchcraft and the Act of 1604* (Leiden, 2008).

Behringer, Wolfgang, *Witches and Witch-Hunts* (Cambridge, 2004).

Bell, Karl, *The Magical Imagination: Magic and Modernity in Urban England 1780–1914* (Cambridge, 2012).

Bergin, John, Eoin Magennis, Ní Mhunghaile Lesa, and Patrick Walsh (eds), *New Perspectives on the Penal Laws: Eighteenth-Century Ireland/Iris an dáchultúr*, special issue no. 1. (Dublin, 2011).

Berman, David, 'Enlightenment and Counter Enlightenment in Philosophy', *Archiv für Geschichte der Philosophie*, 54 (1982): 148–65.

Bonzol, Judith, 'The Medical Diagnosis of Demonic Possession in an Early Modern Community', *Parergon*, 26/1 (2009): 115–40.

Borsje, Jacqueline, *The Celtic Evil Eye and Related Mythological Motifs in Medieval Ireland* (Paris, 2012).

Bostridge, Ian, *Witchcraft and its Transformations, c. 1650–c. 1750* (Oxford, 1997).

Bourke, Angela, *The Burning of Bridget Cleary: A True Story* (London, 1999).

Briggs, Robin, *Witches and Neighbours: The Social and Cultural Context of Witchcraft* (Oxford, 2nd ed., 2002).

Brown, Michael, *Francis Hutcheson in Dublin, 1719–30* (Dublin, 2002).

——— with, Seán Patrick Donlan (eds), *The Laws and Other Legalities of Ireland, 1689–1850* (Farnham, 2011).

Bushaway, Bob, 'Tacit, Unsuspected, but still Implicit Faith: Alternative Belief in Nineteenth-Century Rural England', in Tim Harris (ed.), *Popular Culture in England, 1500–1850* (Basingstoke, 1995): 189–215.

Byrne, Patrick F., *Witchcraft in Ireland* (Cork, 1967).

Cameron, Euan, *Enchanted Europe: Superstition, Reason and Religion, 1250–1750* (Oxford, 2010).

Clark, Stuart, *Thinking with Demons: The Idea of Witchcraft in Early Modern Europe* (Oxford, 1997).

Cohn, Norman, *Europe's Inner Demons: The Demonisation of Christians in Medieval Christendom* (London, 2nd ed., 1993).

Connolly, S.J., 'The "Blessed Turf": Cholera and Popular Panic in Ireland, June 1832', *Irish Historical Studies*, 23/91 (1983): 214–31.

———, *Religion, Law and Power: The Making of Protestant Ireland, 1660–1760* (Oxford, 1992).

———, *Religion and Society in Nineteenth Century Ireland* (Dundalk, 1985, repr. 1994).

———, '"Ag Deanamh Commanding": Elite Responses to Popular Culture, 1650–1850', in J.S. Donnolly and Kerby A. Millar (eds), *Irish Popular Culture, 1650–1850* (Dublin, 1998): 1–29.

———, *Priests and People in pre-Famine Ireland, 1780–1845* (1982, repr. Dublin, 2001).

———, *The Oxford Companion to Irish History* (Oxford, 2nd ed., 2002).

———, *Divided Kingdom: Ireland 1630–1800* (Oxford, 2008).

———, *Contested Island, Ireland 1460–1630* (Oxford, 2009).

Corish, P.J., *The Catholic Community in the Seventeenth and Eighteenth Centuries* (Dublin, 1985).

Correll, Timothy Corrigan, 'Believers and Sceptics, and Charlatans: Evidential Rhetoric, the Fairies and Fairy Healers in Irish Oral Narratives and Beliefs', *Folklore*, 116 (2005): 1–18.

Curran, Bob, *Ireland's Witches: A Bewitched Land* (Dublin, 2005).

Davies, Owen, 'Methodism, the Clergy, and the Popular Belief in Witchcraft and Magic', *History*, 82/266 (1997): 98–112.

———, 'Charmers and Charming in England and Wales from the 18th to 20th Centuries', *Folklore*, 109 (1998): 41–52.

———, *Witchcraft, Magic and Culture 1736–1951* (Manchester, 1999).

———, *Popular Magic: Cunning-folk in English History* (London, 2003, repr. 2007).

———, *The Haunted: A Social History of Ghosts* (Basingstoke, 2007).

———, 'A Comparative Perspective on Scottish Cunning-folk and Charmers', in Julian Goodare, Lauren Martin, and Joyce Miller (eds), *Witchcraft and Belief in Early Modern Scotland* (Basingstoke, 2008): 185–205.

———, 'Decriminalising the Witch: The Origin and Response to the 1736 Witchcraft Act', in Jo Bathand John Newton (eds), *Witchcraft and the Act of 1604* (Leiden, 2008): 207–32.

———, *Grimoires: A History of Magic Books* (Oxford, 2009).

———, *America Bewitched: The Story Witchcraft after Salem* (Oxford, 2013).

——— with, De Blécourt, Willem, (eds), *Beyond the Witch Trials: Witchcraft and Magic in Enlightenment Europe* (Manchester, 2004).

———, with, Willem De Blécourt (eds), *Witchcraft Continued: Popular Magic in Modern Europe* (Manchester, 2004).

Elmer, Peter, '"Saints or sorcerers": Quakerism, Demonology and the Decline of Witchcraft in Seventeenth-century England', in Jonathan Barry, Marianne Hester, and Gareth Roberts (eds), *Witchcraft in Early Modern Europe: Studies in Culture and Belief* (Cambridge: 1996): 145–79.

———, 'Towards a Politics of Witchcraft in Early Modern England', in Stuart Clark (ed.), *Languages of Witchcraft: Narrative, Ideology and Meaning in Early Modern Culture* (Hampshire, 2001): 101–18.

———, 'Medicine, Witchcraft and the Politics of Healing in Late-Seventeenth-century England', in Ole Peter Grell and Andrew Cunnigham (eds), *Medicine and Religion in Enlightenment Europe* (Aldershot, 2007): 223–42.

———, *The Miraculous Conformist: Valentine Greatrakes, the Body Politic, and the Politics of Healing in Restoration Britain* (Oxford, 2013).

Empey, Mark, '"We are not yet Safe, for they Threaten us with More Violence": A Study of the Cook Street Riot, 1629', in William Sheehan and Maura Cronin (eds), *Riotous Assemblies: Rebels, Riots and Revolts in Ireland* (Dublin, 2011).

Garnham, Neal, *The Courts, Crime and the Criminal Law in Ireland, 1692–1760* (Dublin, 1996).

———, 'How Violent was Eighteenth-century Ireland?', *Irish Historical Studies*, 30/119 (1997): 377–92.

———, 'Local Elite Creation in Early Hanoverian Ireland: The Case of the County Grand Juries', *Historical Journal*, 42/3 (1999): 623–42.

———, 'Crime, Policing and the Law, 1600–1900' in, Liam Kennedy and Philip Ollerenshaw (eds), *Ulster Since 1600: Politics, Economy and Society* (Oxford, 2013): 99–105.

Gaskill, Malcolm, 'The Devil in the Shape of a Man: Witchcraft, Conflict and Belief in Jacobean England', *Historical Research*, 71 (1998): 142–71.

———, *Crime and Mentalities in Early Modern England* (Cambridge, 2000).

———, *Witch finders: A Seventeenth-Century English Tragedy* (London, 2006).

———, 'Witchcraft and Evidence in Early Modern England', *Past and Present*, 198 (2008): 33–70.

Geary, Laurence M., *Medicine and Charity in Ireland, 1718–1851* (Dublin, 2004).

Gibson, Marion, *Reading Witchcraft: Stories of Early English Witches* (London and New York, 1999).

———, *Possession, Puritanism and Print: Darrell, Harsnett, Shakespeare and the Elizabethan Exorcism Controversy* (London, 2006).

———, *Witchcraft Myths in American Culture* (New York, 2007).

Gijswijt-Hofstra, Marijke, and Roy Porter (eds), *The Athlone History of Witchcraft and Magic in Europe: Volume 5, the Eighteenth and Nineteenth Centuries* (London, 1999).

Gillespie, Raymond, 'Women and Crime in Seventeenth-Century Ireland', in Margaret MacCurtain, Mary and O'Dowd (eds), *Women in Early Modern Ireland* (Edinburgh, 1981): 43–52.

———, *Devoted People: Belief and Religion in Early Modern Ireland* (Manchester, 1997).

———, 'The Burning of Ellen NíGilwey, 1647: A Sidelight on Popular Belief in Meath', *Journal of the County Meath Historical Society*, 10 (1999): 71–77.

———, *Reading Ireland: Print, Reading, and Social Change in Early Modern Ireland* (Manchester, 2005).

———, 'Imagining Angels in Early Modern Ireland', in Peter Marshall and Alexandra Walsham (eds), *Angels in the Early Modern World* (Cambridge, 2006): 214–32.

————, *Seventeenth-Century Ireland* (Dublin, 2006).

————, 'Ireland', in Richard M. Golden (ed.), *Encyclopaedia of Witchcraft: The Western Tradition* (4 vols, Denver and Oxford, 2007).

Godbeer, Richard, *The Devil's Dominion: Magic and Religion in Early Modern New England* (Cambridge, 1992, repr. 2002).

Golden, Richard M., (ed.), *Encyclopaedia of Witchcraft: The Western Tradition* (4 vols, Denver and Oxford, 2007).

Goodare, Julian, 'The Aberdeenshire Witchcraft Panic of 1597', *Northern Scotland*, 21 (2001): 17–38.

———— (ed.), *The Scottish Witch-hunt in Context* (Manchester, 2002).

————, 'The Scottish Witchcraft Act', *Church History*, 74/1 (2005): 39–67.

———— with, Lauren Martin, and Joyce Miller (eds), *Witchcraft and Belief in Early Modern Scotland* (Basingstoke, 2008).

Gribben, Crawford, *God's Irishmen: Theological Debates in Cromwellian Ireland* (Oxford, 2007).

Griffin, Brian, *TheBulkies: Police and Crime in Belfast 1800–1865* (Dublin, 1997).

Hayton, David, *Ruling Ireland, 1685–1742: Politics, Politicians, and Parties* (Woodbridge, 2004).

———— with, Kelly, James and Bergin, John (eds), *The Eighteenth-century Composite State: Representative Institutions in Ireland and Europe, 1690–1800* (Basingstoke, 2010).

Henderson, Lizanne, 'Witch-hunting and Witch-belief in the Gàidhealtachd', Julian Goodare, Lauren Martin, and Joyce Miller (eds), *Witchcraft and Belief in Early Modern Scotland* (Basingstoke, 2008): 95–118.

Holmes, Andrew R., *The Shaping of Ulster Presbyterianism Belief and Practice, 1770–1840* (Oxford, 2006).

Hunter, Michael, 'The Royal Society and the Decline of Magic', *Notes and Records of the Royal Society*, 65 (2011): 103–119.

————, 'The Decline of Magic: Challenge and Response in Early Enlightenment England', *Historical Journal*, 55/2 (2012): 399–425.

Hutton, Ronald, 'Witch-hunting in Celtic Societies', *Past and Present*, 212/1 (2011): 43–71.

Jenkins, Richard P., 'Witches and Fairies: Supernatural Aggression and Deviance among the Irish Peasantry', *Ulster Folklife*, 23 (1977): 33–56.

————, 'The Transformations of Biddy Early: From Local Reports of Magical Healing to Globalised New Age Fantasies', *Folklore*, 118 (2007): 162–82.

Jones, Norman, 'Defining Superstitions: Treasonous Catholics and the Act Against Witchcraft of 1563', in Charles Carleton, Robert L. Woods, Mary L. Robertson, and Joseph L. Black (eds), *States, Sovereigns, and Society* (Stroud, 1998): 187–203.

Karlsen, Carol F., *The Devil in a Shape of a Woman: Witchcraft in Colonial New England* (New York, 1989).

Kelly, James, 'The Emergence of Scientific and Institutional Medical Practice in Ireland, 1650–1800', in Greta Jonesand Elizabeth Malcolm (eds), *Medicine, Disease and the State in Ireland* (Cork, 1999): 21–39.

Kenny, Gillian, *Anglo-Irish and Gaelic Women in Ireland, c. 1170–1540* (Dublin, 2007).

Kieckhefer, Richard, *European Witch Trials: Their Foundations in Popular and Learned Culture, 1300–1500* (London, 1976).

Knights, Mark, *The Devil in Disguise: Deception, Delusion and Fanaticism in Early Enlightenment Period* (Oxford, 2011).

Lapoint, Elwyn C., 'Irish Immunity to Witch-Hunting, 1534–1711', *Eire Ireland*, 27 (1992): 76–92.

Larner, Christina, *Enemies of God: The Witch-Hunt in Scotland* (London, 1981).

———, *Witchcraft and Religion: The Politics of Popular Belief* (Oxford, 1984).

Lenihan, Edmund, *In Search of Biddy Early* (Cork and Dublin, 1987).

Levack, Brian P., *The Witch-hunt in Early Modern Europe* (Harlow, 3rd ed., 2006).

———, *Witch-hunting in Scotland: Law, Politics and Religion* (Abingdon, 2008).

———, *The Devil Within: Possession and Exorcism in the Christian West* (Yale, 2013).

——— (ed.), *Oxford Handbook of Witchcraft in Early Modern Europe and Colonial America* (Oxford, 2013).

Cuarta, Brian Mac, *Ulster 1641: Aspects of the Rising* (Belfast, 1993, rev. ed. 1997).

Macfarlane, Alan, *Witchcraft in Tudor and Stuart England: A Regional and Comparative Study* (London, 1970, 2nd ed., 1999).

Marshall, Peter, *Mother Leakey and the Bishop: A Ghost Story* (Oxford, 2007, repr. 2008).

——— with, Alexandra Walsham (eds), *Angels in the Early Modern World* (Cambridge, 2006).

Maxwell-Stuart, Peter, *Witchcraft in Europe and the New World, 1400–1800* (Basingstoke, 2001).

———, *Satan's Conspiracy: Magic and Witchcraft in Sixteenth-century Scotland* (East Linton, 2001).

———, 'Witchcraft and Magic in Eighteenth Century Scotland', in Owen Davis and Willem De Blécourt (eds), *Beyond the Witch Trials: Witchcraft and Magic in Enlightenment Europe* (Manchester, 2004): 81–99.

———, *Witch-hunters* (Stroud, 2006).

———, *Astrology from Ancient Babylon to the Present* (Stroud, 2010, repr. 2012).

McAuliffe, Mary, 'Gender, History and Witchcraft in Early Modern Ireland: A Re-Reading of the Florence Newton Trial', in Mary Ann Gialenella Valiulis (ed.), *Gender and Power in Irish History* (Dublin, 2009): 39–58.

McCafferty, John, *The Reconstruction of the Church of Ireland: Bishop Bramhall and the Laudian Reforms, 1633–1641* (Cambridge 2007, repr. 2010).

Narvaez, Peter, (ed.), *The Good People: New Fairylore Essays* (Kentucky, 1991).

Neary, Anne, 'The Origins and Character of the Kilkenny Witchcraft Case of 1324', *Proceedings of the Royal Irish Academy*, 83C (1983).

Newton John, and Jo Bath (eds), *Witchcraft and the Act of 1604* (Leiden, 2008).

Giolláin, Diarmuid Ó, 'The Fairy Belief and Official Religion in Ireland', in Peter Narvaez, (ed.), *The Good People: New Fairylore Essays* (Kentucky, 1991): 199–214.

Ohlmeyer, Jane, *Civil War and Restoration in the Three Stuart Kingdoms: The Political Career of Randal MacDonnell First Marquis of Antrim, 1609–83* (Cambridge, 1993).

Oldridge, Darren, (ed.), *The Witchcraft Reader* (Abingdon, 2nd ed., 2008).

Porter, Classon Emmet, *Witches, Warlocks and Ghosts* (Belfast, 1885).

Purkiss, Dianne, *The Witch in History* (London, 1996).

———, 'Desire and its Deformities: Fantasies of Witchcraft in the English Civil War', *The Journal of Medieval and Early Modern Studies*, 27 (1997): 103–32.

Roper, Lyndal, 'Evil Imaginings and Fantasies: Child Witches and the end of the Witch-Craze', *Past and Present*, 167/1 (2000): 107–39.

———, *Witch-Craze: Terror and Fantasy in Baroque Germany* (New Haven, 2004).

Rosen, Barbara, *Witchcraft in England, 1558–1618* (Massachusetts, 1969, repr. 1991).

Rowlands, Alison, 'Witchcraft and Old Women in Early Modern and Germany', *Past and Present*, 173/1 (2001): 50–89.

——— (ed.), *Witchcraft and Masculinities in Early Modern Europe* (Basingstoke, 2009).

Ryan, David, *Blasphemers and Blackguards: The Irish Hellfire Clubs* (Dublin, 2012).

Ryan, Meda, *Biddy Early –Wise Woman of Clare* (Dublin, 1978, repr. 1991).

Sands, Kathleen R., *Demon Possession in Elizabethan England* (London, 2004).

Sawyer, Ronald C., 'Strangely Handled in All Her Lyms': Witchcraft and Healing in Jacobean England', *Social History*, 22/3 (1989): 461–85.

Schwartz, Hillel, *Knaves, Fools, Madmen and that Subtile Effluvium: A Study of the Opposition to the French Prophets in England, 1706–1710* (Gainesville, 1978).

———, *The French Prophets: The History of a Millenarian Group in Eighteenth-Century England* (California, 1980).

Seymour, St. John D., *Irish Witchcraft and Demonology* (Dublin, 1913, repr., London, 1989).

Sharpe, James, 'Women, Witchcraft and the Legal Process', in Jenny Kermode and Garthine Walker (eds), *Women, Crime and the Courts in Early Modern England* (London, 1994): 106–24.

———, *Instruments of Darkness: Witchcraft in Early Modern England* (Philadelphia, 1996, repr. 1997).

———, 'Disruption in the Well-Ordered Household: Age, Authority and Possessed Young People', in Paul Griffiths, Adam Fox and Steve Hindle (eds), *The Experience of Authority in Early Modern England* (London, 1996): 187–212.

———, *The Bewitching of Anne Gunter* (London, 1999).

———, *Crime in Early Modern England, 1550–1750* (Edinburgh, 1999).

———, *Witchcraft in Early Modern England* (Harlow, 2001).

———, 'Witchcraft in the Early Modern Isle of Man', *Cultural and Social History*, 4/1 (2007): 11–28.

Sneddon, Andrew, *Witchcraft and Whigs: The Life of Bishop Francis Hutchinson* (Manchester, 2008).

———, 'Legislating for Economic Development: Irish Fisheries as a Case Study in the Limitations of "Improvement"', in David Hayton, James Kelly, and John Bergin (eds), *The Eighteenth-Century Composite State: Representative Institutions in Ireland and Europe, 1689–1800* (Basingstoke, 2010): 136–59.

———, 'What the Witchcraft Bishop did in Ireland: The Controversial Career of Francis Hutchinson, 1660–1739', *History Ireland*, 18/1 (2010).

———, 'Witchcraft Belief and Trials in Early Modern Ireland', *Irish Economic and Social History*, 39 (2012): 1–25.

———, *Possessed by the Devil: The Real History of the Islandmagee Witches and Ireland's only Mass Witchcraft Trial* (Dublin, 2013).

——— with, John Privilege (eds), 'The Supernatural in Ulster Scots Folklore and Literature Reader': 41–50, http://www.arts.ulster.ac.uk/ulsterscots/works/supernatural/.

Suggett, Richard, 'Witchcraft Dynamics in Early Modern Wales', in Michael Roberts and Simone Clarke (eds), *Women and Gender in Early Modern Wales* (Cardiff, 2000): 75–103.

———, *A History of Magic and Witchcraft in Wales* (Port Stroud, 2008).

Thomas, Keith, *Religion and the Decline of Magic: Studies in Popular Beliefs in Sixteenth and Seventeenth Century England* (London, 1971, repr. 1997).

Valletta, Frederick, *Witchcraft, Magic and Superstition in England, 1640–70* (Aldershot, 2000).

Wasser, Michael, 'The Mechanical World-view and the Decline of Witch-beliefs in Scotland', Juliane Goodare, Lauren Martin and Joyce Miller (eds), *Witchcraft and Belief in Early Modern Scotland* (Basingstoke, 2008): 206–26.

Whan, Robert, *The Presbyterians in Ulster, 1680–1730* (Woodbridge, 2013).

Wilby, Emma, *Cunning-folk and Familiar Spirits: Shamanistic Visionary Traditions in Early Modern British Witchcraft and Magic* (Brighton, 2005, repr. 2010).

Yates, Nigel, *The Religious Condition of Ireland, 1770–1850* (Oxford, 2006).

Young, Francis, *English Catholics and the Supernatural, 1553–1829* (Farnham, 2013).

Index

Printed and bound in the United States of America